always up to date

The law changes, but Nolo is on top of it! We offer several ways to make sure you and your Nolo products are up to date:

1 **Nolo's Legal Updater**
We'll send you an email whenever a new edition of this book is published! Sign up at **www.nolo.com/legalupdater**.

2 **Updates @ Nolo.com**
Check **www.nolo.com/update** to find recent changes in the law that affect the current edition of your book.

3 **Nolo Customer Service**
To make sure that this edition of the book is the most recent one, call us at **800-728-3555** and ask one of our friendly customer service representatives. Or find out at **www.nolo.com**.

please note

We believe accurate, plain-English legal information should help you solve many of your own legal problems. But this text is not a substitute for personalized advice from a knowledgeable lawyer. If you want the help of a trained professional—and we'll always point out situations in which we think that's a good idea—consult an attorney licensed to practice in your state.

The Essential Guide to
Family and Medical Leave

By Attorneys Lisa Guerin & Deborah C. England

FIRST EDITION   JUNE 2007

Editor   ALAYNA SCHROEDER

Book Design   SUSAN PUTNEY

Proofreading   JOE SADUSKY

Index   BAYSIDE INDEXING SERVICE

Printing   CONSOLIDATED PRINTERS, INC.

Guerin, Lisa, 1964-
    The essential guide to family and medical leave / by Lisa Guerin &
Deborah England.
       p. cm.
    ISBN-13: 978-1-4133-0671-2
    ISBN-10: 1-4133-0671-3
    1. Leave of absence--Law and legislation--United States--Popular works.
2. Parental leave--Law and legislation--United States--Popular works. I. England,
Deborah. II. Title.
    KF3531.Z9G84 2007
    344.7301'25763--dc22

                        2006103269

Quanity sales: For information on bulk purchases or corporate premium sales, please contact the Special
Sales Department. For academic sales or textbook adoptions, ask for Academic Sales. 800-955-4775.
Nolo, 950 Parker Street, Berkeley, CA 94710.

Acknowledgements

The authors would like to thank all of the folks at Nolo who made this book possible, including:

Alayna Schroeder, for her thoughtful, clarifying, and extraordinarily quick editing.

Sigrid Metson and Kelly Perri, for their insights on managing FMLA leave and for their good cheer and hard work in marketing this project.

Janet Portman and Mary Randolph, for their sustained enthusiasm and support.

Susan Putney, for creating a beautiful book design.

Stan Jacobsen, for his research assistance.

The authors would also like to thank their friends, colleagues, and mentors in the field of employment law, including:

Michael Gaitley, senior staff attorney, the Legal Aid Employment Law Center—Employment Law Center

Everyone at Rudy, Exelrod and Zieff

Patrice Goldman

The Honorable John True.

Dedication

To my father, Jim England, who could have used a leave law while raising four kids. And, to my mother, in loving memory.

Deborah C. England

About the Authors

Lisa Guerin is an editor at Nolo specializing in employment law. She is the author or co-author of several Nolo books, including *The Manager's Legal Handbook*, *Dealing With Problem Employees*, *The Essential Guide to Federal Employment Laws*, *The Essential Guide to Workplace Investigations*, *Create Your Own Employee Handbook*, *The Progressive Discipline Handbook*, and *Nolo's Guide to California Law*. Ms. Guerin has practiced employment law in government, public interest, and private practice, where she represented clients at all levels of state and federal courts and in agency proceedings. She is a graduate of Boalt Hall School of Law at the University of California at Berkeley.

Deborah C. England has practiced employment law in San Francisco for 20 years, representing clients in litigation in state and federal courts. In addition to litigation, she regularly advises clients on employment issues and in efforts to informally resolve employment disputes. Ms. England has published numerous articles and essays on employment and civil rights law and has spoken frequently on these topics before legal and employment professional organizations.

Table of Contents

Index

An Overview of Family and Medical Leave

The Family and Medical Leave Act (FMLA) is a law with an undeniably noble purpose: to help employees balance the demands of work with personal and family health needs. Since the FMLA was enacted in 1993, millions of employees have relied on it to protect their jobs while taking time off to recover from a serious illness, care for an ailing family member, or bond with a new child.

Surveys conducted by the Department of Labor (DOL), the federal agency that administers and enforces the law, show that the majority of companies covered by the FMLA find it very or somewhat easy to administer and that it has had little or no impact on company productivity, profitability, or growth. But managers and human resources professionals know that there's another side to this story. Experience has shown that it can be difficult to apply the FMLA when real employees take leave in the real world. For example, do you know what to do in these situations?

- An employee who needs leave is also covered by workers' compensation, a state family and medical leave law, and/or the Americans With Disabilities Act—and the requirements of those laws appear to conflict with the FMLA.

- An employee asks for time off but won't tell you why or is reluctant to reveal personal medical information that might entitle the employee to leave.

- An employee wants to take FMLA leave at your company's busiest time of year.

- An employee wants to take time off as needed for a chronic ailment, rather than all at once, and can't comply with your company's usual call-in procedures.

- An employee doesn't give exactly the right amount or type of notice, forgets to hand in a medical certification form, or can't return to work as scheduled.

- An employee decides, after taking FMLA leave, not to come back to work.

Changes to FMLA Regulations

As this book goes to press, the Department of Labor (DOL) is considering whether to revise its regulations interpreting the FMLA. These regulations provide many of the guidelines for employers to follow when applying the FMLA in the real world, addressing some of the details not addressed in the law itself. In December 2006, the DOL asked the public to comment on a number of key provisions. The DOL is currently considering these comments and may decide to revise the FMLA regulations—which would change the rules you have to follow in applying the FMLA.

Some of the subjects that are up for discussion include:

- **the definition of a "serious health condition"** entitling an employee to FMLA leave, particularly whether the regulations should require a longer absence before the FMLA kicks in

- **rules for using intermittent leave,** including whether employees should be required to take more time off at once (for example, a full or half day) than the current regulations require

- **medical certifications and fitness-for-duty reports** (documents employers can require employees to submit to prove they qualify for FMLA leave) including whether changes are needed to comply with the Health Insurance Portability and Accountability Act (HIPAA) and whether employers should be entitled to more information than the current regulations allow

- **employee notice requirements,** including whether and in what circumstances employees must comply with an employer's usual requirements for using sick or vacation leave, and

- **employer notice requirements,** particularly what happens when an employer fails to designate leave as FMLA leave. We know there will be changes here, because the United States Supreme Court already struck down the existing regulation in *Ragsdale v. Wolverine World Wide Inc.,* 535 U.S. 81 (2002) (see Chapter 7).

If and when the regulations change, some of the information in this book—which relies on the regulations currently in effect—might become outdated. To get the latest information on the regulations, register your purchase according to the instructions at the back of the book, and we'll send you an email notifying you of any changes. You can also check Nolo's website at www.nolo.com for the latest information.

These issues—and many more like them—come up every day, and managers have to figure out how to handle them legally and fairly, while protecting the company's interests. That's where this book comes in: It explains, in plain English, exactly how the FMLA works and what it requires. Although it can be tricky sometimes to figure out what to do in a particular situation, this book's step-by-step approach will help you sort things out and meet your obligations.

This chapter will help you get started. It introduces the law's basic requirements, with special emphasis on your responsibilities as a manager. It explains how other laws and company policies can affect your obligations when an employee needs time off for family or medical reasons. And it provides a roadmap to the rest of the book, so you'll be able to easily find the answers to all your FMLA questions.

What the FMLA Requires

In a nutshell, the FMLA requires companies to allow employees to take time off to fulfill certain caretaking responsibilities or to recuperate from a serious illness. If your company is covered by the law, an eligible employee is entitled to take up to 12 weeks of unpaid leave every 12 months to bond with a new child, care for a family member with a serious health condition, or recover from his or her own serious health condition.

FMLA leave is unpaid, although an employee may choose—or the company may require employees—to use up accrued paid leave, such as sick leave or vacation, during this time off. The employer must continue the employee's group health coverage during FMLA leave. When the employee's leave is over, the employee must be reinstated to the same or an equivalent position, with the same benefits, as the employee had before taking time off. Although there are a few exceptions to this requirement, they apply only in very limited circumstances.

CAUTION

Special rules apply to public employers and schools. The FMLA imposes slightly different obligations on government employers and schools; we don't cover these rules in this book. Similarly, in unionized workplaces, the collective bargaining agreement—the contract between the company and the union—might impose different family and medical leave obligations. Because every collective bargaining agreement is different, we can't cover them here.

Your Obligations as a Manager

The moment an employee comes to your office and says, "My wife is having a baby," "My mother has to have surgery," or "I've been diagnosed with cancer," you'll have to figure out whether the FMLA applies, provide notices and meet other paperwork requirements, manage the employee's time off, and reinstate the employee according to strict rules and guidelines.

Ten Steps to FMLA Compliance

Whenever you're faced with a leave situation that might be covered by the FMLA, you should ask yourself the questions listed below. This checklist will help you make sure that you meet all your legal obligations and don't forget anything important. Each of these topics is covered in detail in this book.

Step 1: Is your company covered by the FMLA? It is if it has had at least 50 employees for at least 20 weeks in this or the previous year. If your company is covered, it has to post a notice and perhaps adopt a written FMLA policy, even before an employee requests leave. Company coverage is explained in Chapter 2.

Step 2: Is the employee covered by the FMLA? An employee who has worked for at least a year, and at least 1,250 hours during the prior year, at a company facility that has at least 75 employees within a 50-mile radius, is covered. Chapter 3 explains how to make these calculations.

Step 3: Does the employee need leave for a reason covered by the FMLA? Leave is available for the employee's own serious health condition or to care for a family member with a serious health condition. Chapter 4 explains what a serious health condition is. Leave is also available to bond with a new child; that's covered in Chapter 5.

Step 4: How much leave is available to the employee? An employee is entitled to take up to 12 workweeks of leave, either all at once or intermittently, in a 12-month period. Chapter 6 will help you figure out how much leave an employee may take.

Step 5: Did you and the employee meet your notice and paperwork requirements? The employee must give reasonable notice and provide certain information; you must designate FMLA leave and give the employee required notices, among other things. Chapter 7 provides the details.

Step 6: Did you request a medical certification—and did the employee return it? You can—and should—ask an employee who needs leave for a serious health condition to provide a medical certification from a health care provider. Chapter 8 explains how.

Step 7: Did you successfully manage the employee's leave? You must continue the employee's health benefits, manage and track intermittent leave, arrange for substitution of paid leave, and more. In addition, you have to make sure the work gets done while the employee is out, whether by distributing the employee's responsibilities to coworkers, hiring a temporary replacement, or outsourcing the job. Chapter 9 covers all of these issues.

Step 8: Did you follow the rules for reinstating an employee returning from leave? You must return the employee to the same or an equivalent position and restore the employee's seniority and benefits, unless an exception applies. Chapter 10 explains these rules, as well as what to do if the employee doesn't return from leave.

Step 9: Have you met your obligations under any other laws that apply? Whether or not the FMLA applies, the employee may be protected by the Americans With Disabilities Act, workers' compensation statutes, state family and medical leave laws, and other laws. To find out about your obligations under these other laws, see Chapter 11.

Step 10: Have you met your record keeping requirements? If your company is covered by the FMLA, you must keep certain payroll, benefits, leave, and other records, and you'll certainly want to keep proper documentation of your decisions and conversations, in case you need to rely on them later. These issues are covered in Chapter 12.

The Compassionate Manager

One of the challenges of implementing the FMLA is that you must meet your legal obligations within a context that can be emotional. After all, employees who qualify for FMLA leave are undergoing major life changes. On the positive side, the employee may be welcoming a new child, with all the joy and excitement that brings. On the more sobering side, perhaps the employee is losing a parent or spouse to a terminal illness, caring for a seriously ill child, or suffering through a painful disease. Although you have to follow the law's requirements and make sure your company's needs are met, no one wants to be the hardhearted administrator who responds to an emotionally distraught employee by handing over a stack of forms to be completed in triplicate.

The FMLA recognizes that employees who need time off for pressing family or health concerns might not always be able to dot every "i" and cross every "t." The law provides guidance on what to do if, for example, an employee is too ill or injured to communicate with you, can't return to work on time because of continuing health problems, or doesn't complete forms on time. These rules will help you balance your legal obligations with the natural human desire to be compassionate during a difficult time.

And, as we'll remind you from time to time, you have little to gain from imposing strict deadlines and paperwork requirements on employees who are truly in dire straits. Judges and juries are people, too, and they can find ways to enforce the spirit of the law in favor of an employee who needed its protection—even if the employee failed to meet deadlines, give adequate notice, hand in forms on time, or provide required information.

LESSONS FROM THE

Real World

An employee who didn't give notice of need for leave can still sue for violation of the FMLA.

For four years, John Byrne worked as a stationary engineer on the night shift at Avon Products. By all accounts, he was a model employee until November 1998, when a coworker reported finding him asleep in a break room. The company checked its security logs and found that Byrne had been spending a lot of time in the break room lately. So the company installed a camera, which filmed Byrne sleeping for three hours one night and six hours the next.

Byrne's managers planned to talk to him about the problem on November 16, but Byrne left work early. He told a coworker that he wasn't feeling well and would be out the rest of the week. A manager called Byrne's house, where his sister answered the phone and said he was "very sick." When Byrne came to the phone, he mumbled some odd phrases and agreed to come to a meeting at work the following day. When he didn't show up for the meeting, he was fired.

It turns out that Byrne was unable to attend the meeting because he had been hospitalized for severe depression, after relatives convinced him to come out of a room where he had barricaded himself. Byrne had begun hallucinating and having panic attacks and required two months of treatment. When Byrne felt better, he asked Avon to take him back. The company refused, and Byrne sued for violation of the FMLA.

Avon argued that Byrne never gave adequate notice that he needed FMLA leave, so the court should throw out his FMLA claim. The court didn't see it that way, however. Although Byrne never mentioned the FMLA or said that he needed medical leave, the court found that his marked change in behavior might have been sufficient to put Avon on notice that he needed FMLA leave. The court also found that Byrne might have been unable, because of his mental state, to give notice that he needed leave. Either way, the court found that Byrne should be able to present his claims to a jury.

Byrne v. Avon Products Inc., 328 F.3d 379 (7th Cir. 2003).

Of course, people have different comfort levels when dealing with emotional subjects. Some can easily offer support and a shoulder to cry on; others would rather volunteer for a root canal. If you fall on the more stoic end of this spectrum, take heart: You don't need to become a therapist—or the employee's best friend—to show some understanding in a difficult situation. Just remember that a little kindness goes a long way. Acknowledge what your employees are dealing with, cut them some slack if necessary, and work with them to make the law serve its purpose.

Why You Need to Get It Right

Properly managing your FMLA obligations is a win-win situation. Employees win because they get time off when they really need it, with the assurance that their jobs will be waiting for them when they come back. You and your company win because helping employees balance work and family leads to greater employee loyalty to the company and all of the other benefits that flow from it, including better morale, stronger retention, and even improved productivity.

That's the carrot—and here's the stick: Violating the FMLA can lead to serious trouble. And we don't just mean the morale problems and associated woes that can crop up if employees feel that their needs aren't important to the company. Mishandling family and medical leave issues can also give rise to lawsuits—not just against your company, but against you, individually, as the manager who made the flawed decision. Of course, this is the ultimate worst-case scenario, and chances are good that you'll never have to face it. If you're one of the unlucky few, however, your personal assets—such as your home, your car, and your bank accounts—could be on the line, not to mention your career and reputation.

How Other Laws and Company Policies Come Into Play

The FMLA isn't the only law you need to consider when employees need time off for family or medical reasons. Other federal and state laws might also come into play, depending on the circumstances. In addition, a company's own policies often affect family and medical leave—by, for example, providing paid sick, vacation, or family leave; requiring employees to follow certain procedures before taking time off; or dictating how seniority, benefits, and other issues are handled when an employee is on leave.

This possibility of overlap means two very important things to managers:

- Whenever an employee requests time off pursuant to any law or company policy, you must ask yourself whether the FMLA applies. The employee isn't required to explicitly ask for "FMLA leave"; it's your responsibility to determine whether the employee's time off is FMLA-qualified. An employee on workers' comp leave, temporary disability leave, parental leave, or even vacation might be protected by the FMLA, if the employee meets all of the criteria. And you will certainly want to count that time off as FMLA leave, not only to make sure the employee's rights are protected, but also to put some limit on the total amount of time an employee can take off in a year.

- When the FMLA and another law or policy both apply, you may have to provide more than the FMLA requires. If other laws or your company's policies give employees additional rights, you must honor them as well. The employee is entitled to every protection available, whether it is provided by the FMLA, another law, or your company's policies.

Overlapping Laws

The basic rule about what to do when the FMLA and another law overlap is easy to state: You must follow every applicable provision of every applicable law. In other words, you may not focus solely on the FMLA and ignore your company's obligations under other state or federal laws. If both laws apply to the same situation, this means that you must give the employee the benefit of whichever law is more generous or provides greater rights.

Here are some of the other laws that might also apply to an employee who takes FMLA leave (Chapter 11 explains each in detail; you can find information on each state's leave laws in Appendix A):

- **Antidiscrimination laws,** which prohibit discrimination based on certain protected characteristics. The Americans With Disabilities Act (ADA) and similar state laws might come into play if an employee's serious health condition is also a protected disability. Laws that prohibit gender and pregnancy discrimination sometimes also overlap with the FMLA.

- **Workers' compensation statutes,** which require most employers to carry insurance that pays for medical treatment and partial wage replacement for employees who suffer work-related injuries or illnesses. An employee who needs workers' compensation leave almost always has a serious health condition under the FMLA, as explained in Chapter 11.

- **State leave laws,** which require employers to give time off for specified reasons. Some states give employees the right to take pregnancy disability leave, parental leave, or other types of family and medical leave. If the employee takes leave for a reason that's covered by both state law and the FMLA, you can count that time off against the employee's allotment of FMLA hours. However, if state law provides leave that isn't covered by the FMLA, you can't count those types of leave against the employee's FMLA entitlement—which means that the employee might be legally allowed to take more than 12 weeks off. (See Appendix A for detailed information on state family and medical leave laws.)

- **State insurance programs,** which provide some wage replacement, usually funded by payroll deductions, for employees who are unable to work due to a temporary disability (including pregnancy and childbirth). California also has a paid family leave insurance program, which provides similar benefits to employees who take time off to bond with a child or care for a family member. An employee on FMLA leave might be entitled to some compensation from this type of program.

Company Policies

Company policies interact with the FMLA in a slightly different way. For the most part, the employee gets the benefit of whichever provision, law or policy, is more generous. If your company's policies give more rights to employees than the FMLA does, you must follow your policies. For example, if your company has a family and medical leave policy that allows employees to take up to 16 weeks of leave, you cannot disregard that policy and give employees only the 12 weeks required by the FMLA. If your company's policies are less generous, however, the company must follow the FMLA: It must, for example, give employees a full 12 weeks of FMLA leave, even if the company's policies provide for only six.

Employees are also entitled to use whichever applicable provisions—from the FMLA or from your company's policies impose less strict requirements. For example, many companies require employees to follow certain procedures to take advantage of company benefits. A company might require employees to request vacation time a month in advance, to call in at least an hour before missing a shift due to illness, or to provide a doctor's note for sick leave lasting more than a couple of days. If these types of policies conflict with—or are stricter than—the FMLA, you cannot enforce them against an employee who needs FMLA leave. On the other hand, if your policies require less of employees than the FMLA does, you may require the employee to comply only with your policies, not with the stricter requirements of the FMLA.

In addition to these general rules, the FMLA also makes explicit reference to particular types of employer policies. For example, the FMLA says that you can fire an employee for substance abuse, even if the employee takes FMLA leave to go to rehab, but only if your company has a policy allowing it to do so.

Because this is a potentially confusing area, we've devoted Appendix B to company policies that can affect your FMLA rights. This appendix identifies the most common areas in which company policy might come into play and provides some sample policy language that will help you maximize your company's rights. In addition, you'll find policy alert icons throughout the book. These icons let you know that your company's policy could determine your rights and obligations regarding that topic.

How to Use This Book

This book explains every aspect of the FMLA, from figuring out whether your company is covered by the law to reinstating an employee returning from FMLA leave. We cover these topics in the order in which you will generally encounter them as you administer an employee's leave. In addition, we provide helpful appendixes that explain how your state's laws and your company's policies could affect your company's FMLA rights and obligations.

We strongly advise you to read the whole book, even if you are already familiar with some aspects of the FMLA. Because the FMLA imposes fairly tight deadlines on employers—and because the way you handle initial issues can affect your company's rights down the road—you'll find it very helpful to understand the whole picture before you have to handle a leave request. Once you've reviewed every chapter, you can use the book as a reference, to quickly look up the information you need.

Each chapter includes features that will help you meet your obligations, including:

- **Chapter Highlights,** which explain the main topics to be covered
- **Lessons From the Real World,** which show how courts have handled particular issues in the real world
- **Examples,** which will help you understand how to apply the material to real-life situations
- **Sample Forms,** which allow you to request information from, and provide information to, employees about FMLA leave (all forms are included in Appendix C and on the CD-ROM at the back of the book)
- **Manager's Checklists and Flowcharts,** which you can use to make sure you've considered every important factor when making decisions about key FMLA issues, and
- **Common Mistakes—And How to Avoid Them,** which will help you steer clear of legal trouble in applying the FMLA.

Complying with the FMLA can be a challenge, but the materials in this book will help you handle your responsibilities legally, fairly, and confidently. The first step is to figure out whether your company is covered by the law—and, if so, to give employees notice of their rights under the law—using the guidelines in Chapter 2. If you already know that your company is covered and has met its posting and policy obligations, move on to Chapter 3, which will help you figure out which employees are eligible for leave.

Is Your Company Covered by the FMLA?

CHAPTER HIGHLIGHTS

Your company is covered by the FMLA if it employed 50 or more employees for 20 or more weeks in the current or preceding year.

Employees to count toward the 50 or more minimum include:

- all full-time employees

- all part-time employees

- employees on leave if they are expected to return to work, and

- employees who work jointly for your company and another company.

These workers don't count towards the 50-employee minimum:

- independent contractors

- employees working outside the U.S or its territories

- employees hired or terminated during a calendar week (for that week), and

- employees who are not expected to return from leave.

For purposes of the FMLA's 20-week minimum, employees are employed by your company in any week in which they are on payroll.

The 20 weeks of employing 50 or more employees don't have to be consecutive, as long as they occur in the current or preceding year.

When your company is a joint employer, your company's responsibilities under the FMLA depend on whether it is a "primary" or "secondary" employer.

If your company is a covered employer, you must:

- post general FMLA information at every worksite, and

- include information about the FMLA in your company's personnel handbook or other written personnel policies.

B efore you get your first request for FMLA leave, you have to figure out whether the law applies to your company. The reason? Companies subject to the FMLA are required to post notices about the FMLA and include FMLA information in employee handbooks or company policies. You don't have the luxury of waiting for an employee to raise the issue; you are legally required to inform your employees of their rights under the law. If your company doesn't provide this information, it can't deny FMLA leave to employees who fail to meet their obligations under the law (for example, to provide advance notice of the need for leave or a medical certification from a health care provider, confirming the need for leave). Your company may also have to pay penalties to the government.

This chapter will help you figure out whether the FMLA applies to your company. It covers:

- whether your company is directly covered by the FMLA
- whether your company is covered by the FMLA as a joint employer, and
- what actions you must take, right away, if your company is covered.

Calculating the Size of Your Company

Your company is covered by the FMLA if it employed 50 or more employees for each working day during 20 or more weeks in the current or preceding year. The purpose of this 50-employee rule is to exempt small businesses from the FMLA: Congress recognized that these businesses might not be able to afford to provide the leave and benefits—and bear the administrative burdens—mandated by the law.

Most companies won't be splitting hairs: Companies with more than 50 employees know they are subject to the FMLA, and very small companies know they aren't. However, for companies that are close to that 50-employee dividing line, the details about which employees count towards the minimum become very important. For example, managers sometimes aren't sure whether part-time employees count toward the minimum, or whether to count temporary workers who are placed—and technically employed—by an outside agency. To evaluate whether the FMLA applies to your company, we'll walk through each of these factors, step by step.

Step 1: Does Your Company Employ 50 or More People?

It seems like a simple calculation—anyone can add to 50, right? However, when you're making the calculation, you'll need to take each of these employees into account:

- every full-time employee
- every part-time employee
- employees on leave, whether paid or unpaid, including medical leave, FMLA leave, vacation, and disciplinary or workers' compensation leaves, as long as your company reasonably expects them to return to work, and
- employees, such as temps, who work jointly for your company and another company (called "joint employees," and discussed below).

 SKIP AHEAD

If your company has fewer than 50 employees. If your company has not employed 50 people at any given time in the last two years, your company will not be directly subject to the FMLA and you can skip the rest of this section. However, if you're a joint employer with a company that is subject to the FMLA, you will still have some legal responsibilities (For more information, see "Joint Employers and the FMLA," below).

If your company has employed at least 50 people at any time in the last two years, keep reading to find out if the FMLA applies to your company.

Step 2: Did Your Company Employ 50 or More Employees for 20 or More Workweeks?

The FMLA applies only to companies that have employed 50 or more employees for 20 or more weeks of the current or preceding year. Employees whose names appear on your company's payroll at any time in a calendar week count as employed for the whole workweek. However, employees hired or terminated during a calendar week don't count for that week, nor do independent contractors or employees working outside the U.S. or its territories.

EXAMPLE: You are the HR manager of Blue Lagoon Pool Maintenance and Repair Service in Scottsdale, Arizona, which has 34 year-round employees but hires extra part-time employees when pool season heats up. Blue Lagoon hires 25 part-time employees the first week of May. When calculating whether Blue Lagoon has enough employees to be subject to the FMLA, you don't count the new part-time employees for the first week of May, but you do count them for every week they work after that, even if they only work one day a week. As of the middle of October, all the part-time employees still work for Blue Lagoon, so you correctly determine that Blue Lagoon will have at least 50 employees for 20 or more weeks of the year. Blue Lagoon will be subject to the FMLA.

The 20 weeks don't have to be consecutive. For example, if your company is a seasonal employer and has more than 50 employees during all of spring and fall (six months of the year), but only ten employees during summer and winter, your company will be covered by the FMLA. And a company that has reduced its workforce from at least 50 employees to less than 50 employees within the last year is still covered by FMLA if it employed 50 or more employees for any 20 weeks in the current or preceding calendar year.

EXAMPLE: Your company, Razberry Jam Productions, employs 62 field workers from March 15 to May 1 every year, and 53 seasonal cannery workers from June 1 to October 15. The rest of the year, your company maintains a bare-bones staff of 15 shipping and administrative employees. In April, Wendy, a shipping clerk, asks for leave to take care of her husband as he recovers from surgery. Her manager denies the leave, telling Wendy that he has counted back 20 calendar weeks and the cannery was closed for most of that period, so the FMLA doesn't apply to Razberry Jam Productions.

You correctly step in and reverse the manager's decision. What did he do wrong? The manager should have looked at the entire current and preceding year for the company. If he had done that, he would have seen, as you did, that your company employed over 50 employees for more than 20 weeks in that period. Your company was covered by the FMLA.

If your company didn't employ 50 employees for at least 20 weeks in the current or preceding year, it isn't covered by the FMLA. But, if your company is a "secondary" joint employer (as discussed in "Joint Employers and the FMLA," below), it may still have to comply with certain FMLA requirements.

Covered Companies May Not Have Eligible Employees

To be eligible for leave under the FMLA, it's not enough that employees work for a covered company; they must also meet certain individual eligibility requirements, as explained in Chapter 3. One of these requirements is that the employee must work within a 75-mile radius of 50 or more company employees.

As a result of this rule, a company that's covered by the FMLA might not have a single eligible employee. For example, a nationwide company might have outlets in a hundred major metropolitan areas, each employing 20 to 30 employees. Yet, if none of those outlets are with 75 miles of another, none of the company's employees would be eligible to take FMLA leave. In this situation, the company would still have to post notices and provide information on the FMLA (see "If Your Company Is Covered," below), but it wouldn't have to provide leave.

Joint Employers and the FMLA

Even if it doesn't meet the criteria described above, your company could still be subject to the FMLA if it is a "joint employer." A joint employer shares control with another company over the working conditions of the other company's employees. This happens when your company contracts with temporary agencies or shares employees with a contractor or subcontractor, for example. If, counting joint employees, your company meets the requirements described above, your company is subject to the FMLA. However, its FMLA responsibilities to the joint employees depend on whether it's a "primary" or a "secondary" employer, as we explain below.

Is Your Company a Joint Employer?

There are no hard and fast rules that determine whether your company is a joint employer. Instead, you must look at all the circumstances of the relationship between the two companies to determine whether your company acts like an employer. The main factors to consider are whether your company:

- has the power to hire and fire some employees of the other company
- has the power to set rates and methods of pay of employees of the other company
- has the right to supervise the work and work schedules of employees of the other company, and
- is responsible for maintaining employment records for employees of the other company.

These factors are hallmarks of a joint employer relationship. No one factor or combination of factors automatically creates a joint employer relationship. But as a practical matter, if your company uses temps or employees supplied by another company, it is probably a joint employer.

EXAMPLE: Your company, Internet Service Solutions (ISS), operates a customer call center to service the accounts of customers of an Internet service provider, Internet View. To find new customer service representatives, ISS hires temporary employees through a placement service, Techno Temps. ISS supervisors interview prospective Techno Temps candidates for their departments, choose which to hire, and decide how much to pay them. If the supervisor likes the Techno Temp employee's work, the employee might later be offered a job directly by ISS. If a Techno Temps placement doesn't work out, ISS can terminate employment. Currently, 20 of ISS's customer service representatives are Techno Temps employees.

In this situation, ISS is a joint employer with Techno Temps because ISS has the power to hire and fire Techno Temps employees working at ISS, sets their pay rate, and supervises them on a day-to-day basis. As a result, all joint employees have to be counted by both ISS and Techno Temps to determine whether the two companies are covered by the FMLA.

Depending on the circumstances, ISS might also be a joint employer with Internet View. For example, if ISS is a subsidiary of Internet View, and human resources operations like recruiting, payroll, and personnel files are all managed by Internet View, ISS and Internet View are probably joint employers.

LESSONS FROM THE

Real World

If your company doesn't control the working conditions of another company's workers, it doesn't have to count them as "joint employees."

Stephane Moreau worked as an assistant station manager for a foreign airline in a major U.S. airport. When his father became ill, Stephane asked for FMLA leave to take care of him. But the airline refused to give him the leave. Even though the airline was covered by the FMLA, Stephane only met individual eligibility requirements if the company employed 50 or more employees within 75 miles of Stephane's worksite. The airline claimed that it didn't.

Stephane knew that ground handling companies serviced the airline's planes at the airport. He argued to the employer that the employees of the ground handling companies were "joint employees," because they provided services to the airline's planes at the airport where he worked. The airline disagreed and told Moreau that he would be fired if he took the time off— and when he did, they kept their promise.

Stephane sued, but he lost. The court decided that the airline wasn't a joint employer because, among other things, it didn't have the power to hire or fire the ground crew, set the pay rates for the workers, keep their employment records, set their work schedules, or control their work conditions.

Moreau v. Air France, 343 F.3d 1179 (9th Cir. 2003).

Primary and Secondary Employers

Figuring out whether your company is a joint employer is just your first task; it tells you whether you have any obligations under the FMLA. To find out what those obligations are, you must figure out whether your company is the "primary" or a "secondary" employer.

Is Your Company a Primary or Secondary Employer?

If your company is a joint employer, use the criteria below to determine whether your company is a primary or secondary employer.

A primary employer is one who has authority to:

- hire and fire the employee seeking leave
- place the employee in a particular position
- assign work to the employee
- make payroll, and
- provide employment benefits.

If your company is responsible for these tasks, your company is the primary employer. If not, your company is the secondary employer. Once again, these factors give guidance but are not hard and fast rules.

EXAMPLE: Your company has 33 employees on its regular payroll. Aaron works for IS-2, a temporary agency that directly employs 21 IT technicians placed at your company. IS-2 hires and fires these technicians, issues their paychecks, and provides medical insurance coverage for them. Aaron needs to take time off for the birth of his child.

Who is Aaron's primary employer? Because IS-2 handles all of the employment obligations for the IT technicians, IS-2 is Aaron's primary employer. Your company is the secondary employer because it uses Aaron's services but is not otherwise responsible for his employment.

TIP

When in doubt, act like the primary employer. If you aren't sure whether your company is a primary or secondary employer, the best practice is to assume that it is a primary employer and give employees the required notices, as discussed below. If a court is later asked to decide the issue, you'll have met your company's obligations either way.

Primary and Secondary Employers' Responsibilities

So what are the responsibilities of the primary and secondary employers? Well, the primary employer's responsibilities are pretty much the same as those of any company subject to the FMLA. It must provide FMLA notices to joint employees, grant and administer their FMLA leaves, and restore them to their jobs when FMLA leave is over. The primary employer can't interfere with employees' FMLA rights or discriminate against employees for asserting those rights or the rights of others. We'll discuss how to implement all these requirements in future chapters.

The secondary employer's responsibilities are a little less onerous. As long as the secondary employer is still jointly employing anyone with the primary employer when the employee's leave ends, the secondary employer must let any joint employee on FMLA leave return to the same position he or she held before the leave. Additionally, the secondary employer can't interfere with a joint employee's exercise of FMLA rights and can't retaliate or discriminate against the employee for asserting FMLA rights or for assisting other employees in asserting those rights. Even a secondary employer that would not otherwise be covered by the FMLA (for example, because it employs less than 50 employees even counting joint employees) is bound by these obligations.

EXAMPLE: At the end of his leave, Aaron wants to return to his IT technician position with your company. Your company still has 10 of the IS-2 technicians placed through the temporary agency. Must your company return Aaron to his technician position even though it no longer employs 50 employees including the joint employees?

Yes. As a secondary employer of a joint employee, your company must return Aaron to his position.

Is Your Company an Integrated Employer?

A parent and subsidiary company or two or more affiliated companies (sometimes called "sister companies") must each count all of the other company's (or companies') employees, even those who work only for one company, when calculating whether it meets the 50-employee test. These "integrated" companies are viewed under the FMLA as a single employer. Companies are "integrated employers" when there is:

- common management
- interrelation between operations
- centralized control of labor relations, and
- common ownership or financial control.

So, if your company is integrated with another company, it must include all of the other company's employees in the FMLA count—even if your company shares no staff with the other company and has entirely separate work facilities

CAUTION

A successor in interest might have FMLA obligations to "inherited" employees. If your company bought or merged with another company, the company that's left after the merger or sale may be a "successor in interest." If so, the transferred employees will have the same FMLA rights as if they had been continuously employed by a single company. So if your company is not covered by the FMLA and it buys another company that is, it must honor the FMLA rights of the employees of the other company who become its employees after the sale. If you think your company might be a successor in interest, you may wish to get the help of an attorney to determine your company's responsibilities under the FMLA.

✓ Managers' Checklist	**Does the FMLA Apply to My Company?**

❏ My company had 50 or more employees on payroll during each of 20 workweeks in this or the last calendar year.

   ❏ I included all employees on leave in this count.

   ❏ I included all part-time employees on payroll during any workweek.

   ❏ I did not include employees hired or fired during any workweek in the count for that workweek.

   ❏ I did not include employees working outside the U.S. or its territories in this count.

   ❏ I counted all employees jointly employed by my company and joint employer(s), including temp agency employees.

   ❏ I counted all employees of my company and any other company that is integrated with it.

If Your Company Is Covered

Once you determine that your company is covered by the FMLA, you must immediately provide information to employees about their rights and obligations under the law. You'll have to post a notice explaining the FMLA and, if your company has written policies it distributes to employees (for example, in an employee handbook), you'll need to include information about the FMLA in those policies.

Posting Requirements

Employees rely on you to provide information about the FMLA. That obligation begins with the requirement to hang a poster explaining employees' FMLA rights. The poster must be in a "conspicuous" place where it can be readily seen by employees and job applicants, and in writing that is large enough to read easily. Your company has to hang this poster even if it doesn't have any FMLA-eligible employees on site. The reason for this is that currently ineligible employees may become eligible under the FMLA and will need to know their rights.

Fortunately, you probably won't have to put together a poster from scratch. That's because the U.S. Department of Labor (DOL) has an approved poster that you can download and use. We've provided copies of this poster, in both English and Spanish versions, in Appendix C and on the CD-ROM at the back of this book.

What Must Be Included in Your FMLA Poster

The poster must include the following information:

- Employees who have worked 1,250 hours and for at least one year are eligible for FMLA leave.
- Eligible employees are entitled to 12 weeks of unpaid leave.
- FMLA leave is job-protected leave.
- FMLA leave is available for certain family and medical reasons.
- The reasons for which employees can take FMLA leave (for example, for a serious health condition, for the birth of a child, etc.).
- Employees may be required or allowed to take certain types of FMLA leave as paid leave.
- What advance notice of leave is required from employees.
- Your company may require medical certification from the employee, including, possibly, second or third opinions.
- Certain benefits (such as health insurance) are protected.
- How benefits are protected (for example, by your company continuing employees' health coverage).
- What acts the FMLA bars your company from doing (for example, interfering with FMLA rights, discriminating against employees taking leave).
- Employees can complain to the DOL if they believe that your company has violated the FMLA.
- The contact information for the DOL.

(29 U.S.C. §2619(a); 29 C.F.R. §825.300(a).)

If a "significant portion" of your company's workforce doesn't speak English, the poster must be in the language in which those employees are literate. The family leave laws of some states may also require a poster written in the language in which a specific number or percentage of your company's employees are literate. Additionally, some states have additional posting requirements under their own family, medical, or pregnancy leave laws. For example, California requires employers covered by its family leave law to post a notice alerting employees to their rights under the FMLA, the state family leave law, and the state's pregnancy disability leave law.

TIP

Post the FMLA information in every language that your company's employees speak, including English. That way, you will not have to worry that some employees are not getting the required information.

SEE AN EXPERT

Get legal help with your posting requirements. Consult an attorney with expertise in the laws of every state in which your company employs workers to find out the state-specific poster requirements.

If your company doesn't post the general FMLA information discussed above, it can't deny leave, discipline, or take any action against an employee because the employee has not complied with FMLA requirements. And, the DOL could penalize your company $100 for each violation of the posting requirement. If your company's failure to post the FMLA information interferes with an employee's FMLA rights, the employee could sue the company.

EXAMPLE: Delia has worked for your company for two years. Your company doesn't post FMLA information, even though it is covered by the FMLA. Your company also has its own 16-week maternity leave policy. Delia gets pregnant and requests and takes the full 16 weeks of leave. When she tries to return to her original position after the leave ends, you tell her that you filled her position two weeks earlier because she hadn't returned within 12 weeks, which is all she is entitled to under the FMLA. Delia objects and says that the FMLA protects her right to return to her original job. You point out to Delia that the FMLA does provide for reinstatement, but only following leaves of up to 12 weeks. You tell Delia you have assigned her to a downgraded position. Delia threatens legal action. Should you be worried?

You should be quite worried! You were right about the FMLA protecting employee reinstatement rights only for the 12-week FMLA leave period (as discussed in Chapter 6). But, the FMLA information wasn't posted for Delia and other employees to see, your company effectively interfered with her FMLA rights.

Written FMLA Policies

Before any individual employee even asks for FMLA leave, your company must notify all employees of their FMLA rights. In addition to the FMLA poster discussed above, your company must include information about FMLA entitlements and employee obligations in its employee handbook, written personnel policies, or any other such document that describes "leave, wages, attendance, and similar matters." (29 C.F.R. § 825.301(a).)

The FMLA information that you have to include in these documents must accurately describe employees' FMLA rights and can't leave out any significant provision of the FMLA. The documents also have to include your company's own policies regarding FMLA leave. Make sure that your company's leave policies don't contradict the FMLA's terms.

EXAMPLE: Your company's employee handbook states that an employee needing leave must call in at least 30 minutes prior to the start of his or her shift. Jaye suffered a seizure that caused her to lose consciousness early one morning. She was scheduled to start work at 8:00 a.m. Because she was en route to the hospital and in the process of being admitted, she was unable to call until 9:30 a.m. Should you discipline Jaye for violating company policy?

Better not. The 30-minute call-in policy may violate the FMLA, because the FMLA allows employees to give notice of an unforeseeable need for leave "as soon as practicable" (see Chapter 7). Jaye was unable to call in until 9:30. You need to revise your company handbook to conform to the FMLA notice requirement.

If your company doesn't have an employee handbook or written policies, then you have to give a written description of FMLA rights and obligations to each employee who requests FMLA leave. We've included a sample FMLA general information form approved by the DOL in Appendix C and on the CD-ROM at the back of this book.

> **TIP**
>
> **Write up an FMLA policy.** Rather than giving general FMLA information to employees each time they ask for FMLA leave, it's better to create an FMLA policy and distribute it to every employee. Not only is this more efficient, but having a standard policy also ensures that you're giving each employee the same information.

Finally, if you do already have a policy, you'll want to make sure that it has all the information that's legally required. We've included a sample FMLA policy in Appendix B, which you can use to draft or modify your own company policy.

FMLA Information That Must Go in Your Company's Handbook or Policy

Your company's handbook or other written policies must describe the following about the FMLA:

- what is a serious health condition, with examples
- which family members an employee can take leave to care for (spouse, child, parent)
- the method of calculating FMLA leave, including how you calculate the leave year (discussed in Chapter 6)
- pregnancy leave procedures
- how an employee should request leave (for example, by using a particular form)
- that employees should request leave 30 days prior to the start of leave when the need for leave is foreseeable
- that employees should request leave as soon as practicable, if a leave his unforeseeable, which usually means within one or two business days
- the information the employee should provide when requesting leave (for example, a statement that the leave is needed for a serious health condition)
- what intermittent and reduced schedule leave means
- medical certification requirements
- any requirements that the employee provide information (such as medical status) during leave
- that FMLA leave is unpaid
- whether your company requires allows employees to take paid leave concurrently with FMLA leave
- your company's substance abuse policy, if one exists, providing for possible termination for violation even on FMLA leave
- return to work requirements, including fitness-for-duty certification, and
- company policies regarding continuation of nonhealth benefits (such as life insurance) during leave.

If your company fails to include FMLA information in its employee handbook or benefits policies or to provide the information to an employee requesting leave, it won't be able to take action against an employee who doesn't comply with the requirements of the FMLA or your company's own leave policies. And, it may be liable for interfering with employee FMLA rights in the same way we discussed in "Posting Requirements," above.

LESSONS FROM THE

Real World

An employer that didn't notify an employee in writing of his FMLA obligations couldn't argue that he didn't meet them.

Invacare Corporation employed Isaiah Taylor in its shipping department. Taylor requested leave to care for his wife after back surgery. His supervisor denied the leave, but Taylor took time off anyway and Invacare fired him. He sued Invacare for violating the FMLA.

Invacare argued that Taylor's need for leave was foreseeable and he'd failed to give 30 days' notice as the FMLA required. Taylor and a coworker testified that Invacare hadn't provided employees with FMLA notice information—including the requirement to provide 30 days' advance notice of foreseeable leave.

Taylor won the case because Invacare had failed to inform its employees of their obligations and rights under the FMLA. As a result, Invacare couldn't fire Taylor because he didn't give the notice required by the FMLA.

Taylor v. Invacare Corp., 64 Fed.Appx. 516 (6th Cir. 2003).

Your company's handbook or policies should include all company leave policies that interact with FMLA rights, such as attendance policies, notice requirements, and the like. We'll discuss these policies, and how they interact with the FMLA, in subsequent chapters.

Common Mistakes Regarding Employer Coverage— And How to Avoid Them

MISTAKE 1: Your company is covered by the FMLA, but no one knows it so managers deny leave to eligible employees.

AVOID THIS MISTAKE BY:

- Figuring out if your company is covered by the FMLA.
- Reevaluating FMLA coverage when there is a change in your company's workforce or structure, such as a merger or expansion.
- Counting all employees the FMLA requires (for example, employees on leave, part-time employees, and joint employees).
- Counting only those employees the FMLA requires you to count (for example, do not count independent contractors).

MISTAKE 2: Your company doesn't meet its obligations as a joint employer.

AVOID THIS MISTAKE BY:

- Keeping track of all workers who are "joint" employees of your company and another company, including all temps and any employees your company shares with a contractor or subcontractor.
- Figuring out whether your company is the primary or the secondary employer of joint employees.
- Fulfilling your company's responsibilities as a primary or secondary employer.

MISTAKE 3: Failing to give all employees general FMLA information.

AVOID THIS MISTAKE BY:

- Immediately posting the required FMLA notice in a conspicuous location at every worksite.
- Making sure that your company's employee handbook includes a detailed and accurate description of employee FMLA rights and duties (use the sample FMLA policy in Appendix B).
- Making sure that any written company benefits policies include a detailed and accurate description of employee FMLA rights and duties.

Is the Employee Covered by the FMLA?

CHAPTER HIGHLIGHTS

Employees are entitled to FMLA leave if they:

- work for your company at a worksite with 50 or more employees within a 75-mile radius

- have worked for your company for at least 12 months, and

- have worked at least 1,250 hours in the 12-month period preceding the leave.

You must determine whether there are 50 employees within 75 miles on the date the employee requests leave—not the date the employee's leave is scheduled to begin.

Time that counts towards the 1,250-hour minimum includes:

- any hours the employee worked, whether or not paid

- work-related travel time during the workday

- continuing education or other required work-related activities, and

- time spent on military leave.

These hours don't count towards the 1,250-hour minimum:

- time spent on suspension

- travel time from home to work, and

- time on leave other than for military service (unless your company counts leave time for overtime purposes).

You must carefully track employees' hours to determine eligibility; if you don't keep accurate records, the employee's records will be used to resolve eligibility disputes.

Now that you know that the FMLA applies to your company, it's time to figure out which employees the law protects. Not every employee who works for a covered employer is entitled to leave. An employee must have worked for your company for at least one year, and at least 1,250 hours during the preceding year, to be entitled to leave. In addition, your company must have at least 75 employees within a 50-mile radius of the employee's worksite.

Keeping all these numbers can get complicated. There are detailed rules on which hours count toward the minimum, how you measure the 75 miles, and when you make these determinations. And it's not a one-time calculation: An employee who was eligible for—and took—FMLA leave in the past might no longer qualify later; similarly, an employee who isn't entitled to FMLA leave today might become eligible sometime in the future. You'll have to decide whether an employee is entitled to FMLA leave on a case-by-case basis, every time an employee requests leave.

This chapter explains each part of the eligibility process: how to do the necessary calculations, how to track an employee's eligibility, and how to keep proper records that will allow you to quickly determine whether an employee meets these requirements.

Employee Eligibility, Step by Step

To be eligible for FMLA leave, an employee must:

- work at a worksite with 50 or more employees within a 75-mile radius
- have worked for your company for at least 12 months, and
- have worked at least 1,250 hours in the 12 months immediately preceding the leave.

If an employee doesn't meet all three of these requirements, the employee is not entitled to FMLA leave.

Step 1: Are There 50 Employees Within 75 Miles?

To figure out whether a specific employee is entitled to FMLA leave, you first need to figure out whether there are 50 or more employees at the employee's worksite or within a 75-mile radius of the worksite. If your company employs thousands of FMLA-eligible workers, but has several employees who work in a remote satellite office that's more than 75 miles from any other company worksite, the employees in the satellite office won't be entitled to FMLA leave.

TIP

Don't forget to count joint employees. When figuring out whether there are 50 employees within 75 miles of the employee's worksite, make sure to count all employees—including joint employees.

Measuring the 75-Mile Radius

If your company has a "campus" of buildings grouped together, they count as one worksite. Similarly, unconnected buildings used by your company within a reasonable geographic vicinity (for example, within the city limits) are considered a single worksite. This means that the 75-mile radius can be measured out from any of the related buildings: If there are 50 employees within 75 miles of any related building, all employees who work in one of the related buildings meet this part of the eligibility test.

EXAMPLE: Petra has worked full time at the Main Street outlet of your company, the Grande Baguette bakery chain, for the last four years. Grande Baguette employs 20 people at the Main Street outlet and another 20 people at another location in the city, the First Street outlet. It employs another 20 people at an outlet in a suburban mall that's 77 miles away from Petra's outlet but only 72 miles from the First Street store. Petra is pregnant and has requested leave to begin on the date of her scheduled C-section. Is Petra entitled to FMLA leave?

Yes. Even though there are only 20 employees at the Grande Baguette outlet where Petra works, the two city locations count as one worksite. There are 40 employees at the citywide worksite, and an additional 20 employees at the mall outlet. Because the mall outlet is within 75 miles of one of the city locations, those employees count when determining Petra's eligibility—even though they don't work within 75 miles of her actual worksite. Because there are 60 employees within 75 miles under the FMLA definition, Petra is eligible for leave.

To measure the 75-mile radius, you must use the shortest route on public streets, roads, highways, and waterways from the worksite. Although employees have tried to argue that the 75 miles should be measured "as the crow flies," courts have determined that this distance must be measured using actual routes that could be used between worksites.

When to Make Your Count

You must determine whether the company has the minimum number of employees at or within 75 miles of the employee's worksite on the day the employee requests leave, not the date the employee's leave will begin. If your company had the requisite number of employees on the day the employee requested leave, the employee has met this eligibility requirement, regardless of later reductions in your local workforce.

EXAMPLE: Your company has five stores in downtown Omaha, employing a total of 63 employees. Next month, it plans to close two stores that employ a total of 21 people; after those closures, the company will have only 42 employees. Ted works at one of the stores that will remain open. He asks his supervisor, Margo, for three weeks off beginning six weeks from now, to look after his mother following hip replacement surgery. Margo, who knows about the store closure plans, tells you she is going to deny FMLA leave because there will be only 42 employees when Ted's leave starts.

Fortunately, Margo speaks to you before making this mistake. You correctly point out that the company must determine whether this eligibility requirement is met on the date an employee requests leave, not the date leave is scheduled to begin. Because the company had more than 50 employees in the city at the time Ted made his FMLA request, he is entitled to leave as long as he meets the other eligibility requirements.

Determining Where an Employee Works

It's not hard to identify the employee's worksite when he or she works in the same cubicle every day. Figuring out the worksite for employees who travel or telecommute presents more of a challenge, however. For employees with no fixed company worksite, the worksite where the employee reports or where work is assigned to the employee is that employee's worksite for FMLA purposes. This is true even if the reporting worksite is temporary and the company's headquarters are many miles away.

EXAMPLE: You are the Human Resources Manager for Nice Catch, a company that owns several fishing vessels operating out of Dutch Harbor, Alaska. Nice Catch is headquartered in Anacortes, Washington. Nice Catch employs more than 75 workers on its boats in Dutch Harbor and assigns crews from its small dockside office there. In the Anacortes headquarters, Nice Catch employs 22 people. Nice Catch has never employed more than 25 employees in the Anacortes office at one time.

Maria works on a fishing boat out of Dutch Harbor and has requested leave to care for a baby that she and her partner are adopting. Richie is an accountant in the Anacortes office and has to have shoulder surgery to repair a torn rotator cuff, which has interfered with his ability to work. Assuming they meet the other eligibility requirements, are Maria and Richie entitled to FMLA leave?

Yes and no, respectively. Because the boat crews are assigned work out of the Dutch Harbor office, that's their worksite for purposes of calculating FMLA eligibility—even if their fishing boats operate hundreds of miles apart. So Maria works at a site with more than 75 employees, and she is entitled to leave. There are only 22 employees at Richie's worksite, however, so he isn't an eligible employee under the FMLA.

Step 2: Has the Employee Worked for the Company for 12 Months?

To be eligible for FMLA leave, an employee must have worked for your company for at least 12 months. These months need not be consecutive. An employee who has put in a total of 12 months meets this eligibility requirement, regardless of when the work took place.

EXAMPLE: Horacio works on one of your company's construction crews. He worked eight months for your company last year, from the beginning of April through the end of November, before he was laid off because of lack of work during the winter. The company rehired Horacio on April 1. On August 1, Horacio has a heart attack and takes several weeks off work for treatment and recovery. Has Horacio met the 12-month requirement for FMLA eligibility?

Yes. Although Horacio has only worked for your company in eight of the last 12 months, he has worked 12 months total: Eight months during his first stint with your company, and four months immediately before his heart attack. He has met this eligibility requirement.

When to Make Your Count

The employee must have worked the 12 months as of the date that he or she will start using FMLA leave, not as of the date the employee requests leave. Note that this is a different from the first eligibility requirement, discussed above: You must determine whether there are 50 employees within a 75-mile radius on the date the employee requests leave, not the date leave will start.

EXAMPLE: Anna began working for your company fulltime 11 months ago. Anna requests leave to undergo back surgery beginning in one month. Is Anna entitled to FMLA leave?

Yes, Anna is entitled to FMLA leave as of the date the leave will start. If she had gone out for back surgery after working for your company for 11 months and needed immediate time off to recuperate, she wouldn't be covered by the FMLA.

Which Time Counts

If an employee works at all during a week, that week counts toward the 12-month requirement. Unlike the hours worked requirement (discussed below), the 12-month requirement measures how long the employee has been with your company, not how many hours he or she has actually worked.

When determining whether an employee has worked at least 12 months, you should count every week in which the employee shows up on the payroll. It doesn't matter whether the employee works full time or part time, or whether the employee works intermittently (that is, the employee works some weeks and not others): Once the employee reaches 52 weeks on the payroll, the employee has met the requirement.

If you have joint employees—that is, employees who are employed both by your company and by another company (such as a temp agency)—count all of the weeks when they have been employed by either joint company. For example, if an employee of a temporary agency was placed with your company six months ago and worked for the temporary agency for a year before that, that employee has satisfied the 12-month employment requirement.

Time employees spend on leave counts towards the 12-month minimum only if:

- the employee took leave for military service (see Chapter 11 for more information), or

- your company provided compensation or benefits during the employee's leave.

EXAMPLE: Brett has worked full time for your company for one year but spent two months of that year on company-approved, paid disability leave. Brett now requests leave for a serious health condition. Is Brett entitled to FMLA leave?

Yes, because he has worked at least 12 months, including the paid leave time.

However, there are a couple of time periods that don't count toward the 12-month requirement. These include:

- **Suspensions.** If an employee was suspended, that suspension period doesn't count toward the 12 months.

- **Layoff periods.** If you lay off an employee and then recall that employee later, you don't usually count the layoff period when calculating whether the employee has worked for 12 months.

Step 3: Has the Employee Worked Enough Hours?

In addition to simply being employed with your company for at least 12 months, an employee seeking FMLA leave must have worked at least 1,250 hours in the 12-month period immediately preceding the leave. As with the 12-month requirement, you must calculate whether an employee has worked 1,250 hours as of the date leave is scheduled to begin—not the date the employee requests leave.

Which Hours Count

You must count every hour worked towards the 1,250-hour minimum. These include:

- hours worked for which the employee was not paid (for example, overtime hours worked by an employee exempt from receiving overtime pay)
- work-related travel time during the workday (for example, when an employee has to travel from his or her usual worksite to a meeting in another location; see 29 C.F.R. § 785)
- continuing education or other required work-related activities, and
- time spent on military leave (see Chapter 11).

The following hours don't count:

- time during which the employee was suspended
- time the employee spends traveling from home to office and back, unless:
  - your company has an agreement or practice of paying for such time (29 C.F.R. §785.35), or
  - state law treats such travel time as paid time under certain circumstances (for example, when the employee travels from home to a temporary worksite away from his or her usual worksite)
- time spent on leave other than military leave, unless your company counts leave time as "hours worked" for overtime pay purposes.

POLICY ALERT

Your company's overtime policies could determine whether employees are eligible for FMLA leave. As noted above, if your company counts leave time as hours worked in determining whether an employee has worked overtime, it must also count leave time towards an employee's total hours worked in the 12-month FMLA period. See Appendix B for more information on how your company's policies can affect its FMLA obligations.

LESSONS FROM THE

Real World

An employee who didn't actually work 1,250 hours in the preceding year is not entitled to FMLA leave, even if the employer granted it by mistake.

In May 1995, Jayson Sepe, a builder for McDonnell Douglas Corp., requested and was granted a 12-week leave in connection with the birth of his daughter. Because of medical leave Sepe had already taken in the last year, he had worked only 822 hours in the 12 months preceding his daughter's birth.

While on the May 1995 leave, Sepe worked for an excavating company he and his wife had started a few years earlier, in violation of McDonnell Douglas's policy prohibiting employees from working while on leave. McDonnell Douglas fired Sepe for violating the policy.

Sepe sued the company for, among other things, violating the FMLA. Sepe argued that McDonnell Douglas could not challenge his eligibility after (mistakenly) granting his request for FMLA leave. The court disagreed. Because Sepe had not worked the required 1,250 hours in the 12 months prior to requesting leave, he was not qualified for FMLA protection from termination.

Sepe v. McDonnell Douglas Corp. (8th Cir. 1999) 176 F.3d 1113.

If Intermittent FMLA Leave Reduces an Employee's Hours

Sometimes, an employee seeking FMLA leave needs occasional days or hours (rather than whole weeks) off or reduced work hours (for example, from full time to part time). The employee may be entitled to intermittent or reduced-schedule leave under the FMLA. Chapter 6 covers reduced schedule and intermittent leave in detail.

An unintended consequence of taking leave this way can be that the employee's hours fall below the 1,250-hour minimum. But you can't deny FMLA leave as a result: As long as the employee still needs the reduced schedule for the same condition that necessitated FMLA leave in the first place, the employee remains eligible.

EXAMPLE: Though her regular schedule requires her to work 25 hours per week, Yvonne has been on an FMLA-qualified reduced schedule of ten hours per week for the past 12 weeks. Yvonne notifies you that she needs to continue her reduced schedule. She has all the necessary paperwork and has not used up all her FMLA leave time.

In preparation for meeting with Yvonne, you count up her hours for the past 12 months. Because of her reduced schedule, Yvonne has worked less than 1,250 hours in the last 12 months. Can you deny Yvonne's request for a continued reduced schedule?

No. As long as Yvonne was qualified when she started leave and needs the reduced schedule for the same condition, she has a right to take the full 12 weeks of leave, as calculated for a part-time employee (discussed in Chapter 6).

The rules are different if an employee needs FMLA leave for a different condition. In this situation, you must redetermine the employee's eligibility. If the employee's previous intermittent leave has reduced the employee's hours below the 1,250-hour threshold, the employee is not eligible for leave for an unrelated condition.

EXAMPLE: Let's go back to Yvonne, whose regular work schedule calls for 25 hours a week, but who has been working only ten hours a week for the last three months. Yvonne needed this intermittent leave to care for her father, who had a serious health condition. Yvonne's father is on the mend, but now Yvonne requests two weeks of FMLA leave so she can have knee surgery. Is she entitled to this leave?

No. In the last 12 months, Yvonne has worked 10 hours a week for 12 weeks (120 hours), plus 25 hours a week for 40 weeks (1,000 hours), for a grand total of 1,120 hours. If she needed to stay on her reduced-leave schedule to continue caring for her father, she would still be entitled to FMLA leave. Because she wants leave for an unrelated condition, however, you must recalculate her hours—and she hasn't met the 1,250-hour threshold for FMLA eligibility.

Keeping Track of Employees' Work Hours

Because employees' eligibility for FMLA leave depends on how long they've worked for the company and how many hours they've worked, you must keep track of all employees' work hours. After all, an employee's eligibility can change over time. A newly hired full-time employee, for example, won't be eligible until he or she has worked for the company for at least 12 months. After a year, however, the employee may be eligible.

And it's not just that employees who weren't eligible can become eligible in the future: An employee who qualified for FMLA leave in the past may no longer be eligible later. Maybe the employee hasn't worked enough hours in the previous year or has already used up all his or her FMLA leave.

To make sure that an employee who requests leave is actually entitled to it, keep good records of actual hours worked—and leave taken—for all of your company's employees. If your company's records and/or a compensation agreement with the employee don't accurately reflect actual hours worked, the actual hours (as shown by the employee's records, calendars, and so on, or by other employees' recollections) will be used to determine eligibility. Even unpaid time worked by an employee (for example, overtime worked by an exempt employee not entitled to overtime pay) counts toward the 1,250-hour requirement, so it is important to keep thorough records of all time employees actually work, whether paid or not.

Most payroll systems provide a running total of hours worked by employees, so you may already have adequate records of hours worked. If your company keeps time sheets or requires employees to punch a time clock, these records may provide all the documentation you need.

If you don't have some readily available source of documentation, the best practice is to keep a separate chart of hours worked for each employee. This isn't as complicated as it sounds. You can create a simple spreadsheet, like the one below, and update each employee's hours at the end of each pay period. If you have a payroll system, you may even be able to export those numbers directly. There is a blank copy of the form for your use in Appendix C and on the CD-ROM at the back of this book.

SAMPLE	FMLA Hours Worked			
	EMPLOYEE NAME	START DATE	HOURS WORKED IN THE 12 MONTHS PRIOR TO REQUESTED LEAVE	DATES FMLA LEAVE TAKEN
	Employee A	1/14/05	3,000	3/22/06 – 5/10/06

SAMPLE	FMLA Hours Worked			
	EMPLOYEE NAME	START DATE	HOURS WORKED IN THE 12 MONTHS PRIOR TO REQUESTED LEAVE	DATES FMLA LEAVE TAKEN
	Employee B	4/25/07	300	Not eligible

Don't forget to track hours worked by employees who aren't entitled to earn overtime pay (called "exempt employees"). Many companies don't routinely record hours worked by exempt employees. After all, these employees are not typically paid by the hour, but instead must put in as many hours as it takes to get the job done.

Unless you have records showing the actual hours worked by exempt employees, however, you must assume that they have worked the required 1,250 hours as long as they've been employed for 12 months. You may also need to know the exact hours worked by an exempt employee if he or she wants to take intermittent or reduced-schedule leave. This type of leave is calculated as a reduction in the hours or days the employee typically works, so you can't figure out how much FMLA intermittent or reduced-schedule leave time an exempt employee is entitled to unless you know how many hours the employee has worked.

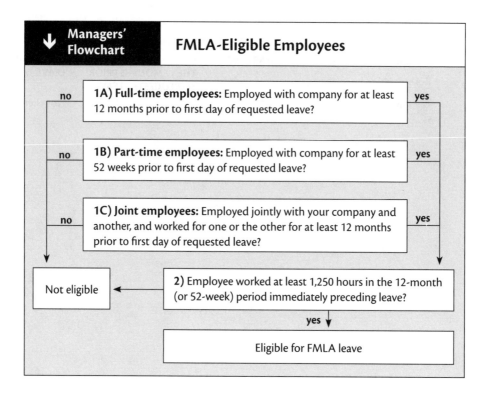

> **TIP**
>
> **Tracking exempt employees' hours won't change their exempt status.** One of the cardinal rules of wage and hour law is to avoid treating exempt employees like nonexempt employees. For example, if you dock an exempt employee's pay for showing up an hour late, you are treating that employee like an hourly worker—and the Department of Labor may require you to pay overtime to that employee and others who hold the same position. When it comes to tracking hours for FMLA purposes, however, you don't have to worry: You can keep records of an exempt employee's hours without inadvertently changing that employee's exemption status.

Common Mistakes Regarding Employee Coverage— And How to Avoid Them

MISTAKE 1: Denying FMLA leave to employees who are eligible, or granting it to those who are not eligible, because work hours aren't properly documented.

AVOID THIS MISTAKE BY:

- Keeping accurate records of employee work hours, including all time that counts towards the FMLA 1,250-hour minimum (military leave, hours for which the employee is not paid, and so on).
- Tracking hours for exempt employees, even if you don't do so for any other purpose.
- Creating a chart that keeps a running total of each employee's hours that count towards FMLA eligibility, if your company doesn't have other records you can use for this purpose.

MISTAKE 2: Misjudging an employee's eligibility by calculating company size, months worked, and hours worked at the wrong time.

AVOID THIS MISTAKE BY:

- Calculating whether the employee works within a 75-mile radius of at least 50 employees on the date the employee requests leave, not the date the employee's leave is scheduled to begin.

- Computing the months and hours worked by an employee requesting FMLA leave as of the date the requested leave will start, not the date the employee requests leave.

MISTAKE 3: Miscalculating how many months an employee has worked.

AVOID THIS MISTAKE BY:

- Counting any week in which the employee showed up on your company's payroll as a week worked.

- Counting all months worked towards an employee's 12-month minimum; these months don't have to be consecutive.

- Counting time the employee spent on leave as time worked if your company paid compensation or provided benefits during the leave or the employee was on military leave.

MISTAKE 4: Miscounting hours worked.

AVOID THIS MISTAKE BY:

- Including all hours that count towards FMLA eligibility, including unpaid hours worked, compensable travel time, and time spent in continuing education.

- Excluding time spent on leave unless the employee was on military leave or your company counts leave time as hours worked for overtime purposes.

- Allowing employees whose hours have dropped below the minimum required due to intermittent leave to continue taking leave for the same condition; if the employee needs leave for a new condition, you must redetermine the employee's eligibility.

| ✓ | Managers' Checklist | **Is the Employee Eligible for FMLA Leave?** |

❑ There are 50 or more employees working within 75 miles of the leave-seeking employee's worksite.

    ❑ I counted telecommuting or other employees not physically present at the worksite where they report or where they receive work assignments.

    ❑ I measured the 75-mile radius based on the most direct surface travel routes, like roads, highways, and waterways.

    ❑ I counted all buildings within a reasonable geographic vicinity as a single worksite and measured the 75-mile radius from those buildings.

❑ The employee worked for the company for at least 12 months (or 52 weeks) prior to the first day of the requested leave.

    ❑ I counted the employee as working in any week when the employee was on company payroll, even if the employee worked intermittently or part time.

    ❑ I counted the employee as working in any week when the employee was on leave and getting pay or benefits from my company.

    ❑ I did not count the employee as working in any week when the employee was suspended or should otherwise have been working but wasn't.

❑ Company records show that the employee worked at least 1,250 hours in the 12 months prior to the first day of the requested leave.

    ❑ I counted only the hours that the employee actually worked, whether paid or not.

    ❑ Because my company does not count time on leave when calculating hours for overtime pay purposes, I did not count any hours that the employee was on leave.

Leave for a Serious Health Condition

CHAPTER HIGHLIGHTS

The FMLA allows an eligible employee to take time off for his or her own serious health conditions or to care for a family member who has a serious health condition.

It's not your responsibility to diagnose employees—you just have to know enough about what qualifies as a "serious health condition" to realize when an employee requests or takes time off that might qualify for FMLA protection.

There are six categories of serious health conditions:

- inpatient care
- incapacity for more than three days with continuing treatment by a health care provider
- incapacity relating to pregnancy or prenatal care
- chronic serious health conditions
- permanent or long-term incapacity, and
- certain kinds of conditions requiring multiple treatments.

To take time off for his or her own serious health condition, an employee must be unable to perform the functions of his or her job.

An employee may take time off to care for a spouse, parent, or child with a serious health condition; in-laws, domestic partners, siblings, grandparents, and other family members don't count under the FMLA (but may under state law).

An employee is caring for a family member when the employee provides physical or psychological care, arranges for care or changes in care, provides necessary transportation, or fills in for other care providers.

E ligible employees are entitled to take FMLA leave for their own serious health conditions or to care for a family member with a serious health condition. Sounds simple enough, right? In the real world, however, this has proven to be a fairly complicated standard to apply. Most of the controversy involves the definition of a serious health condition: which illnesses or conditions qualify, how long an employee has to be incapacitated to be eligible for leave, in what situations a minor problem might turn into a "serious" condition, and so on.

This chapter will help you untangle these complications and understand what qualifies as a serious health condition. We'll explain the definitions and eligibility criteria, and we'll provide checklists and charts that will help you sort through the issues and figure out whether an employee might qualify for this type of FMLA leave.

Your Role in Identifying a Serious Health Condition

After learning that an employee's (or family member's) health condition must be serious—and that there's a complex legal definition for that word—before an employee can take FMLA leave, some managers start to worry. After all, most managers aren't doctors, and their job responsibilities don't include diagnosing employees, let alone their family members. Is every manager going to have to learn how to read x-rays and lab results just to administer the FMLA?

Happily, the answer is no. It's not your job to decide whether an employee really does have a serious health condition—that's a job for doctors and other health care providers. You simply have to know enough about how the FMLA defines a serious health condition to recognize when an employee asks for or takes time off for what might be an FMLA-protected reason. If the FMLA applies, you'll need to give the employee required notices (see Chapter 7), formally designate the time off as FMLA leave (also covered in Chapter 7), and ask the employee to provide a medical certification from a health care provider confirming that the leave is for a serious health condition (see Chapter 8). But you'll only know that it's time to start this process if you're familiar enough with the categories of serious health condition to recognize that the FMLA might be in play when an employee needs time off for health reasons.

EXAMPLE: Cari tells you that she is pregnant. After congratulations and small talk, Cari says she has been having severe morning sickness and might need to take some time off—or, at least, come in late when she's really feeling crummy. Because you're reading this book, you immediately realize that the time off Cari is requesting could be FMLA-protected. Should your next step be to question Cari closely about her symptoms, so you can decide whether she is truly incapacitated by her morning sickness?

No. You don't have the right to insist that Cari discuss this type of personal health information with you. (It could even be illegal under the laws of some states.) Instead, you should give Cari the required notices and paperwork to designate her time off as FMLA leave and ask her to provide a medical certification from her health care provider.

This doesn't mean that you have to blindly accept whatever the employee and his or her health care provider tell you, however. If, based on the information you receive, you question whether the employee (or family member) really has a serious health condition, you can request a second opinion (Chapter 8 explains how).

TIP

When an employee takes sick leave, workers' compensation leave, disability leave, or leave to care for a family member, always ask yourself whether the FMLA applies. An employee doesn't have to specifically request "FMLA" leave to be protected by the law: As long as the employee is eligible and takes time off for a covered reason, the FMLA applies and you should designate the time as FMLA leave. Chapter 7 explains how much information an employee has to provide and how to designate leave; for now, just remember that an employee who is taking another type of leave might also covered by the FMLA.

What Is a Serious Health Condition?

To qualify for FMLA leave, an employee—or his or her family member, if the employee wants leave to care for someone else—must have a serious health condition. To be eligible, the employee or family member must have an illness, injury, impairment, or physical or mental condition that involves:

- **inpatient care** at a hospital, hospice, or residential medical care facility
- **incapacity for more than three calendar days** with continuing treatment by a health care provider
- incapacity due to **pregnancy or prenatal care**
- incapacity or treatment for a **chronic serious health condition**
- **permanent or long-term incapacity** for a condition for which treatment may not be effective (such as a terminal illness), or
- absence for **multiple treatments** for either restorative surgery following an injury or accident, or a condition that would require an absence of more than three days if not treated.

Multiple and Undiagnosed Conditions Count

The FMLA applies to ailments for which health care providers have been unable to offer a definitive diagnosis, as well as to incapacitation that is caused by multiple ailments. As long as the condition meets the definition of one of the categories described above, it's a serious health condition—even if it doesn't (or doesn't yet) have a name.

Inpatient Care

This is probably the easiest category to recognize as a serious health condition. A condition that involves inpatient care—in other words, an overnight stay—at a hospital, hospice, or residential medical care facility qualifies as a serious health condition covered by the FMLA. An employee is entitled to FMLA leave for the actual time the employee (or his or her family member) is receiving inpatient care and for any period of incapacity or subsequent treatment connected to that inpatient care.

A person is incapacitated by a serious medical condition if he or she is unable to work, attend school, or perform other regular daily activities due to the condition, treatment for the condition, or recovery from the condition. This means, for example, that an employee who was hospitalized for an appendectomy would be entitled to FMLA leave not only for the period of time spent in the hospital before, during, and after the operation, but also for time spent at home recuperating from the procedure.

Follow-up treatment after an inpatient stay is also protected. For example, if a person was hospitalized for surgery, return visits to the doctor for post-operative care would also be covered under the FMLA. The person doesn't have to be incapacitated by the treatment or be out for more than three days: As long as the subsequent treatment is connected to the condition requiring inpatient care, it's covered.

EXAMPLE: Jesse takes a nasty fall while cleaning the gutters on his roof and suffers a major concussion. He goes the emergency room, where they keep him overnight for observation. He spends the next day at home resting, then returns to work. By midmorning, he has a crashing headache. He calls his doctor, who advises him to come in immediately to be checked for complications. All of Jesse's time off—in the hospital, at home, and at the doctor's office—is covered by the FMLA.

If Jesse had never suffered a concussion but simply got a bad headache at work and decided to go to the doctor, his time off might not be FMLA-protected. Because it isn't subsequent treatment following an inpatient stay, it doesn't qualify as this type of serious health condition. Depending on what the medical cause is, how long the problem lasts, and what type of treatment he gets, however, it might fall into one of the other categories of serious health conditions.

Incapacity for More Than Three Days Plus Continuing Treatment

Someone who is incapacitated for more than three days *and* requires continuing treatment from a health care provider also has a serious health condition under the FMLA. This category of serious health condition has been the most difficult for employers to understand and administer, and it's easy to see why. It covers a lot of grey areas, because it marks the dividing line between minor ailments such as colds and stomachaches (which are usually not covered by the FMLA—see "Conditions That Are Not Typically

Covered," below) and more serious problems that are obviously protected (like a terminal illness or required surgery).

To figure out whether an ailment fits into this category, you must understand how to measure the three-day requirement, who qualifies as a health care provider, and what constitutes continuing treatment.

The Three-Day Requirement

To qualify under this category, the employee (or employee's family member) must be incapacitated for *more* than three consecutive days. These three days must be consecutive, but they need not be business days: An employee who is incapacitated for Friday through Monday would qualify, for example.

It's not entirely clear what constitutes "more than" three days. Some courts have found that an employee must be incapacitated for at least four days to qualify; others have found that an employee who is sick for any more than 72 hours is covered. Because of this confusion, the best practice is to assume that an employee who is incapacitated for more than 72 hours is covered.

Who Is a Health Care Provider?

Health care providers are defined quite broadly by the FMLA. They include not only medical doctors, but also:

- doctors of osteopathy
- podiatrists
- dentists
- optometrists
- chiropractors (only for manual manipulation of the spine to treat a subluxation of the spine—that is, misalignment of vertebrae—identified by x-ray)
- clinical psychologists
- nurse providers
- nurse midwives
- clinical social workers, and
- Christian Science providers.

(See 29 CFR § 825.118.)

Health care providers who practice outside of the United States also qualify, as long as they are authorized to practice within the laws of the country where they work and the services they provide are within the scope of that authorized practice.

Finally, any health care provider from whom the employer or the employer's group health plan will accept certification of a serious health condition for purposes of substantiating a claim for health care benefits also qualifies. In other words, if your company treats someone as a health care provider for purposes of allowing or disallowing benefits claims, it must treat that person as a health care provider under the FMLA.

EXAMPLE: Your company's health care plan accepts certifications from chiropractors documenting a wide variety of employee injuries and ailments, including repetitive stress disorders, spinal problems, and neck injuries. Steven sees his chiropractor for pain in his wrists and forearms. After performing a series of tests and physical manipulations, the chiropractor determines that Steven has carpal tunnel syndrome. The chiropractor gives Steven some exercises, provides him with braces to wear, and advises him not to do any typing or other activities that will cause strain for three weeks.

Steven asks for FMLA leave and gives you a medical certification from his chiropractor. Because Steven's chiropractor didn't take any x-rays and isn't treating Steven for subluxation of the spine, you intend to tell Steven that he has to get a medical certification from a different type of health care provider.

But wait—your company's health care plan accepts certifications from chiropractors not just regarding subluxation of the spine, but on a broader variety of conditions and ailments. As a result, Steven's chiropractor qualifies as a health care provider under the FMLA, even though he doesn't meet the usual criteria for chiropractors. If you question whether Steven's condition qualifies as a serious health condition, you are free to request a second opinion (as explained in Chapter 8).

How Much Treatment Is Required

An employee who's out sick for more than three days does not necessarily have a serious health condition under the FMLA. To qualify in this category, the employee's (or family member's) condition must also involve continuing treatment by a health care provider.

Because "continuing treatment" is open to some interpretation, the FMLA's regulations define it as either:

- at least two treatments by a health care provider; nurse or physician's assistant acting under the direct supervision of a health care provider; or provider of health care services acting on the orders of, or referral by, a health care provider, or

- at least one treatment by a health care provider that results in a regimen of continuing treatment under the provider's supervision.

"Treatment" means an actual visit to the health care provider—not a telephone consultation. It includes examinations to determine if a serious health condition exists, evaluations of that condition, and actual treatment to cure or alleviate the condition.

LESSONS FROM THE
Real World

Leave necessary to determine that a condition isn't serious might be FMLA-protected.

James Woodman was a truck driver for Miesel Sysco Food Services. When Woodman suffered chest pains, he went to his doctor, who recommended a series of tests to determine their source and whether Woodman had suffered a heart attack. The doctor also recommended that Woodman take time off until the problem was diagnosed.

Ultimately, the tests showed that Woodman had not suffered a heart attack. His celebration was short-lived, however: Shortly thereafter, the company fired him for taking unauthorized leave. Because he didn't have a heart attack, the company said, he also didn't have a serious health condition, so his absence wasn't covered by the FMLA.

The Michigan Court of Appeals disagreed with the company's conclusion, however. The FMLA's definition of treatment includes examinations to determine whether a serious health condition exists—precisely what Woodson required, as determined by his doctor.

Woodman v. Miesel Sysco Food Service Co., 8 W & H 2d 619 (Mich. Ct. Apps 2002).

A continuing regimen of treatment refers only to treatments that require the participation of a health care provider. For example, taking prescription medications or engaging in therapies that require special equipment (such as an oxygen tank) qualify as a regimen of continuing treatment. However, taking over-the-counter medications or staying in bed does not—even if that's just what the doctor ordered—because you could have made these decisions on your own.

EXAMPLE 1: John has a sore throat, stuffy nose, and cough. He calls his HMO's advice line to find out whether he should see a doctor. The nurse provider who answers his call tells him that there's a nasty cold going around and that he should stay in bed and drink lots of water—there's no need to come in. John doesn't have a serious health condition under the FMLA—he didn't visit the doctor at all, and he isn't following a continuing regimen of treatment.

EXAMPLE 2: Consuela has the same symptoms as John and goes home sick late Tuesday morning. Her symptoms worsen, and she decides to visit her doctor on Thursday. The doctor finds that she has strep throat and prescribes a ten-day course of antibiotics. Consuela is down for the count until Saturday evening, when she starts to feel better. Consuela has a serious health condition: She was incapacitated for more than three days, visited her doctor once, and had a continuing regimen of treatment.

EXAMPLE 3: Because most of her employees have been sick, Marta finally comes down with the dreaded bug. Marta had several bouts with pneumonia as a child, so she goes to her doctor as soon as she realizes that she's sick. The doctor finds that she doesn't yet have pneumonia, but he also doesn't like the way her lungs sound. Marta doesn't want to take antibiotics unless it's absolutely necessary, so her doctor asks her to come back for a follow-up appointment in several days to make sure her lungs have cleared up. At the second visit, Marta sounds fine; she returns to work after four days off. Marta has a serious health condition. She was incapacitated for more than three days, and she made two visits to the doctor.

Pregnancy or Prenatal Care

Incapacity due to pregnancy or for prenatal care qualifies as a serious health condition. The employee need not be out for more than three days nor actually visit a doctor to fall into this category—as long as she is unable to work or perform other regular, daily activities because of her pregnancy, she has a serious health condition. So, for example, a woman who suffers severe morning sickness or is ordered by her doctor to spend the last month of her pregnancy on bed rest qualifies under this part of the definition.

Visits to the doctor for prenatal care also fall within this category. The woman need not be incapacitated or suffering from medical complications to qualify; even routine check-ups qualify for leave.

Chronic Serious Health Condition

Chronic serious health conditions are also covered by the FMLA. A chronic serious health condition:

- requires periodic visits for treatment
- continues over an extended period of time, and
- may cause episodic, rather than continuing, incapacity.

These conditions needn't cause incapacity for more than three days, nor must they involve continuing treatment. Instead, this category is intended to encompass long-lasting conditions that require ongoing management and treatment, such as diabetes, epilepsy, or asthma.

EXAMPLE: Raymond has multiple sclerosis (MS), a disease of the central nervous system that can cause loss of vision, extreme fatigue, muscle weakness, loss of coordination, and other neurological problems. He is generally able to care for himself and work, with the help of a cane to walk steadily and medications to control his symptoms. On occasion, however, his symptoms become more severe and confine him to his bed. Raymond's daughter, Cheryl, requests time off to care for her father when his symptoms become exacerbated. Is her leave protected by the FMLA?

Most likely, assuming she met the requirements for caring for a family member (discussed below). Because Raymond's MS requires periodic treatment, is a permanent condition, and causes episodic incapacity, it qualifies as a chronic serious health condition.

Some mental conditions—such as major depression and bipolar disorder—might also qualify under this part of the definition. Often, these conditions are long-term, episodic, and require ongoing treatment but can be largely controlled with medication. Again, you won't have to make the final call—you'll just need to recognize the possibility when the employee requests leave.

Permanent or Long-Term Incapacity

Someone who is incapacitated permanently or for the long term by a condition that is not necessarily amenable to treatment has a serious health condition, as long as he or she is under the supervision of a health care provider. Actual treatment is not required to qualify under this part of the definition; it is enough that the person's care is supervised by a health care provider.

Examples of conditions that might fall into this category are Alzheimer's disease, terminal cancer, or advanced amyotrophic lateral sclerosis (also known as ALS or Lou Gehrig's disease).

Multiple Treatments

Someone who is absent for multiple treatments has a serious health condition if the treatments are for

- restorative surgery after an accident or injury, or
- a condition that would require an absence of more than three days if not treated.

Examples of conditions that might qualify in the first subcategory include surgery to reset a broken limb or repair a torn ligament. The second subcategory includes treatments for severe arthritis, dialysis for kidney disease, and cancer treatment. (Of course, cancer might qualify as a serious health condition under other categories as well—for example, if hospitalization and/or surgery were required.)

EXAMPLE: Geri has been diagnosed with breast cancer. She had a lumpectomy and is undergoing chemotherapy. Every Tuesday afternoon, she goes in for treatment. The treatment takes several hours, and she often feels too nauseated to return to work afterward. As her therapy progresses, her reaction to the treatment becomes more severe; she sometimes has to take all or part of Wednesday off, and sometimes she even feels sick Monday afternoon and Tuesday morning, in anticipation of her treatment. All of this time—the time she actually spends getting chemotherapy and the time during which she is incapacitated by her treatment—is FMLA-protected leave.

Conditions That Are Not Typically Covered

The FMLA does not create hard-and-fast rules that particular illnesses or diseases are always, or never, serious health conditions. Instead, the facts of each situation are considered individually. After all, one person might breeze through a bout of bronchitis without missing more than a day of work; another with the same illness might have to be hospitalized for complications. In this situation, the first person would not have a serious health condition, but the second would.

Nevertheless, there are certain ailments that don't typically qualify as serious health conditions. These include:

- cosmetic treatments (other than for restorative purposes) unless complications arise or inpatient care is required
- colds and flu
- ear aches
- upset stomachs and minor ulcers
- headaches other than migraines, and
- routine dental or orthodontic problems or periodontal disease.

This doesn't mean you can automatically exclude these conditions from FMLA coverage. Again, it depends on the facts. One person's headache might be the result of eye strain or sinus congestion; another's might be a symptom of a brain tumor. Breast enhancement plastic surgery would not be covered if it is purely cosmetic; reconstructive surgery after a mastectomy or breast reduction surgery necessary to relieve severe back pain, on the other hand, is likely covered.

Substance Abuse

Substance abuse may qualify as a serious health condition, if it meets one of the definitions described above. However, the employee may not take FMLA-protected leave for the effects of substance abuse (for example, because the employee is using drugs or hung over). The company is required to provide FMLA leave for treatment only.

An employee who takes FMLA leave while getting treatment for substance abuse may not be fired solely for taking FMLA leave; that would violate the law. However, if the employer has an established, communicated policy providing that employees may be fired for substance abuse, and it applies the policy consistently to all employees, it may fire an employee for substance abuse—even if the employee is out on FMLA leave while seeking treatment. In other words, the simple fact that an employee is using the FMLA may not protect that employee from termination for substance abuse, depending on the employer's policies.

 POLICY ALERT

If your company has a policy of terminating employment for substance abuse, the FMLA doesn't prevent you from enforcing it. If your company has an established, communicated policy that employees may be fired for substance abuse and applies it consistently to all employees, the company may rely on that policy to fire an employee who is on FMLA leave while seeking treatment.

Is It a Serious Health Condition?

CATEGORY	REQUIREMENTS	EXAMPLES
Inpatient treatment	Overnight stay in a hospital, hospice, or residential medical care facility	Inpatient surgery Hospitalization Overnight hospital stay for observation
Incapacity for more than 3 days and continuing treatment	Incapacity for more than three days and either: • at least two visits to a health care provider, or • one visit to a health care provider and an ongoing regimen of treatment	Pneumonia Migraine Chicken pox Mononucleosis Viral infection
Pregnancy/prenatal care	Incapacity due to pregnancy or prenatal care	Severe morning sickness Doctor's appointments for prenatal care, including OB-GYN visits, sonograms, visits or treatment for complications of pregnancy Medically required bed rest
Chronic serious health conditions	Condition that: • requires periodic visits for treatment • continues over an extended period of time, and • may cause episodic, rather than continuing, incapacity.	Epilepsy Asthma Diabetes Multiple sclerosis Sickle cell anemia
Permanent/long-term incapacity	Permanent or long-term incapacity, under the supervision of a health care provider	Cancer Alzheimer's disease Stroke ALS
Multiple treatments	Treatments for: • restorative surgery after an accident or injury, or • a condition that would require an absence of more than three days if not treated.	Arthritis treatment Dialysis Chemotherapy Radiation therapy Surgery to reset a broken bone, repair a torn ligament, or treat burns

Leave for Employee's Own Serious Health Condition

When an employee takes time off for his or her own serious health condition, an additional qualification applies: The employee must not only have a serious health condition as defined above, but must also be unable to perform the functions of his or her job.

An employee is unable to perform the functions of the position if the employee cannot work at all or cannot perform one or more of the essential functions of the job, as defined by the Americans With Disabilities Act (ADA). Under the ADA, essential functions are the fundamental duties of the position—those things that the person holding the job absolutely must be able to do.

It can be tough to figure out which job duties are essential, unless you already have a job description that designates the essential functions of the position. If you don't, you'll need to consider which functions are absolutely necessary to doing the job successfully and which are not.

 RESOURCE

Need help drafting job descriptions? For detailed guidance on identifying a job's essential functions and using them to create a legal, effective job description, see *The Job Description Handbook*, by Margie Mader-Clark (Nolo).

The Equal Employment Opportunity Commission (EEOC), the federal agency that enforces the ADA, looks at these factors in determining whether a function is essential:

- the employer's own assessment of which functions are essential, as demonstrated by job descriptions written before the employer posts or advertises for the position (this caveat is intended to discourage employers from designating essential functions solely to disqualify particular applicants with disabilities from holding the job)
- whether the position exists to perform that function
- the experience of workers who actually hold that position
- the time spent performing that function

- the consequences of not performing that function
- whether other employees are available to perform that function, and
- the degree of expertise or skill required to perform the function.

 TIP

An employee on intermittent or reduced-schedule leave must be able to perform the essential functions of the job. The FMLA permits eligible employees to take intermittent or reduced-schedule leave when medically necessary. Unlike employees on full-time leave, employees taking this type of leave must be able to perform the essential functions of their jobs because they'll still be working. Chapter 6 discusses this in greater detail.

If an employee must be out of work to receive treatment for a serious health condition (for example, for prenatal care, required surgery, or a doctor's appointment for follow-up care), the employee is considered unable to work for that period of time.

EXAMPLE: Clara tore a ligament in her leg while playing soccer. She had surgery to repair the ligament, and her doctor told her not to walk much on that leg for several weeks. Clara is a receptionist for a large company. Her job involves greeting visitors, answering phones, receiving packages and mail, and so on. Because Clara can perform the essential functions of her job while seated at her desk, she probably isn't eligible to take several weeks off under the FMLA. Although the time she actually spends in surgery and follow-up care would be covered, the weeks of recovery would not.

If Clara's job duties required her to walk around the building—for example, to collect or deliver mail, get refreshments for visitors, and so on—the company would have to decide whether these are essential duties or not, using the criteria listed above. If Clara held a much more physical job (for example, if she worked as a bike messenger or a laborer in a warehouse), she would clearly be unable to perform her job's essential duties and would be entitled to FMLA leave.

CROSS-REFERENCE

Other laws may apply. An employee's serious health condition might also qualify as a disability under the Americans With Disabilities Act (ADA) and similar state law, and/or it might be the result of an on-the-job injury that's covered by workers' compensation. Chapter 11 explains what these laws require and how they might overlap with the FMLA.

Leave for a Family Member's Serious Health Condition

An employee is also entitled to take leave to care for a family member who has a serious health condition, as defined above. To figure out whether an employee qualifies for this type of leave, however, you must also understand which family members are covered by the law and how the FMLA defines "caring for" a family member.

Who Is a Family Member Under the FMLA

An employee may take time off to care for a spouse, child, or parent with a serious health condition. Here is how the FMLA defines each of these terms (see 29 C.F.R. § 825.113):

- **Spouse.** A spouse is a husband or wife to whom the employee is legally married—domestic partners or live-in partners aren't covered. In the handful of states that recognize common-law marriage, a couple that meets the state's requirements may take FMLA leave to care for each other. However, same-sex couples are not entitled to take FMLA leave to care for each other, even if legally married in Massachusetts (the only state that currently recognizes same-sex marriage) or in a country that allows same-sex couples to wed.

CAUTION

The FMLA doesn't cover domestic partners, but state law might. Some states' family and medical leave laws include more family members. For example, the California Family Rights Act (CFRA) allows employees to take time off to care for a domestic partner. Consider both the FMLA and your state's law when evaluating an employee's request for leave. Chapter 11 and Appendix A cover this issue in more detail.

- **Child.** An employee may take FMLA leave to care for his or her biological child, adopted child, stepchild, foster child, or legal ward. An employee may also take time off to care for a child whom the employee has the day-to-day responsibility to care for and support financially, even if the employee does not have a legally recognized relationship with that child. (In legal terms, this is called serving "in loco parentis," or in the place of a parent.) Children are covered only until they reach the age of 18, unless they are incapable of taking care of themselves because of a physical or mental disability.

EXAMPLE: Sarah's sister, Francis, is a single mother. After being convicted of selling drugs, Francis was sentenced to three years in prison. While Francis is serving her time, Sarah is taking care of Francis's son, Terry. Terry gets the measles, and Sarah asks for FMLA leave to care for him. Because Sarah is Terry's aunt, and nephews aren't covered by the FMLA, you deny her request. Did you do the right thing?

Nope. Although Sarah is Terry's aunt, she is also acting as his legal guardian and parent while Francis is in prison. This relationship is covered by the FMLA.

- **Parent.** An employee may take FMLA leave to care for his or her legal parent or for someone who served in loco parentis when the employee was a child. This might include, for example, a stepparent, grandparent, adopted parent, legal guardian, or foster parent. In-laws are not covered.

We Are Family—Not!

Contrary to the famous song by Sister Sledge, sisters and brothers do not qualify as family members under the FMLA. This means an employee may not take FMLA leave to care for a seriously ill sibling unless the employee has acted as a child or parent to the sibling. For example, an employee who raised her younger brothers and sisters after their parents died would probably be entitled to take FMLA leave to care for them.

Proving a Family Relationship

Employers are entitled to request reasonable documentation confirming that a familial relationship exists when an employee takes leave to care for a family member. This proof might be in the form of a birth certificate, papers documenting the placement of a foster child, or simply a written statement from the employee (this might be the only documentation an employee has regarding a common law spouse or a child for whom the employee acts as a parent, for example). (See 29 C.F.R. § 825.113(d).) If the employee provides an official document as evidence, the company must return it to the employee.

We have provided a form you can use to request this confirmation. A sample appears below; you'll find a blank copy in Appendix C and on the CD-ROM at the back of this book.

FMLA Leave to Care for a Family Member

I, _____Jerry Singer_____, have requested time off work to care for _____Melissa Singer_____.
I have read the definitions below and I confirm that this person qualifies as my child.

I have attached a copy of the following documents confirming this relationship:

Birth certificate

(*List any documents you can provide, such as a birth certificate, papers confirming an adoption or foster care placement, a marriage certificate, and so on. If you don't have any documents, please write that in the space provided.*)

Date: _10-10-07_ Signature: _____Jerry Singer_____

Definitions

Spouse: A husband or wife to whom you are legally married.

Parent: Your legal parent, or someone who had day-to-day responsibility for supporting you financially and taking care of you when you were a child.

Child: Your biological child, adopted child, stepchild, foster child, or legal ward, or a child whom you have the day-to-day responsibility to support financially and take care of. Children are covered only until they reach the age of 18, unless they are incapable of taking care of themselves because of a physical or mental disability.

Caring for a Family Member

To take FMLA leave to care for a family member, it isn't enough that the employee takes time off to spend with a family member, even if the family member is gravely ill: The employee must actually provide care. For purposes of the FMLA, care includes:

- **physical care** (such as changing bandages, administering medication, preparing meals, helping with hygiene, assisting with physical therapy or exercise, and so on)

- **psychological care** (providing comfort and reassurance to a family member who is hospitalized or bedridden at home, for example)

- **providing necessary transportation** (to doctor's appointments, for example)

- **arranging for care or changes in care** (for example, making arrangements for a family member to move into an assisted living facility or hiring home health care aides to care for a family member), and

- **filling in for others providing care** (an employee might provide care two days a week, when the family member's usual caregiver takes time off, or might share caretaking responsibilities with other family members). (See 29 CFR § 825.116.)

Unless it is needed for the family member's comfort and assurance, simply spending time with a family member does not qualify as care. For example, an employee who takes time off to visit his ailing parents would not be entitled to FMLA leave unless he was needed to actually care for his parents while there.

LESSONS FROM THE

Real World   **Calling on the phone does not constitute care.**

H. Charles Tellis worked for Alaska Airlines in Seattle as a maintenance mechanic. He told his manager that he needed a couple of weeks off because his wife was having difficulties with her pregnancy. The manager suggested that he take FMLA leave and told him to pick up the appropriate forms at the company's benefits office.

Tellis started his leave and requested the forms. The next day, his car broke down. He decided to fly to Atlanta, where he owned another car, and drive back home. This trip took him four days. While he was gone, his wife gave birth; his sister-in-law took care of the family while he was gone. Alaska Airlines eventually terminated Tellis's employment, based in part on his absence.

Tellis sued, arguing that his time off was covered by the FMLA because he was caring for his wife. The 9th Circuit Court of Appeals disagreed: It found that he did not provide any actual care while he was on his trip. Although Tellis claimed that he gave his wife moral support and comfort by phoning her from the road, the court found that this was not what the FMLA means by care taking.

Tellis v. Alaska Airlines, 414 F.3d 1045 (9th Cir. 2005).

TIP

"Kin care" laws may also apply. Some states allow employees to take time off to care for a seriously ill family member or to take a family member to appointments with the doctor or dentist. Often called "kin care" laws, some of these statutes allow an employee to take unpaid leave for this purpose, while others require employers to allow employees to use their own sick leave for these types of time off.

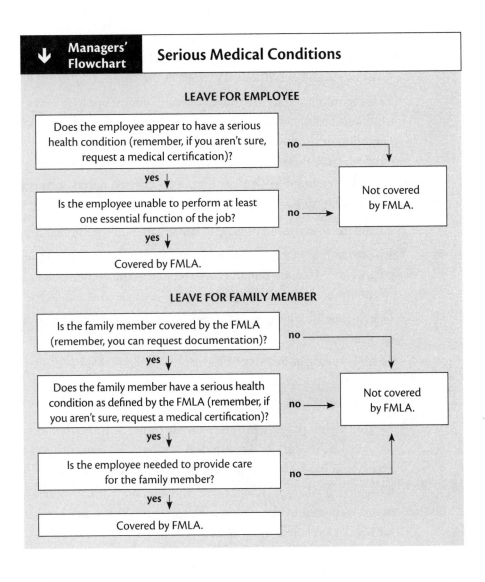

↓ Managers'
Flowchart

Serious Medical Conditions

LEAVE FOR EMPLOYEE

Does the employee appear to have a serious health condition (remember, if you aren't sure, request a medical certification)?

no → Not covered by FMLA.

yes ↓

Is the employee unable to perform at least one essential function of the job?

no →

yes ↓

Covered by FMLA.

LEAVE FOR FAMILY MEMBER

Is the family member covered by the FMLA (remember, you can request documentation)?

no → Not covered by FMLA.

yes ↓

Does the family member have a serious health condition as defined by the FMLA (remember, if you aren't sure, request a medical certification)?

no →

yes ↓

Is the employee needed to provide care for the family member?

no →

yes ↓

Covered by FMLA.

Common Mistakes Regarding Serious Health Conditions—And How to Avoid Them

MISTAKE 1: Denying FMLA leave for conditions that are covered.
AVOID THIS MISTAKE BY:

- Asking an employee to get a medical certification (see Chapter 8) whenever a serious health condition might be present. It's not your job to diagnose a serious health condition: Leave that up to the health care provider.

- Remembering that seemingly minor ailments can be serious health conditions. Even colds, stomachaches, and dental problems can qualify as serious health conditions if they meet the criteria.

- Keeping in mind that the "three-day rule" doesn't apply to every type of serious health condition. An employee with a chronic serious health condition or pregnancy complications is entitled to leave even if the employee isn't incapacitated for more than three days in a row.

MISTAKE 2: Denying FMLA leave to care for covered family members.
AVOID THIS MISTAKE BY:

- Asking the employee to provide documentation of the familial relationship.

- Understanding that "parents" and "children" refers not only to legal parents and children, but also to those whom the employee takes care of or who took care of the employee when he or she was a child.

- Not distinguishing between biological children and adopted or foster children.

MISTAKE 3: Failing to designate time off for an illness, injury, or disability as FMLA leave, if appropriate.
AVOID THIS MISTAKE BY:

- Making it your practice to automatically think of the FMLA when an employee takes time off for any physical or mental ailment. If it is a serious health condition, you will want to designate that time as FMLA leave.

- Considering whether an employee who goes out with a workers' comp injury is covered by the FMLA. (The answer will almost always be "yes," for reasons explained in Chapter 11.) ●

Leave for a New Child

CHAPTER HIGHLIGHTS

Eligible female and male employees are equally entitled to take parenting leave under the FMLA for the birth, adoption, or foster placement of a child.

Female or male employees who adopt or serve as foster parents of a child may take FMLA leave to:

- attend adoption or foster proceedings

- attend counseling sessions

- meet with attorneys

- meet with doctors

- attend court hearings, or

- attend to other placement-related matters.

You can request documents certifying an employee is a new biological, adoptive, or foster parent before granting parenting leave. Any employee must conclude his or her parenting leave within one year of the date of birth, adoption, or foster placement of the child.

Married parents who work for the same company are entitled to a combined 12 weeks of leave for the birth, adoption, or foster placement of their child; this limit doesn't apply to unmarried parents, who are each entitled to a full 12 weeks of parenting leave.

Your professional experience likely confirms what studies show: Providing parenting leave enhances employee loyalty, morale, and productivity. Perhaps this is one reason why the parenting leave provisions of the FMLA have generated so little controversy and opposition and have resulted in relatively few complaints to the Department of Labor. Employers and employees alike benefit when employees are able to take some time off to care for a new child.

That nearly everyone agrees on the value of parenting leave doesn't mean that everyone understands exactly how the rules work, however. The basic parenting leave provision of the FMLA provides that qualifying employees of either sex are entitled to up to 12 weeks of leave for the birth, adoption, or foster placement of a child. As with other parts of the FMLA, however, things get complicated when you take a closer look at the details.

Some of the confusion surrounds the definition of "parent" and "spouse," while some is a result of the interplay between parenting leaves and medical leaves related to pregnancy or caring for ill children. For example, a female employee may request leave for the birth of her child, as well as leave for a pregnancy-related medical condition—two different categories under the FMLA, which can affect when the female employee is entitled to take leave. On top of these complications, if both parents work for the same company, the FMLA treats married parents and unmarried parents differently.

This chapter explains the FMLA's parental leave entitlement. It covers leave for birth, adoption, and placement of a foster child; timing requirements for parenting leave; and how to calculate leave rights when an employee needs both parenting leave and leave for a serious health condition. This chapter also describes the rules that apply when both parents work for your company.

Leave for Birth

Under the FMLA, biological mothers and fathers are entitled to leave for the birth of a child. Parenting leave for the birth of a child isn't limited to the birth itself—it's also for bonding with and caring for the newborn. And in contrast with leave for a serious medical condition, employees requesting parenting leave don't have to show that the child is ill or requires care.

At times, it can be hard to distinguish between parenting leave and leave for a serious medical condition, such as when an employee needs leave because of a serious medical condition associated with her pregnancy or childbirth or when a newborn becomes ill. This chapter shows you how to draw this distinction in situations when you might have to do so.

Multiple Births in the Same Year

An employee who has more than one child in the same year does not get more leave. For example, if an employee gives birth to twins, she does not get 12 weeks of FMLA parenting leave for each child—just 12 weeks total.

As discussed further below, employees taking parenting leave are not entitled to intermittent or reduced-schedule leave, so a parent can't divide up his or her leave time, either. For example, a father who had two children at different times in the year (perhaps with two different mothers) can't take six weeks of leave for each birth—he would be entitled only to 12 weeks at once.

Conditions That Don't Count

When an employee's child is stillborn or the mother miscarries, the FMLA does not provide for parenting leave. Of course, if the employee is the mother, she may have serious medical and/or psychological conditions that entitle her to take FMLA leave.

TIP

It's okay to show compassion, as long as you are consistent. When you know that an employee has suffered a loss or trauma, it is both decent and natural to extend sympathetic treatment. Some companies voluntarily offer bereavement leave, for example, even though it isn't required by the FMLA. If your company offers extra leave or benefits in difficult times, such as relaxation of attendance or punctuality rules, just be sure to offer such treatment to all employees in similar circumstances.

If an employee needs leave to care for a sick newborn or for a wife who is suffering pregnancy-related illness, that's a request for leave to care for a family member with a serious health condition, not a request for parenting leave. Leave for serious health conditions is covered in Chapter 4.

Leave for Adoption

The FMLA's parenting leave provisions don't protect just employees who have biological children—an adoptive parent is also entitled to leave to spend time with his or her new child (as with a biological newborn) or to deal with the adoption process. Often an employee in this situation needs time off before the adoption is finalized, for example, to attend court proceedings, meetings with attorneys, counseling sessions, consultations with doctors, or for other matters related to the adoption process. The FMLA allows an employee to take this time off (provided other eligibility requirements are also met). The employee is entitled to adoption leave whether the adoption is conducted through a licensed placement agency, private arrangement, or otherwise.

LESSONS FROM THE

Real World

An employee was entitled to FMLA leave when trying to get custody of his biological daughter in an adoption proceeding.

Dwayne Kelley worked for Crosfield Catalysts. He had raised Shaneequa Forbes as his daughter, even though her birth certificate listed Barbara and Michael Forbes as her parents. Kelley "had reason to believe" that the girl was his biological daughter.

When the state child welfare department filed a court action to take custody of Shaneequa away from him, Kelley requested time off work to pursue custody. Crosfield denied the request based on the belief that Kelley could not "adopt" his own child and so was not entitled to adoption leave. Kelley took four days off anyway to appear at the custody hearing. Crosfield fired him, and he filed a lawsuit under the FMLA.

Kelley won the lawsuit. The court of appeals agreed that Crosfield had violated the FMLA. It determined that Kelley was entitled to take leave in connection with an adoption, regardless of whether or not the child in question was his biological child.

Kelley v. Crosfield Catalysts (7th Cir. 1998) 135 F.3d 1202.

Leave for Placement of a Foster Child

A new or soon-to-be foster parent is also entitled to FMLA leave to spend time with the foster child and to deal with the foster placement process. Foster care is 24-hour care of a child by someone other than the child's parent or guardian. Foster placement is made either by an agreement between the state and the foster parent or by court order. In either case, the state must be involved for a child placement to qualify as foster care under the FMLA: Informal custody arrangements, even for emergency childcare, don't qualify unless the state plays a role in the placement.

As with the adoption of a child, an eligible employee is entitled to take FMLA leave to attend to matters related to the placement of a foster child with that employee, whether the need for leave arises before or after the actual placement. A foster parent may need time off to attend hearings, examinations, and other proceedings, and that time is protected.

Parental Certifications

When an employee requests parenting leave, you can ask that employee to give you documentation showing that he or she is in fact the biological, adoptive, or foster parent of a newborn or newly placed child. Such documentation might include:

- a birth certificate
- an adoption decree or court order, or
- a foster placement certification or court order.

See "Proving a Family Relationship," in Chapter 4, for more information on these certifications, including a sample form you can use for this purpose. (A copy of the form, "FMLA Leave to Care for a Family Member," is also in Appendix C and on the CD-ROM at the back of this book.)

Timing of Parenting Leave

Although a parent is entitled to leave to bond with a new child, the child must indeed be "new." That means the employee must conclude the leave for the birth, adoption, or foster placement of a child within one year of the child's birth or adoptive or foster placement. (29 C.F.R. § 825.201.) "Placement" occurs when the parent gets the right to custody of the child. The one-year deadline is not extended when legal or governmental action has delayed the adoptive or foster parent from getting physical custody of the child.

This is a rigid deadline. Even a legitimate need for leave that arises more than one year after birth, adoption, or foster placement will not qualify under this provision of FMLA. Of course, if the child has a serious health condition that requires the parent's care, the parent may still qualify for FMLA leave after the first year is over—just not parenting leave.

EXAMPLE 1: Your employee, Pang, took custody of a foster child on May 2, 2006. On March 28, 2007, Pang asks to take ten weeks of FMLA parenting leave. You grant the request.

You really shouldn't have granted that much time, because Pang had only a little over four weeks of time left in the one-year period following the child's placement. That was all the time off that she was entitled to within the FMLA deadline for parental leave.

EXAMPLE 2: Your employee Jess and his partner had a baby on March 5, 2006. On March 27, 2007, Jess informs you that he needs to take three weeks off to care for the baby, who has developed severe bronchitis. Because more than a year has passed since the child's birth, you inform Jess that he has no leave time available for the birth of his child.

You blew it! The baby's illness is not "birth-related" and is not subject to the one-year deadline for such leave. Rather, the baby's illness is a serious medical condition, and Jess may qualify to take FMLA leave as long as he meets other eligibility requirements.

LESSONS FROM THE

Real World

An employee is not entitled to FMLA leave to travel to retrieve adopted children more than one year after adoption.

Bernardo Bocalbos, a naturalized U.S. citizen who was born in the Philippines, worked as an assistant actuary for National Western Life Insurance Co. In 1992, Bocalbos adopted his brother's children, who lived in the Philippines. In March 1995, after finally receiving the necessary visas for the children, Bocalbos requested FMLA leave to travel to the Philippines to retrieve the children. The request was granted. Prior to Bocalbos's departure, his supervisor informed him that he had to take certain actuarial exams by May 1995 or he would be terminated. Bocalbos signed a memorandum stating he understood this requirement. In April 1995, Bocalbos left for the Philippines and returned to work in June 1995. Bocalbos did not sit for the required exams prior to his departure. National Western terminated him for failing to take the exams by May 1995. Bocalbos sued National Western for retaliating against him for taking FMLA leave.

The court of appeals sided with National Western, holding that the leave Bocalbos took three years after the adoption of the children was outside the FMLA deadline for adoption-related leave, so he was not protected.

Bocalbos v. National Western Life Ins. Co. (5th Cir. 1998) 162 F.3d 379.

Foreign adoptions like the one in the above "Lesson" are increasingly common. Madonna and Angelina Jolie are just the most famous people who have adopted children born in foreign countries, but your company's employees may choose to add to their families in this fashion, too. If an employee must take time off to travel to take custody of a newly adopted child and does so within one year of the finalization of the adoption, the FMLA protects the employee's right to do so.

Where an employee has already taken leave for the placement of a foster child and later adopts that child, the FMLA does not give the employee additional leave time for the adoption. The FMLA permits leave only for the "newly placed" foster or adoptive child within one year of the original placement. So even if the adoption doesn't happen for more than a year, the employee can't get additional parenting leave time.

Intermittent or Reduced-Schedule Leave

The FMLA does not require your company to offer intermittent and reduced-schedule parenting leave to employees, with one possible exception: Employees who become foster parents can take leave for each child that is placed with them. Although such employees still have a maximum of 12 weeks of leave to use in a year, they may take this leave in separate increments if more than one child is placed with them within a single year.

EXAMPLE 1: Brenda, whose delivery date is December 21, 2007, requests four weeks of parenting leave following the birth of her child. She then plans to return to work for a couple of weeks and wants an additional three weeks of leave to bond with the baby in February 2008. You grant the leave immediately following the birth but deny the additional leave. Have you done the right thing?

Yes. As long as Brenda has a normal pregnancy and delivery and no post-delivery complications, she is not entitled to the February leave, because that would be intermittent leave.

EXAMPLE 2: Tomas becomes a foster parent on February 1, 2008, and takes six weeks of FMLA leave to spend with his foster child. He enjoys the experience so much that he decides to take in another foster child, who will be placed with him on August 5, 2008. He asks for another six weeks of parenting leave. You deny his request because he has already taken parenting leave during the year, and you don't have to allow him to take intermittent leave for this purpose. Was this the right call?

Not in this situation. Even though parents usually can't divide up their parenting leave, an exception applies when they receive more than one foster child in a year. Although the employee's total leave entitlement doesn't increase, the employee can take this leave in separate parts for multiple foster child placements, each part corresponding to a newly placed child.

However, your company has the option of agreeing to provide intermittent or reduced-schedule parenting leave at the employee's request, even though the FMLA does not require it. In fact, if you have a company policy allowing that type of leave, you should follow the policy. Your company may impose restrictions on this type of leave that are different from those mandated by the FMLA, because you're agreeing to provide more than the law requires. For example, although the FMLA requires employers to allow intermittent leave in increments of one hour or less, you may require employees who use intermittent leave for parenting to take it in larger increments (for example, a full day at a time).

POLICY ALERT

If your company has a policy of offering intermittent or reduced schedule leave for parenting leave, follow it. Your company is bound to follow its own leave policies, even if they exceed FMLA obligations.

EXAMPLE: A few years after her first request, Brenda makes a request similar to the one described in the example above, but this time your company has a policy of granting occasional days off or reduced workdays to employees with newborns. Brenda specifically requests FMLA leave in two time segments, one in December and one in February. You deny Brenda the second block of time off because it is not available under the FMLA. Are you correct?

No. Where your company policy allows for intermittent leave for childbirth, you must abide by the policy.

This limitation doesn't apply to a woman who has a serious health condition as a result of pregnancy or childbirth or a spouse caring for a woman with such a condition. In those situations, the leave is not parenting leave, so the employee is entitled to intermittent and reduced-schedule leave. Likewise, if a child has a serious health condition, the employee isn't restricted by this provision and is eligible for intermittent or reduced-schedule leave (see Chapter 6, "Intermittent and Reduced-Schedule Leave").

SEE AN EXPERT

State family and medical leave laws may require your company to provide intermittent or reduced-schedule parenting leave. Appendix A includes information on each state's family and medical leave laws. If you have questions about how to comply with your state's requirements for parenting leave, consult with an employment attorney.

Substitution of Paid Leave

Your company can require its employees who request parenting leave to substitute paid accrued paid vacation, personal leave, or family leave under its own policies and to count the time against the employee's FMLA available leave time. So, for example, an employee with two weeks' vacation time on the books could be required to use it up, and that time off would count against the employee's 12-week entitlement to FMLA leave.

However, the rule is different for sick or medical leave, because parenting leave is not "sick" time. So, your company can't require employees requesting parenting leave to use up accrued sick leave. If the leave requested is to care for a spouse, newborn, or newly placed child with a serious health condition, on the other hand, paid medical leave may be substituted if your policy allows sick leave to care for family members.

Even if your company doesn't require an employee to substitute paid vacation, personal, or family leave for parenting leave, it must allow an employee to use this time to get paid during FMLA leave, upon the employee's request.

Parents Who Work for the Same Company

Parents who work for the same company are entitled to parenting leave, but the amount of time they get depends on their marital status. If the parents are married, they get a combined 12 weeks of leave in connection with the birth, adoption, or foster placement of their child or to care for a seriously ill parent. This rule applies even to spouses who work at different worksites or in different divisions of your company. (29 C.F.R. § 825.202(b).) Spouses are allowed to use the combined leave at the same time.

If the parents are not married, they each get 12 weeks of leave. This rule seems to favor unmarried couples, but the reason for the rule is actually to avoid discouraging employers from hiring married couples by lessening the burden on those employers when their married employees have children together.

EXAMPLE: Dan and Anabelle both work for your company and are married to each other. Dan works in the downtown headquarters, while Anabelle works in the warehouse in a nearby suburb. They are both eligible for FMLA leave. Three months ago, Dan and Anabelle adopted a child. Anabelle requests seven weeks of leave in connection with the adoption. You grant the requested leave.

During Anabelle's leave, Dan asks for five weeks off to bond with the child, two weeks of which will overlap with Anabelle's leave. You grant his request. Were you right to do so?

Yes. You accurately noted the time off for each of the parents and calculated the total combined FMLA parenting leave to be taken. Dan was entitled to the five weeks of parenting leave that was left after Anabelle's leave was subtracted from the combined 12 weeks.

Unmarried couples are each entitled to the full 12 weeks of FMLA parenting leave. However, unlike married couples, they are not entitled to FMLA leave to care for each other when one has a serious medical condition. So if an unmarried pregnant employee needs care for a serious medical condition and you also employ her partner, her partner is not entitled to FMLA leave to provide that care. Your state's family and medical leave law might require you to grant leave to care for a domestic partner, however. (Appendix A provides information on each state's family and medical leave laws.)

EXAMPLE 1: Jared and Betsey are domestic partners who are both employed by your company. The couple has announced that Betsey is pregnant. Before Betsey's due date, Jared requests 10 weeks of parenting leave to begin after the baby's birth. You grant his request and wish the couple well.

Shortly after the baby's birth, Betsey calls in and asks for 5 weeks of parenting leave. You deny that request, telling Betsey that she and Jared get a combined 12 weeks of parenting leave and he has already been granted 10 weeks.

Wrong. Since they are not married, Jared and Betsey are each entitled to 12 weeks of FMLA leave in connection with the birth of their child.

EXAMPLE 2: Jared phones in two months after the baby's birth to ask to take two weeks of FMLA leave to take care of Betsey, who has developed severe postpartum depression and been prescribed medication that affects her ability to function.

Because you have read this guide, you know that you can deny this request and tell Jared that unmarried partners are not entitled to leave to care for each other under the FMLA.

In the last example, if Jared and Betsey had been married, Jared would be entitled to the requested leave to care for his spouse during her illness. However, that means that in the first example, Betsey would be entitled to only 2 weeks of parenting leave, because Jared already took 10 weeks.

 CROSS-REFERENCE

State laws may also apply. Several types of state laws might also protect employees who take parenting-related leave. For example, some states require employers to offer parenting leave (similar to that provided by the FMLA) to a wider range of employees than does the FMLA. And some state family leave laws cover the same territory as the FMLA. Appendix A provides a summary of each state's laws; Chapter 11 explains what to do when a state law overlaps with the FMLA.

Combining Parenting Leave With Leave for a Serious Health Condition

As you've now learned, employees are entitled to two types of leave under the FMLA: leave for a serious health condition, and parenting leave to care for and bond with a new child. Sometimes, these two rights may seem to overlap. For example, a pregnant mother may need time off before her pregnancy, when she experiences morning sickness or is confined to bed. Or a newborn may become ill, requiring a parent's care.

Pregnancy

Incapacity due to pregnancy including leave needed for prenatal care is itself considered a serious health condition under the FMLA. In fact, all leave before delivery that a pregnant woman takes because of her pregnancy is leave for a serious medical condition, not parenting leave. (See Chapter 4 for more information on pregnancy leave).

There are a couple of reasons it's important to figure out whether an employee is taking leave for pregnancy (a serious health condition) or parenting:

- **Unlike parenting leave, FMLA leave for pregnancy incapacity may be taken on an intermittent or reduced-schedule basis.** If you lump pregnancy and parenting leaves together and deny a request for intermittent leave for pregnancy as a result, you violate the FMLA.

- **If married parents both work for you, they are subject to the combined 12-week "cap" on parenting leave, as explained above.** However, an employee's leave for her own pregnancy doesn't count towards this combined 12 weeks, nor does a husband's leave to care for his pregnant wife. For example, if a pregnant employee took five weeks off due to incapacity, she and her husband would still be entitled to a combined total of 12 weeks off for parenting leave. There is a limitation, though—each person still has an overall cap of 12 weeks of FMLA leave. In this example, the pregnant employee could take a maximum of seven weeks of parenting leave, because she already used five weeks of her annual allotment.

EXAMPLE 1: Back to your married employees, Dan and Anabelle. A few days after Dan's request for parenting leave, Anabelle asks for three weeks off to care for the child, who has developed pneumonia. You deny this request and tell Anabelle that she and Dan have taken all 12 weeks of parenting leave available under the FMLA.

Oops! Your mistake was assuming that Anabelle's request for time to care for the sick child was part of the 12-week combined parenting leave, instead of leave for a serious health condition. With a medical certification, Anabelle is entitled to three weeks off, because it is less than difference between her total FMLA leave for the year (12 weeks) and the time she actually took off during the combined parenting leave (seven weeks).

EXAMPLE 2: A few weeks after returning from his final week of parenting leave, Dan develops a severe cough. He calls in one morning to inform you that his doctor has diagnosed him with bronchitis and ordered him to stay home and off his feet for at least a week to give the antibiotics a chance to work. You ask for a note from his doctor and grant the leave on the condition that you receive the medical certification.

Congratulations. You learned from your earlier error. Dan's illness is an FMLA-qualifying condition separate and apart from the parenting leave he took earlier and he, too, has 12 weeks of FMLA leave, less the time he actually took off already (five weeks). So, Dan has seven weeks of leave left for any FMLA-qualifying reason except parenting leave.

In addition to granting leave to a pregnant woman incapacitated by a pregnancy-related medical condition, the FMLA also requires your company to allow a husband to take time off to care for his wife who is suffering such incapacitation. As with any other leave for a serious medical condition, the spouse must provide care to the pregnant employee and should provide a medical certification (see Chapter 4, "Leave for a Family Member's Serious Health Condition"). Of course, this means that a normal pregnancy that doesn't incapacitate the mother doesn't entitle her spouse to take leave to be with her.

LESSONS FROM THE

Real World

An employee was not entitled to FMLA leave to be with his pregnant wife when she had not suffered medical complications.

After his pregnant wife experienced false labor, Steve Aubuchon orally requested leave from his job with Knauf Fiberglass to be with her. Aubuchon did not inform Knauf that his wife had any medical complications or that she was incapacitated. Knauf denied the request. Aubuchon nevertheless missed several weeks of work, and Knauf fired him for unauthorized absence. He filed a lawsuit claiming that Knauf violated the FMLA.

The court of appeals ruled in the company's favor. Because Aubuchon failed to provide notice to Knauf that his wife had experienced complications during her pregnancy or that she was incapacitated, Aubuchon's leave was not protected and Knauf did not violate the FMLA by firing him.

Aubuchon v. Knauf Fiberglass, GmbH (7th Cir. 2004) 359 F.3d 950.

LESSONS FROM THE

Real World

Even if an employee wasn't entitled to take FMLA leave to care for his common-law wife, he was entitled to take leave to care for his premature infant.

Ingram Construction Company fired Mark Willard for taking time off to care for his common-law wife and newborn child following the baby's premature birth. Willard sued Ingram for violating the FMLA.

The court of appeals held that, while Willard may or may not have met the requirements of a common-law marriage, he was entitled to take FMLA leave to care for his newborn. The legal relationship between Willard and the mother of the child didn't affect his right to take parental leave.

Willard v. Ingram Constr., Co., Inc. (6th Cir. 1999) 194 F.3d 1315.

Because domestic partners and other unmarried couples don't qualify as family members under the FMLA, an employee isn't entitled take FMLA leave to care for a nonmarital pregnant partner even if she has a serious medical condition. But the employee is entitled to take FMLA leave to care for a newborn child, even if the mother of the child isn't the employee's spouse.

Caring for a Child

Leave to care for an ill newborn or newly adopted or foster child is separate and apart from parenting leave, because it is to care for a family member with a serious health condition. So if a child becomes ill, you assess the employee's entitlement to leave under the FMLA in the same manner as any other leave request for a serious health condition. For more information, refer to Chapter 4.

Common Mistakes Regarding Leave for a New Child— And How to Avoid Them

MISTAKE 1: Miscalculating the FMLA leave available to spouses who both work for your company.

AVOID THIS MISTAKE BY:

- Making sure both parents are eligible for FMLA leave in the first place— for example, that they have worked enough hours in the past year. See Chapter 3 for more on these requirements.
- Making sure the two married parents get no more, and no less, than 12 weeks of combined parenting leave.
- Calculating the FMLA leave time each parent has left for other purposes after the combined parenting leave is taken.
- Distinguishing between parenting leave and other types of leave that a soon-to-be or new parent might take (for pregnancy disability, to care for a pregnant spouse, for disability relating to childbirth, or to care for a seriously ill new child, for example). Leave for a child's or spouse's serious health condition doesn't count towards the combined 12-week cap.

MISTAKE 2: Denying FMLA leave because the employee has already taken parenting leave.

AVOID THIS MISTAKE BY:

- Allowing intermittent parenting leave only if your company's policies allow it or the employee is entitled to separate increments of parenting leave for multiple foster child placements in a single year.

- Recognizing the difference between parenting leave and leave for a serious health condition. If a child becomes seriously ill, leave to care for that child does not qualify as parental leave under the FMLA; it's leave to care for a family member with a serious health condition.

MISTAKE 3: Discriminating against fathers in granting or denying parenting leave.

AVOID THIS MISTAKE BY:

- Granting parenting leave to FMLA-eligible fathers for birth, adoption, or foster placement, just as you would to female employees.

- Making no assumptions about who will or should actually be providing care for a new child. Remember, an employee doesn't have to show that he is required to provide care for a new child, as he would have to show to care for a family member with a serious health condition— and you can't deny parenting leave simply because the child's mother is already at home.

✓ Managers' Checklist	Leave for a New Child

❑ I confirmed that the employee requesting parenting leave is eligible for FMLA leave (see Chapter 3).

❑ I have informed the employee that he or she must substitute paid company vacation, personal, or family leave for unpaid FMLA leave, and

  ❑ I have subtracted the paid leave from the employee's available FMLA leave for the leave year.

❑ I have noted the deadline by which the employee must take the full 12 weeks of parenting leave (365 days after birth, adoption, or foster placement).

For Pregnancy Leave:

❑ If the employee is requesting leave for her own pregnancy before delivery, I have:

  ❑ requested medical certification of a serious medical condition

  ❑ designated the leave as leave for the employee's own medical condition and notified the employee

  ❑ noted in the employee's FMLA file that the employee may still request parenting leave within the one-year deadline.

❑ If a pregnant employee is requesting leave to begin before delivery, I have:

  ❑ asked if the leave is for her own medical condition (including prenatal care) or for parenting, and

  ❑ if for her own medical condition, I have followed the steps in the preceding list entry, and

  ❑ if for parenting, I have denied the request for leave prior to delivery.

❑ If an employee is requesting leave to care for his pregnant spouse, I have:

  ❑ requested appropriate certification of serious medical condition

  ❑ designated the leave as leave for the spouse's serious medical condition and notified the employee, and

  ❑ noted that the employee may still request parenting leave within the 365-day deadline.

For Parenting Leave:

❏ If the employee is requesting parenting leave, I have confirmed that the leave is:

    ❏ to begin after the birth of the child

    ❏ not for the employee's own medical condition, and

    ❏ full time and not intermittent or reduced-schedule leave, unless company policy or state law permits such leave.

❏ If the employee is requesting parenting leave for the birth of a child, I have requested appropriate certification (birth certificate).

❏ If the employee is requesting parenting leave for adoption or foster placement, I have:

    ❏ requested appropriate certification of adoption or placement (for example, a court order)

    ❏ allowed time off before adoption or foster placement if necessary to attend proceedings or meetings related to placement.

Where Both Parents Work for Your Company:

❏ For parents who are married and are both seeking parenting leave, I have:

    ❏ confirmed in writing to the parents that they get no more than a combined total of 12 weeks of parenting leave, and

    ❏ subtracted the parenting time from each employee's FMLA time and noted the remainder for use for other types of FMLA leave.

❏ For parents who are not married and are both seeking leave, I have:

    ❏ confirmed in writing to the parents that each parent has a full 12 weeks of parenting leave available

    ❏ subtracted the parenting time from each employee's FMLA time and noted the remainder for use for other types of FMLA leave.

How Much Leave Can an Employee Take?

CHAPTER HIGHLIGHTS

Eligible employees are entitled to 12 weeks of FMLA leave in a 12-month "leave year."

The 12-month "leave year" may be measured in one of four ways:

- the calendar year

- any fixed 12-month period, such as the fiscal year, the year starting on the anniversary of the employee's hire, and so on

- twelve months counted forward from the date an employee begins FMLA leave, or

- twelve months counted backward from the date an employee uses any FMLA leave.

Your company must use the same calendaring method for all employees.

Your company may change calendaring methods with 60 days' advance notice.

Each week of leave is based on the employee's normal workweek, including any overtime the employee is required to work.

Only leave time the employee actually needs can be counted against the employee's available FMLA leave time.

If needed for a serious health condition, FMLA leave may be taken intermittently or on a reduced schedule.

Employees may take intermittent or reduced-schedule leave in the shortest increments of time used for payroll calculations.

You've come a long way: You've determined that your company is covered by the FMLA. You've confirmed that the employee seeking leave is FMLA-qualified and that the reason for leave falls within the FMLA. Now it's time to figure out how much leave the employee has—or has left—to use.

The FMLA requires your company to give eligible employees up to 12 workweeks of leave in a 12-month period. But when does that period start and end? What if the employee took leave last December and wants more leave this July—does the employee get another 12 weeks of leave because it's a new calendar year, or does the employee have to wait a full 12 months? How much leave is available to an employee who works odd hours, part time, or overtime? What if the employee wants to take only one day—or one hour—off a week, not 12 weeks at once?

If you don't know the answers to these questions off the top of your head, you aren't alone. In this chapter, we'll give you the information you need to determine exactly how much FMLA leave is available to your employees. We explain how to choose the right 12-month leave year for your company, how to measure 12 weeks of leave in the 12-month leave year, how to handle requests for intermittent leave or reduced-schedule leave, how to calculate leave for employees who work part time, and more.

Counting the 12-Month Leave Year

Each eligible employee is entitled to 12 weeks of FMLA leave per year. But what constitutes a "year"? Believe it or not, it's up to your company, at least in part: Employers may choose one of four different methods for defining the "leave year" in which an eligible employee may take leave. Whichever method you choose, it's important to apply the same method to all employees. If you don't, employees can use whichever method is most advantageous to them.

TIP

FMLA leave cannot be carried over from one leave year to the next. No matter how your company measures the 12-month leave year, employees can't carry over FMLA leave. An employee is never entitled to more than 12 weeks of FMLA leave in a given leave year.

Four Methods of Defining the Leave Year

The FMLA gives companies four different ways to define the leave year. They are:

- the calendar year
- any fixed 12-month period, such as the company's fiscal year, a year starting on the anniversary of an employee's hire, or a year defined by state law
- the 12-month period counted forward from the date that the employee begins FMLA leave, or
- a "rolling" 12-month period counted backward from the date that the employee uses any FMLA leave.

(29 C.F.R. § 825.200(b).)

The Calendar Year or a Fixed-Period Year

If your company chooses to measure the leave year by either a calendar year or another fixed 12-month period (like the fiscal year), an eligible employee is entitled to up to 12 weeks of FMLA leave at any time in the selected leave year. A major disadvantage for companies that use one of these methods is that an employee could take 24 weeks of continuous leave in a row, if the leave spans the end of one year and the beginning of the next. It's difficult for many employers to have an employee out for that long.

EXAMPLE: Your company measures the FMLA leave year by the calendar year: From January first to December 31, each eligible employee is entitled to 12 weeks of FMLA leave. Your employee, Megan, begins her 12-week FMLA leave on October 1. As of January 1, Megan is entitled to 12 weeks of FMLA leave for the new leave year. This means she will be able to take a solid 24 weeks of FMLA leave in a row.

Counting Forward

If your company chooses the third method, an eligible employee is entitled to up to 12 weeks of FMLA leave in the year beginning on the first day that the employee takes FMLA leave. From that day forward, the employee has 12 months to take the full 12 weeks of FMLA leave. The next 12-month period begins when leave is next taken after the initial 12-month leave year ends. For example, if an employee began leave on February 15, 2008, the employee would have until February 14, 2009 to use up the 12 weeks of leave. If the employee again wanted leave beginning June 20, 2009, the clock would start over.

This is a relatively simple method for your company to use, because you can administer it easily on a case-by-case basis. However, it may allow employees to take more than 12 weeks of leave in a given 12-month period in the same manner that the first two methods do.

EXAMPLE: Your company counts the leave year by going forward one year from the date FMLA leave is first taken. Megan begins a six-week FMLA leave on December 1, 2007. On October 20, 2008, Megan requests to take her remaining six weeks of leave, returning on December 1, 2008. On January 2, 2009, Megan requests a full 12-week FMLA leave. So, Megan will get 18 weeks of FMLA leave between October 20, 2008 and March 27, 2009.

The "Rolling" Leave Year

A "rolling" year is just what it sounds like—an employee's leave eligibility rolls out throughout the year, as leave is taken. If your company calculates the leave year using this method, an eligible employee is entitled to up to 12 weeks of FMLA leave in the year measured backward from the first day that FMLA leave is taken. Each time the employee takes leave, any part of the 12-week entitlement that was not used in the immediately preceding 12 months is available for future leave.

This is less complicated as it sounds. Below is a sample worksheet to keep track of hours used under the "rolling" year method; there is a blank copy in Appendix C and on the CD-ROM at the back of this book

SAMPLE

Chart for Calculating Leave Under "Rolling" Leave Year Method

FMLA Leave Tracking for Jane Edwards			
DATE LEAVE COMMENCED	AMOUNT OF LEAVE TAKEN	DATE ELIGIBLE FOR ADDITIONAL LEAVE	AMOUNT OF LEAVE AVAILABLE
2/12/05	4 wks.	Currently eligible	8 wks.
4/22/05	4 wks.	Currently eligible	4 wks.
9/07/05	4 wks.	2/12/06	4 wks.
3/20/06	4 wks.	4/22/06	4 wks.
7/17/06	2 wks.	9/07/06	6 wks.

The main advantage of this method is that it does not allow employees to take FMLA leave totaling more than 12 weeks in any 12-month period.

EXAMPLE: Mario takes one week of FMLA leave beginning February 12, 2007; four weeks of FMLA leave beginning March 2, 2007; three weeks of FMLA leave beginning May 7, 2007; and four weeks of FMLA leave beginning July 10, 2007. Under the "rolling" 12-month period, Mario's next leave year will begin February 12, 2008. At that time, Mario will be entitled to one week of leave; four more weeks beginning March 2, 2008; three more weeks beginning May 7, 2008; and four more weeks beginning July 10, 2008.

Choosing a Leave Year Method

Be sure to define "leave year" in your company's written FMLA policy and clearly describe which of the four methods the company will use. (See Appendix B for a sample FMLA policy, and Chapter 2 for a general discussion of the FMLA leave information your company should provide employees.) If your company's chosen method is not stated in its policies, employees will be allowed to use the method most favorable to them, whether or not it's the best method for the company.

If, after reading this, your company decides to choose a new calculation method, it can do so. However, if employees are on leave or have requested leave, the company must provide 60 day's notice of the change of method to all employees. During that 60-day period, the employee can continue to utilize the method of his or her choice. Once the 60 days has passed, your company may begin using its selected method for all FMLA leaves. (29 C.F.R. § 825.200(e).)

POLICY ALERT

Your policy determines the leave year. If your company does not select a leave year calculation method, uses different methods with different employees, or changes methods without proper notice, each employee will get to choose his or her favored method.

Applying the Leave Year Consistently

Regardless of which method your company uses to calculate the leave year, it must use the same method for all employees who request FMLA leave. It cannot choose different methods for different employees. If one department uses a different method from another and an employee sues to challenge the method used, a court will use the method most beneficial to the employee.

However, some states require employers to use a particular method for calculating the leave year under their own medical leave laws. If your company has employees in a state with this type of law, it must apply the method required in that state. However, if your company does business in other states that don't have this same requirement, it is free to use a different (but uniform) method for employees in those other states. In this limited situation, using two different methods to calculate the leave year—one in the state where it is mandated and the other in all other locations—won't give employees the right to choose whichever leave method works best for them.

SEE AN EXPERT

Multistate employers may need some expert help. You can find information on each state's family and medical leave laws in Appendix A, but if you have to integrate various state laws with the FMLA, you'll appreciate some advice from a lawyer.

Counting Time Off as FMLA Leave

Under the FMLA, eligible employees are allowed to take off 12 workweeks in the 12-month leave year. If an employee takes FMLA leave all at once, you won't need to consider the employee's hours or schedule in determining how much leave is available. Whether the employee works part time or full time or puts in plenty of overtime, an employee who takes a whole week off at once has used up one week's worth of FMLA leave (subject to the rules set out below).

If an employee takes intermittent or reduced-schedule leave, however, you'll need to figure out how many total hours of FMLA leave are available to the employee. In this situation, the employee's work hours determine how much leave the employee can take. We explain how to make these calculations in "Intermittent and Reduced-Schedule Leave," below.

Whether an employee takes FMLA leave all at once or a little bit at a time, you'll need to know what time off counts against that 12-week entitlement. Here are the rules:

- **Time spent working is not FMLA leave.** If an employee is on full-time FMLA leave but continues to work (perhaps putting in a few hours at home), the hours worked don't count as part of the employee's FMLA leave time. This is true even if your company does not require the employee to work on leave, but the employee voluntarily does it anyway. So, be sure that employees on FMLA leave are not working—follow up with their managers and supervisors to make sure they understand the rule and that they tell employees not to work on leave.

- **Extra time taken off at your request isn't FMLA leave.** If your company gets an employee's agreement to take off more time than he or she actually needs—for example, if an employee agrees to take a full day rather than a couple hours so that you can hire a temporary employee to perform the employee's duties for the day—you can't count the difference between the time off and the time actually needed against the employee's FMLA leave entitlement. These extra hours were a convenience to you and can't be held against the employee.

EXAMPLE: Hal usually works an eight-hour schedule five days a week. Hal requests three hours off every Tuesday to care for his sick father. You instruct Hal to take all of Tuesday off, so that your company can put a different employee into his original schedule. You log Hal's eight hours off as FMLA leave. Was this correct?

Nope. Only the three hours off that Hal needed can be counted as FMLA leave time. The other five hours may be designated as paid time off or other leave under your company's policies but do not reduce Hal's available FMLA leave time.

- **Holidays don't affect the count.** All actual workweeks are counted; it doesn't matter that a holiday falls within one of the weeks that an employee is out on FMLA leave.

- **If the company is closed for at least a week, that time doesn't count as FMLA leave.** If your company shuts down operations entirely and employees are not required to come to work for a week or more, that week will not count as one of the employee's FMLA leave workweeks. For example, a company that closes its doors for two weeks in August can't count those weeks as FMLA leave for any employee.

Intermittent and Reduced-Schedule Leave

Sometimes an employee does not need a full workweek off at a time. An employee may, for example, request permission to take hours or days off "as needed" to care for an ill family member when the usual caretaker is unavailable. This "intermittent leave" is allowed under the FMLA. Intermittent leave is leave taken in separate blocks of time for a single qualifying reason, such as a course of treatment spread over months or flare-ups of a chronic illness.

An employee may instead need a reduced work schedule, for example, during recovery from surgery or illness. The FMLA allows an eligible employee to take "reduced schedule" leave when he or she needs to work fewer hours per week or per day than usual, typically while the employee or a family member is recovering from or being treated for a serious health condition.

When an employee uses one of these forms of leave, figuring out how much leave the employee is entitled to and how long it will take to use up the 12-week allotment can be challenging. The challenge is especially tricky for part-time employees or those with irregular work schedules, because you have to measure the leave taken based on the employee's normal workweek. In this section, we explain how to calculate intermittent and reduced-schedule leave for employees working all types of schedules.

 CROSS-REFERENCE

See Chapter 9 for information on managing intermittent leave, including rules that allow flexibility in scheduling. When it passed the FMLA, Congress recognized that providing intermittent leave could impose a significant burden on employers. The law gives companies a couple of options for easing the load, including the right to transfer an employee who needs intermittent leave to a different position and the right to require employees to schedule foreseeable intermittent leave in a manner that isn't unduly disruptive. These rules—and tips for making sure employees don't abuse the right to take intermittent leave—are covered in Chapter 9.

When Can an Employee Take Intermittent or Reduced-Schedule Leave?

An employee may take intermittent or reduced-schedule leave if it's medically necessary for a serious health condition (the employee's own or that of a family member). As explained in Chapter 5, the FMLA doesn't require you to provide intermittent or reduced-schedule parenting leave, but you're permitted to do so as long as you do it consistently.

Here are some examples of conditions that qualify for intermittent or reduced-schedule leave:

- **An employee is receiving chemotherapy and radiation treatment for cancer.** The weekly treatment renders him unable to work, so he reduces his schedule by one afternoon per week to receive treatment and recover afterward.

- **An employee's mother has multiple sclerosis.** Some days, she is able to care for herself; other days, she needs assistance. The employee can take intermittent leave to care for her mother when necessary.

- **An employee has back surgery to repair a herniated disk.** The employee returns to work part time for several weeks, until he is strong enough to work full time. Afterward, the employee takes a couple of hours off each Friday to go to physical therapy, as well as an hour every other week for a doctor's appointment to check his progress. This employee is using both reduced-schedule leave and intermittent leave.

LESSONS FROM THE

Real World

An employee suffering from flare-ups of a chronic condition is entitled to intermittent leave.

Kathleen Victorelli, an employee at Shadyside Hospital, requested leave when she experienced an episode of stomach pain, nausea, and vomiting as a result of peptic ulcer disease that her doctor had diagnosed two years earlier. The hospital refused the request. Victorelli took the leave anyway and the hospital fired her. She sued, claiming that Shadyside had violated the FMLA.

The court held that Victorelli's peptic ulcer disease was a chronic medical condition that entitled her to intermittent leave when her condition flared up.

Victorelli v. Shadyside Hosp., 128 F.3d 184 (3rd Cir. 1997).

Leave Must Be Medically Necessary

An employee may not take intermittent leave simply because that's what he or she prefers: It must be medically necessary. This means the employee must need time off for a serious health condition (as defined in Chapter 4), and the employee must need that leave in separate increments rather than all at once.

EXAMPLE: Eric tells you that he needs to reduce his work schedule from 40 hours per week to 30 hours per week to recover from surgery. You request medical certification and give him a preliminary designation of the leave as FMLA-qualified, subject to withdrawal if the certification is inadequate (see "Designating Time Off as FMLA Leave" in Chapter 7).

When you get the medical certification, you discover that the surgery is elective cosmetic surgery to reduce eyelid puffiness. You withdraw the preliminary FMLA designation and deny Eric's request for FMLA leave to recover from this surgery. Have you violated the FMLA?

No. Elective surgery and recovery from it don't count as serious health conditions under the FMLA.

Eric has the surgery on a Saturday and returns to work on Monday, a little bruised and bandaged but able to work. However, on Wednesday, Eric calls in to explain that he has a post-operative infection and his doctor has placed him on a regimen of antibiotics and a restricted work schedule of 25 hours per week for two weeks.

Because you have read this book, you send Eric notice that this reduced scheduled leave may qualify as FMLA leave, because the post-surgery complications are FMLA-qualified (even though the initial surgery wasn't).

How can you tell whether intermittent leave is medically necessary? By getting a medical certification. On the certification form, the employee's (or family member's) health care provider must state that intermittent leave is necessary. The provider must also indicate the expected duration of leave and, if intermittent leave is necessary for medical treatment, the dates and duration of the treatment. For more on the medical certification form, see Chapter 8. Chapter 9 explains how to use the information in the form—and in subsequent recertifications, if necessary—to make sure an employee uses intermittent leave appropriately.

Employees Must Be Able to Perform the Essential Functions of the Job

Because an employee on intermittent or reduced-schedule leave continues to work, the employee must still be able to perform the essential functions of his or her job. (See Chapter 4, "Leave for a Serious Health Condition" to learn what an "essential function" is.) In contrast, an employee who takes FMLA leave all at once for a serious health condition must be unable to perform an essential job function. These opposing requirements are based on the different types of leave: An employee on intermittent leave must still be able to do the job while at work, but an employee on full-time FMLA leave won't be working at all.

LESSONS FROM THE

Real World

An employee who cannot perform the job's essential functions is not entitled to intermittent leave or reinstatement.

Minnie Hatchett worked as a business manager for Philander Smith College. A skylight fell on her head, injuring her to such a degree that she couldn't perform certain essential functions of her job. She asked permission to continue working part time, but the college refused the request and told her she had to go on full-time leave. At the end of her FMLA leave, Hatchett still could not perform all the essential functions of her job, so the college offered her some alternative positions. She rejected them, so the college terminated her employment. Hatchett sued the college for violating the FMLA.

The court sided with the college, finding that an employee who cannot perform the essential functions of her job is not entitled to reduced leave schedule or reinstatement under the FMLA.

Hatchett v. Philander Smith Coll., 251 F.3d 670 (8th Cir. 2001).

Applying the 1,250-Hour Eligibility Requirement

An employee on intermittent or reduced scheduled leave doesn't become ineligible for FMLA leave if, because of the FMLA-protected schedule, his or her hours drop below the 1,250-hour requirement. As long as the employee worked 1,250 hours in 12 months at the time of initially requesting the intermittent or reduced-schedule leave, the employee's leave is protected for absences relating to the original condition requiring intermittent leave.

However, the employee must meet the 1,250-hour test at the start of each FMLA leave year. Once the employee has used up the 12-week leave entitlement, you will need to recalculate the employee's leave eligibility as of the next request for leave. When making this calculation, the employee's leave time does not count as hours worked.

This rule applies only to intermittent leave taken for the same condition. If an employee properly qualifies for intermittent leave and then needs FMLA leave for a different reason within the same 12-month period, you should recalculate the employee's eligibility at the time of the second request. In doing so, you needn't count the employee's leave hours as hours worked. The odd result of this rule is that an employee might be eligible for one type of FMLA leave (intermittent leave that began when the employee met the eligibility requirements) but not for others.

EXAMPLE 1: Telly, one of your company's part-time employees, has worked 25 hours per week for five years. For the first 12 weeks of 2007, Telly needs to reduce his hours to 20 per week so he can care for his wife, who is receiving cancer treatment. Your company uses the calendar leave year calculation. In July of 2007, Telly's wife takes a turn for the worse, and he asks to resume his reduced leave schedule effective July 1. You count up his time for the last 12 months and discover that he's only worked 1,240 hours. Should you deny his leave request?

No. Because Telly needs intermittent leave for the same condition, you can't redetermine his eligibility during the leave year. Although his hours have dropped below the eligibility threshold, he is still entitled to leave.

EXAMPLE 2: Now assume that Telly needed to take time off, starting July 1, 2007, for his own health condition. Should you deny this request?

Yes. Because Telly is requesting leave for a different condition, you must redetermine his eligibility. He hasn't worked 1,250 hours at the time his leave is scheduled to begin, so he isn't qualified to take this leave.

Part-Time Employees

Under the FMLA, a part-time employee or an employee with variable hours is entitled to leave in proportion to the amount of time he or she normally works. In other words, the leave time allowed for those employees is prorated. Usually, you will not need to calculate the pro rata time unless the employee is requesting intermittent or partial leave—whether an employee normally works 15 hours in a workweek or 50 hours, if the employee takes a whole week at once, you know that the employee has used one week's worth of leave time. On the other hand, if the employee only uses a few hours here and there, you have to figure how much leave time, in total, the employee is entitled to.

EXAMPLE 1: Leslie, who normally works 30 hours per week, needs 15 hours off each week due to a serious medical condition. Leslie will take half a week of FMLA leave each calendar week and will use up all her FMLA leave in 24 calendar weeks.

EXAMPLE 2: Keith usually works a six-day week. He takes four calendar weeks and two days of leave. Because Keith's workweek is six days long, that equals four and one-third workweeks of leave. If Keith's regular schedule was four days a week, his time off would use up four and one-half weeks of leave.

If a part-time employee's schedule varies from week to week, measure the FMLA workweek by calculating the weekly average hours worked in the 12 weeks prior to the start of the FMLA leave. You can use the employee's timesheet or payroll records to come up with this figure. Make sure the employee agrees to the weekly average in a signed document.

EXAMPLE: Manny works between 20 and 35 hours per week, depending on your company's needs. He requests intermittent leave for his asthma, which flares up periodically. You add up Manny's hours for the past 12 weeks, which total 288 hours. Dividing that by 12, you come up with a weekly average of 24 hours for the past 12 weeks. Manny signs an agreement that his weekly average is 24 hours. Using that as Manny's average workweek, you track his FMLA leave. So, when Manny's asthma acts up at work and he takes four hours off, he has used 1/6 of a workweek of FMLA leave.

> **CAUTION**
>
> **Make sure part-time employees are eligible for leave in the first place.** As explained in Chapter 3, part-time employees must work 1,250 hours in the preceding 12 months to be eligible for FMLA leave. This works out to a bit more than 24 hours a week, 52 weeks a year. You won't have to do the math on intermittent leave availability unless your part-time employees can meet this initial eligibility requirement.

For employees who work irregular hours, the best practice is for you to sit down with the employee and reach an agreement as to the employee's "average" workweek. Calculate the weekly average for the 12 weeks immediately preceding the start of the leave. Put the calculation into a written agreement and have the employee sign it.

Employees Who Work Overtime

If your company requires an employee to work overtime, the overtime hours are considered part of the employee's normal workweek for purposes of calculating the amount of leave time an employee is entitled to. If an employee chooses to work overtime but is not required to, the overtime hours don't count as part of the employee's normal workweek.

EXAMPLE: Claire and her coworkers all have to work four hours of overtime a week, in addition to their regular 40 hours. In this situation, Claire's usual workweek is 44 hours, and she's entitled to 528 total hours of FMLA leave per year (assuming she's otherwise qualified).

If Claire's overtime was voluntary—that is, the company didn't require it but she decided to work it anyway—then she would have a 40-hour week for purposes of calculating her available FMLA leave.

Exempt Employees

It can be tricky to figure out what constitutes a normal workweek for exempt employees—employees who are not entitled to overtime pay. Most companies don't routinely track hours worked by exempt employees, because those employees don't get paid for putting in extra time. However, an exempt employee's FMLA entitlement is based on the hours the employee usually works, just like any other employee.

Because a salaried, exempt employee usually does not "clock in" or "clock out," when an exempt employee requests this type of leave, your company and the employee must agree in writing on the length of the employee's workweek. If you can't reach agreement, your company must track the exempt employee's hours to calculate how many hours are available for leave.

EXAMPLE: Manny is an exempt manager who regularly works 60 hours per week. His FMLA workweek and intermittent time off are calculated according to a 60-hour workweek. When Manny takes four hours of FMLA intermittent leave one week, that counts as 1/15 of a workweek of his overall entitlement.

TIP

Pay docking rules don't apply to FMLA leave. Generally, employers may not dock the pay of an exempt employee for absences of less than a full day (for example, because the employee is tardy or leaves early). Employers who violate this rule might lose the right to exempt these employees from overtime—and, as a result, have to pay them time-and-a-half for every extra hour worked. There are a few exceptions to this rule, however, and one of them is for FMLA leave. You can track—and not pay an exempt employee for—FMLA leave taken in increments of less than a full day without losing the exemption.

Administering Intermittent or Reduced-Schedule Leave

Because intermittent and reduced-schedule leave differs from full-time FMLA leave in several ways, it must be administered more carefully. After all, you'll have to keep track of how much protected time an employee is using and how much time that employee has available. Here are some of the notable differences:

- **Record keeping.** Because the calculations and calendaring required by intermittent and reduced-schedule leave are more complicated than those required by full-time FMLA leave, it is essential to keep accurate and regularly updated records of these leaves. Below is a sample worksheet for keeping track of this leave; there is a blank copy for your use in Appendix C.

Calculating Intermittent/Reduced-Schedule Leave				
REGULAR WORKWEEK	AVAILABLE FMLA LEAVE	LEAVE NEEDED (HRS./WK.)	AVAILABLE LEAVE/LEAVE NEEDED	NUMBER OF CALENDAR WEEKS TO EXHAUST FMLA LEAVE
Employee A: 30 hrs./wk.	X 12 wks. = 360 hrs.	20 hrs./wk.	360 hrs./20 hrs.	= 18 weeks
Employee B: 25 hrs./wk.	X 12 wks. = 300 hrs.	9 hrs./wk.	300 hrs./9 hrs.	= 33 weeks
Employee C: 62 hrs./wk.	X 12 wk. = 744 hrs.	21 hrs./wk.	744 hrs./21 hrs.	= 35 weeks

- **No fitness for duty report.** Under certain circumstances, an employee returning to work after a full-time FMLA leave must submit a "fitness for duty report" confirming that the employee is able to work (see "Fitness for Duty Certifications" in Chapter 10). You can't require an employee returning to his or her original job or regular schedule after an intermittent or reduced-schedule leave to submit this report. (Of course, you don't need this report for employees taking intermittent or reduced-schedule leave, because those employees must be able to perform their jobs throughout such leave.)

- **No minimum time or duration.** Employees may take intermittent or reduced-schedule leave in the shortest periods of time that your company uses for payroll. So, if your company clocks its employees' time by the minute, then an employee's FLMA intermittent leave could be measured in minutes. That means you'll have to track not only the employee's working time down to these small increments, but their FMLA leave time, too.

- **Required overtime versus voluntary overtime.** If an employee on intermittent or reduced-schedule leave is unable to work mandatory overtime, the unworked overtime hours count as FMLA leave time and reduce the employee's 12-week total FMLA leave entitlement by the overtime hours not worked. However, voluntary overtime hours don't count.

EXAMPLE: Your company requires Manny to work eight hours of overtime each week, so his FMLA workweek is 48 hours. If Manny requests a reduced schedule of 40 hours per week, he is taking 1/6 of a workweek of FMLA leave each week.

- **Special rules apply to teachers.** See 29 C.F.R. § 825.601 for special rules that apply to school employees seeking intermittent or reduced-leave schedules.

Flexible Schedules Versus FMLA Leave

Sometimes, an employee who has a medical condition or caretaking responsibilities might request a flexible schedule. In this situation, the employee isn't asking for time off work; instead, the employee wants to work the same total number of hours, but on a different schedule than usual. Because such an employee won't be taking any time off, this does not count as a request for FMLA leave.

EXAMPLE: Your employee Bud normally works a 9-to-5 workday. He has recently requested a change in his work schedule to 11-to-7 because the antidepressants he is taking make him groggy in the morning. Is this a request for FMLA intermittent/reduced-schedule leave?

No, because Bud is not taking any time off and the schedule change is not needed for medical treatment. However, keep in mind that, if Bud's depression is a disability, you may have to accommodate the schedule change under the ADA. (For more information, see Chapter 11.)

Common Mistakes Regarding Leave Duration— And How to Avoid Them

MISTAKE 1: Using inconsistent methods to measure the "leave year."

AVOID THIS MISTAKE BY:

- Making sure everyone in your company uses the same leave year method for all employees seeking FMLA leave.

- If your company changes leave year methods, providing 60 days' notice to all employees before implementing the change. You must allow employees who already started or requested leave prior to your announcement to use whichever method of calculating the leave year is most beneficial to them.

- Applying the new method to all employees as soon as the 60-day notice period passes.

MISTAKE 2: Failing to accurately count employee leave time taken.

AVOID THIS MISTAKE BY:

- Calculating available FMLA leave time at the beginning of leave.

- Tracking all leave time the employee takes—not including time the employee actually spends working, additional time off the employee takes for your company's convenience, and weeks during which your company is shut down.

- Subtracting all leave time taken from the employee's available FMLA leave time.

MISTAKE 3: Failing to accurately calculate available leave time for employees who need intermittent or reduced-schedule leave.

AVOID THIS MISTAKE BY:

- Calculating available leave time based on the employee's usual workweek. Employees who work part time or work overtime hours are entitled to a prorated amount of leave based on their usual hours worked.

- Keeping good records of employee work hours, including hours worked by exempt employees.

- Coming up with the average hourly workweek for employees with irregular schedules, based on the 12-week period before they start their leave.

- Getting written agreements of average workweek hours from employees with irregular schedules and exempt employees who request FMLA leave.

✓ **Managers' Checklist**   **Duration of Leave**

For All Employees Requesting Leave:

❑ I confirmed that my company's method for defining the FMLA leave year is in writing, in our FMLA leave policy.

❑ If our company has not yet defined its leave year or has decided to change methods of defining the leave year, I either

   ❑ provided all employees with notice of this change at least 60 days before they requested leave, or

   ❑ gave employees the benefit of whichever leave year calculation method provided them with the most leave.

❑ I calculated the FMLA leave time available to the employee requesting leave according to my company's leave-year method.

❑ I recorded all FMLA leave the employee has taken, but I have not included the following types of time off as FMLA leave:

   ❑ time the employee actually spent working

   ❑ time taken off for the company's convenience, and

   ❑ weeks during which the company was shut down.

For Employees Requesting Intermittent or Reduced-Schedule Leave

❑ I determined that the employee's requested intermittent or reduced-schedule leave is medically necessary.

❑ I determined that the employee is able to perform the essential functions of his or her job.

❑ If the employee works the same number of hours each week, I used that schedule to calculate the FMLA leave available to the employee.

❏ If the employee's hours are irregular, I calculated the average hours worked per week by the employee requesting FMLA leave, and

    ❏ I have a written agreement of the average workweek signed by the employee, and

    ❏ I calculated the pro rata time off that the employee is entitled to under the FMLA.

❏ If the employee is exempt from overtime, the employee and I reached an agreement as to the employee's average weekly hours, and

    ❏ I have the employee's sign-off on this average.

❏ I included all mandatory overtime hours in the workweek hours of the employee requesting FMLA leave.

Giving Notice and Designating Leave

CHAPTER HIGHLIGHTS

If an employee's requested leave qualifies as FMLA leave, you should designate it as such in writing.

Whenever you have reason to believe that an employee's requested leave may be FMLA-qualified, you can and should preliminarily designate it as FMLA leave, even if the employee does not request it; you can withdraw a preliminary designation if further investigation shows that the FMLA does not apply.

Your company must provide individualized FMLA information to each employee requesting leave that may be FMLA-qualified, explaining the employee's rights under the FMLA and the effect of the employee's failure to comply with the FMLA and company rules.

Employees requesting FMLA leave must give you 30 days' notice of the need for leave, unless:

- the leave is not certain in time
- there is a change in circumstances, or
- your company's leave plan provides for less than 30 days' notice.

An employee requesting FMLA leave that is not foreseeable must provide notice as soon as practicable, usually within two business days after learning that he or she needs leave.

Your company is allowed to discipline an employee for failing to provide proper notice of FMLA leave but can't deny the leave.

The employee requesting FMLA leave must give you sufficient information to determine that the FMLA may apply, but the information doesn't have to be detailed or even refer to the FMLA.

This chapter covers the FMLA's informational requirements: what information you and the employee must give each other when an employee takes or requests time off that might be protected by the FMLA. The heavier burden lies with you, and for good reason: Many employees don't know what the law is or what their rights are. In fact, your employees may never have heard of the FMLA. This means that employees may come to you requesting leave, without knowing that they may be legally entitled to it, and legally obligated to give you information so that you can properly determine whether the FMLA applies.

Your company's informational requirements begin with hanging a poster on the FMLA and providing general information about the law in your policies; Chapter 2 explains how to comply with these obligations. Once an employee requests leave, however, additional requirements kick in. You must know enough about the FMLA to figure out whether it applies, asking the employee for more information if necessary. You must designate the leave as FMLA leave and notify the employee that you've done so. You must also give the employee information on a long list of topics, specially geared toward the employee's leave situation.

Sounds like a lot of meetings and paperwork, doesn't it? While it is a significant responsibility to comply with all these requirements, there are ways to streamline the process. We tell you how below and give you some approved forms to use.

Designating Time Off as FMLA Leave

When an employee comes to you requesting medical or parenting leave, the first important duty that you have is to designate the leave, in writing, as FMLA leave. If you don't, FMLA leave has not started, and you're allowing the employee to take leave without reducing the employee's 12-week entitlement. For example, say an employee takes two weeks off to care for an ill family member. If you don't designate that time as FMLA leave and the employee wants 12 weeks off to bond with a new child later in the same year, you will have to grant the request.

Making a Preliminary Designation

What if an employee comes to you requesting leave, and you're not sure whether the leave is FMLA-qualified? That's what a preliminary designation is for: It allows you to designate the leave as FMLA leave, pending an investigation into whether the leave actually qualifies for the FMLA's protections. The preliminary designation should be in writing, like the sample below. (You can find a blank copy of the form in Appendix C and on the CD-ROM at the back of this book.)

Your investigation into the reason for the leave has limits—you can't go snooping about on your own. Instead, your designation decision has to be based on the information you receive from the employee or from the employee's spokesperson (such as spouse, parent, or child) if the employee is incapacitated, as well as the information in the employee's medical certification for medical leave.

If you make a preliminary FMLA designation and later learn that it is incorrect because, for example, the medical certification doesn't reveal a serious health condition, you must withdraw that designation. Like the preliminary designation, this withdrawal should also be in writing. If you withdraw a preliminary FMLA designation, you can't count any leave time taken against the employee's available FMLA leave time.

However, if you learn that the leave requested falls within the FMLA, you must notify the employee within two business days that you are permanently designating the leave as FMLA leave. As with a preliminary designation, the designation should be in writing. It also has to state that the leave is FMLA leave and will be counted against the employee's available FMLA leave time. If you give the designation orally first, you need to confirm it in writing no later than the following payday. The FMLA does not require you to use a particular form to designate FMLA leave; you can even do it as a notation on the employee's pay stub.

TIP

Use a form to designate leave. Although no particular form is required, it's a good idea to develop an FMLA designation form—such as the sample we provide below (also in Appendix C and on the CD-ROM in the back of this book)—and use it with every request for leave. This will ensure that you're giving the employee all required information and will create a clean written record for you to keep in the employee's file. (See Chapter 12 for more on keeping records relating to FMLA leave.)

SAMPLE

FMLA Designation (Preliminary)

TO: [*Employee's Name*]:

You have requested leave from [*Date*] to [*Date*]. Based on the information you provided, the leave you requested is preliminarily designated as FMLA leave.

Please provide the following additional information:

• [*other information requested, such as medical certification, proof of family relationship, and so on*]

Once you have provided this information, we will determine whether your leave is covered by the FMLA. If so, we will issue a final designation to that effect, and the leave you take will be counted against your available FMLA leave time. If not, we will withdraw this preliminary designation, in writing.

SAMPLE

FMLA Designation (Final)

TO: [*Employee's Name*]:

You have requested leave from [*Date*] to [*Date*]. Based on the information you provided, the leave you requested is designated as FMLA leave and will count against your available FMLA leave time.

Designating FMLA Leave Retroactively

You can designate FMLA leave retroactively if, after an employee has started leave, you learn that the leave is FMLA qualified. You must make this retroactive FMLA designation within two days after you first learn that the leave is FMLA qualified, and you must do it in writing. If you don't, you can designate only subsequent leave—that is, leave taking place after your designation—as FMLA qualified.

You can also retroactively designate FMLA leave when circumstances change so that a leave that wasn't originally an FMLA-qualifying leave becomes qualified. The rules for how much of the original time counts as FMLA leave depend on whether the FMLA-qualifying event developed out of the original reason for leave (for example, when a minor illness takes a serious turn) or not (for example, when an employee suffers an accident during vacation). In the first situation, you may designate all of the employee's time off as FMLA leave; in the second, only leave taken after the FMLA-qualifying event can be designated as FMLA leave.

EXAMPLE 1: Your employee, Ravi, caught a cold that turned into bronchitis. Ravi requests sick leave to recover from the bronchitis. Four days after going out on sick leave, Ravi calls in and says that he's gotten worse and his doctor has diagnosed him with bronchial pneumonia. How do you handle this change of circumstance?

Since you have read this book, you correctly realize that Ravi now has a serious health condition. Because it grew out of Ravi's original health condition, the entire time he has taken off should be designated as FMLA leave for a serious health condition. You give Ravi a written designation within two days of learning of the diagnosis of bronchial pneumonia.

EXAMPLE 2: Selena requests two weeks' vacation time to go snorkeling in Belize. You grant the request. Ten days into the vacation, Selena calls to report that she took a nasty spill on her motorbike and had to be hospitalized for a concussion and broken arm. Does the accident change Selena's leave?

Yes. Selena's leave changed from vacation to FMLA leave for a serious medical condition as soon as she got hurt. Only the time off after her injury counts as FMLA leave. The initial week of time off was true vacation time and does not count against Selena's available FMLA leave time.

Your company may even be able to designate time off as FMLA leave after the employee returns to work—though this is usually prohibited. The three exceptions are:

- The employee was absent for an FMLA-qualifying reason, but you did not learn that reason until after the employee returned to work. When this happens, you must designate the leave as FMLA leave within two business days of the employee's return to work.

- You believe the leave is for an FMLA-qualifying reason but have been unable to confirm that reason. You must preliminarily designate this as FMLA leave as soon as you have reason to believe it is FMLA-qualified, subject to withdrawal following your receipt of a confirmation, certification, or second opinion.

- You are awaiting medical certification or a second opinion that you have requested. Because you already had some idea that the leave might be FMLA leave, you must have preliminarily designated the leave.

Designating Paid Leave as FMLA Leave

The FMLA allows employees to substitute paid time off provided under the employer's policies—such as vacation, sick, or personal leave—for certain types of unpaid FMLA leave. It also sometimes allows employers to require employees to make this substitution, even if the employee doesn't want to.

In addition, you should designate any time off for which the employee is paid from another source as FMLA leave, if it meets the requirements. For example, an employee who suffers an on-the-job injury and takes time off while receiving workers' compensation benefits is probably also qualified for FMLA leave—and you should designate that time off accordingly.

Paid Leave Provided by Your Company

Whether company-provided paid leave can be used during all or part of an employee's FMLA leave depends on the type of leave requested and your company's leave policies.

TIP

It's really overlap, not substitution. Although the regulations interpreting the FMLA, courts, and commentators all refer to "substitution" of paid leave, that's not exactly accurate. The employee isn't using paid leave instead of FMLA leave but is using the two types of leave at the same time.

- **Accrued paid vacation or personal leave.** Either of these can be used for an FMLA leave for a serious medical condition (an employee's or a family member's) or for parenting leave. If your company limits when or for how long employees can take paid vacation, these limits can't be applied to leave that is FMLA-qualified.

- **Paid family leave.** This refers to an employer's policy of allowing employees to take paid leave for birth, adoption, or foster placement or to care for a spouse, child, or parent with a serious health condition. Paid family leave may be substituted for FMLA leave only for conditions that are normally covered by your company's family leave policy.

EXAMPLE: Your company has a paid family leave policy that allows employees to take paid leave to care for ill children and spouses. Your employee, Kurt, has asked for a two-week leave to care for his father following surgery to treat prostate cancer. You give Kurt a written FMLA designation and, in the designation, inform him that he must use accrued paid family leave under your company's policy.

Bad move. Because your company's paid family leave policy does not cover care for a parent, you can't require Kurt to use it during his FMLA leave. The effect is that Kurt has the right to take unpaid FMLA leave to care for his father, and he retains his paid family leave rights under your company's policy.

- **Medical or sick leave.** You can require or permit an employee to use medical or sick leave during an FMLA-qualified leave for the employee's own serious health condition or to care for a spouse, child, or parent with a serious health condition. Again, your company's policy is your guide: An employee is entitled to take medical or sick leave in conjunction with FMLA leave only to the extent that it falls within your company's usual requirements for the use of paid sick or medical leave. For example, sick leave may be substituted for FMLA leave to care for an ailing family member only if your company allows employees to use sick leave to care for family members. Also, the employee can't be required to first exhaust paid sick leave before taking FMLA leave.

EXAMPLE 1: Your company's sick leave policy allows employees to take paid time off only for their own serious health conditions. Following the above example, you withdrew the incorrect designation you initially gave Kurt and gave him a corrected one that designated his leave as FMLA leave but did not require him to use paid leave. Kurt then requested to use accrued, paid sick leave while on leave caring for his father. You have learned your lesson after reviewing this chapter, so you deny the request because your company's paid sick leave policy applies only to the employee's own serious health condition.

EXAMPLE 2: Lourdes is eight months pregnant and requests four weeks of leave following the birth of her child. She also requests that she be allowed to use paid sick leave under the company's sick leave policy. You deny her request, since neither the paid sick leave policy nor the paid family leave policy allows employees to take paid leave to bond with newborns.

Not so fast. Lourdes might need the post-delivery leave for her own serious health condition. You should have preliminarily designated Lourdes's leave as FMLA leave and then investigated. You then could have amended the designation if it qualified under the company's paid sick leave policy.

- **Paid time off.** Many companies don't offer sick leave, vacation leave, and/or personal leave but instead combine all leave into paid time off, or PTO. Because this type of leave is intended to cover any reason the employee might be absent, it is treated like vacation or personal leave under the FMLA. That is, it may be substituted for any type of FMLA leave.

- **Accrued compensatory time off.** Accrued compensatory time off cannot run concurrently with FMLA time, even if the reason for taking the compensatory time is covered by the FMLA.

Paid Leave From Another Source

When an employee takes any type of time off to care for a family member, for parenting, or for the employee's own health, you should always consider whether the FMLA applies—and, if so, designate the leave accordingly. Some types of leave slip through the cracks because the employee is covered by another law or program. But any type of leave that falls within the FMLA's parameters should be designated as such and counted against the employee's 12-week entitlement, no matter how many other laws apply.

Here are some examples:

- **Workers compensation.** As explained in Chapter 11, an employee who suffers a work-related illness or injury may be entitled to partial wage replacement while off work to recuperate. This time will almost always also qualify as FMLA leave.

- **Temporary disability.** The laws of a handful of states provide some income to employees who are temporarily unable to work because of a disability. This time may also qualify as FMLA leave.

- **Paid family leave.** In California, employees can receive some income for time they take off to care for a family member, which might also qualify as FMLA leave.

- **Disability insurance.** If your company provides disability insurance for employees, they might have the right to replacement income while they are out of work. This time off may also be covered by the FMLA.

If an employee is entitled to some compensation from another source, paid leave typically may not be substituted for this time off. For example, an employee may not use paid sick leave while he is also receiving workers' compensation. There are some exceptions to this general rule, however: California's paid family leave program, for example, allows employers to make up the difference between what the program pays (just over half of the employee's regular wages) and the employee's usual pay by taking partial paid leave under the employer's policy.

If You Don't Designate Within the Time Allowed

If you know that an employee's requested leave is for an FMLA-qualified reason but fail to give the employee a written FMLA designation within two business days of learning about it, you can't retroactively designate the leave as FMLA leave. Exactly what this means, however, is an open question.

The regulations interpreting the FMLA say that employers cannot count time off that they fail to designate against the employee's 12-week FMLA leave entitlement. However, the U.S. Supreme Court, in *Ragsdale v. Wolverine World Wide Inc.,* 553 U.S. 81 (2002), invalidated this rule to the extent that it allows the employee to take more than 12 weeks of FMLA-protected leave.

As a result of this case, commentators agree that you can subtract FMLA-qualified time off from the employee's available FMLA leave time, even if you fail to designate it as FMLA leave. But if an employee relies on the failure to designate in some way that harms his or her interests, the employee may still have a claim under the FMLA. The Department of Labor is expected to issue revised regulations to clear up what exactly the effect of this kind of reliance is but has not yet done so.

RESOURCE

Check Nolo's website for updates to DOL regulations. When this book went to print, the FMLA regulations were under review. If new regulations are adopted, we'll explain them at www.nolo.com. (See Chapter 1 for more information.)

Individual Notification Requirements

In addition to the general FMLA information that goes into your company's employee handbook or written policies, when an individual employee requests leave for an FMLA-qualified reason, you must provide written, individualized notice of the company's expectations and the employee's obligations. You also have to respond to any questions that the leave-seeking employee has about the FMLA. If your company doesn't have an employee handbook or other written policies describing FMLA rights and duties, it must give an employee all of the general information described above whenever an employee requests leave for an FMLA-qualified reason.

You must give or send this individualized notice to the employee within two business days after the employee notifies you that he or she needs leave. The written notice must be in a language in which the employee is literate. If the employee is sensory impaired (for example, blind or deaf), be sure to comply with all applicable federal and state laws, such as disability discrimination laws, that require employers to communicate with sensory-deprived employees in a way that they can understand.

The individualized notice may be combined with the written FMLA designation discussed above. You can use the optional DOL notice Form WH-381, "*Employer Response to Employee Request for Family or Medical Leave*," to give the required notice. (Optional Form WH-381 is included in Appendix C and on the CD-ROM at the back of this book.) The form is easy to use, with boxes to check ensuring you've included all the information above, as well as spaces to write in leave and return dates.

In addition to giving an employee individualized notice the first time he or she requests FMLA leave, you must give this employee additional notices in the following circumstances:

- When the employee requests FMLA leave six months or more after the first request for leave. At that point, the employee may no longer remember many of the details you previously provided.

Information That Must Be in an Individualized FMLA Notice

The individualized notice must explain:

- that the leave will be subtracted from the employee's available FMLA leave

- that the employee has to submit medical certification of a serious health condition, if your company requires it

- the consequences if the employee fails to submit medical certification

- that the employee has the right to substitute paid leave for FMLA leave (if that is your company's policy), and that the leave is still subtracted from available FMLA leave

- that your company will require the employee to substitute paid leave for FMLA leave (if that is your company's policy), and that the leave is still subtracted from available FMLA leave

- any conditions related to the substitution of paid leave under your company's policies (for example, that paid sick leave can be used only for the employee's own serious health condition)

- that the employee has to make premium payments during leave to maintain health benefits, if that is your company's policy

- the arrangements for the employee to make health insurance premium payments, if required

- the consequences of the employee's failure to make timely health insurance premium payments (for example, loss of the benefit)

- that the employee must submit a "fitness-for-duty" certificate to return to work, if that is your company's policy

- whether the employee is a "key employee" and, if so, the possibility that return to work may be denied following leave (see Chapter 10)

- the conditions under which a "key employee" will be denied a return to work (see Chapter 10)

- that if the employee isn't a key employee, the employee has the right to return to the same or equivalent job after the FMLA leave ends

- that if the employee fails to return to work after FMLA leave ends, the employee may be liable for payment of health insurance premiums normally paid by your company, and

- any other action by the employee that your company requires (such as periodic reports of the employee's status).

EXAMPLE 1: Your employee, Dev, took a two-week FMLA leave in January. You gave Dev the required individualized notice within a day of learning of his need for the leave. In April, Dev requests another FMLA leave for three weeks. Do you have to give him another notice?

No. Six months have not elapsed since his first leave.

EXAMPLE 2: Dev requests a third FMLA leave for three weeks in July. Do you have to give him another notice?

Yes, because six months have elapsed since Dev's first request for leave (when you gave him the notice).

- Whenever there is a change in the information provided in the original individualized notice. Be sure to refer to the prior notice in the subsequent one and explain how the new notice is different.

EXAMPLE: Dev was required to use accrued paid leave during the July leave, and you informed him of this when you gave him the required notice. In September, Dev requests two weeks of FMLA leave. Pursuant to company policy, this leave will be unpaid. Should you give Dev an additional notice even though six months have not passed since you gave him the previous notice?

Yes. Because his previous leave was paid and this leave is unpaid, you are required to provide an additional notice referring to the prior notice and clearly stating the change in information.

- If your company requires medical certification of a serious health condition or a fitness-for-duty certification to return to work, you must give employees seeking FMLA leave notice of these requirements each time an employee requests leave. You need to include a statement of the consequences if the employee fails to provide the certification. You do not have to give additional notice of the other information required in the original notice.

EXAMPLE: Your company requires all employees seeking FMLA leave for a serious health condition to submit a medical certification. Lourdes took a four-week maternity leave in November and you gave her the required notice. In March of the next year, Lourdes requests a two-week FMLA leave to care for her baby following hernia surgery. Do you give Lourdes an additional notice even though only four months have passed since her last leave?

Yes. Because your company requires medical certification of the serious health condition, it must give Lourdes an additional notice each time she requests leave for a serious health condition.

If you don't give the employee the required FMLA information, you risk being sued for violating the employee's FMLA rights. If your company is found liable, it will have to pay the employee for any losses the employee suffered as a result of the violation.

LESSONS FROM THE

Real World

An employer can be liable for interfering with an employee's FMLA rights because it failed to provide FMLA pregnancy leave information to her.

Marria Saroli was the controller for Automation & Modular Components, Inc. ("A&M"). Upon learning that she was pregnant, Saroli notified A&M and requested leave. A&M didn't respond or provide Saroli with any FMLA information. Instead, A&M told Saroli that it was hiring a man to manage her department and take over her duties.

Saroli's doctor placed her on immediate leave due to a medical condition related to her pregnancy. She again requested pregnancy leave. This time A&M wrote to her, telling her that she could take only six weeks of leave. Saroli had to extend her leave twice, so it exceeded six weeks. When Saroli tried to return to work, A&M told her that the only job she could return to was one with diminished duties. Saroli resigned and sued A&M for interfering with her FMLA rights.

The court ruled that A&M's failure to give Saroli information about her rights under the FMLA and its failure to respond to her requests for information about pregnancy leave interfered with her FMLA rights.

Saroli v. Automation & Modular Components, Inc., 405 F.3d 446 (6th Cir. 2005).

Even failing to give employees accurate and complete information about their FMLA rights and obligations may lead to trouble. In some cases, when employees have been given incorrect information from their employers about their FMLA rights, courts have barred the employers from defending themselves by claiming that the employee failed to comply with the FMLA. For this reason, you'll need to be sure that all the information you provide is accurate.

LESSONS FROM THE

Real World

An employer that led its employee to believe that his whole 24-week leave was covered by the FMLA couldn't later claim that the employee had exhausted his FMLA leave after 12 weeks off.

Sam Duty worked as a maintenance mechanic for Norton-Alcoa Proppants. Duty went out on leave after injuring his back on the job. Norton-Alcoa had a short-term disability policy giving employees 26 weeks of disability leave. Five months after Duty started his leave, Norton-Alcoa sent him a letter stating that his entire leave period was covered by the FMLA. Duty relied on this statement and continued his leave.

When Duty later called in about returning to work, Norton-Alcoa informed him that he had used up his FMLA leave after the first 12 weeks of the disability leave. Duty was terminated for taking unauthorized additional leave.

Duty sued under the FMLA. Norton-Alcoa argued that Duty should not be protected by the FMLA because he did not return to work after 12 weeks of leave.

The court ruled that Norton-Alcoa could not claim that Duty had used up his FMLA leave, because it had led him to believe that his entire leave was FMLA-protected and he had relied on the company's statement by continuing his leave.

Duty v. Norton-Alcoa Proppants, 293 F.3d 481 (8th Cir. 2002).

Employee Notice Requirements

While most of the obligation to administer FMLA leave falls on you, the employee bears some responsibility. Primarily, an employee requesting leave that may be FMLA-qualified must give you enough information so that you can determine whether the FMLA applies.

Methods of Employee Notification

The employee's notice may be either oral (including by telephone) or in writing (including by fax or email). An employee's spokesperson may give the notice if the employee is incapacitated or otherwise unable to give the notice.

What does the employee need to tell you? Not much: only enough information to let you know that the need for leave may be covered by the FMLA. (29 C.F.R. § 208.) The employee doesn't even have to mention the FMLA or the particular rights protected by the FMLA. Nor does the employee have to give you any medical information when making the initial request for leave: It's enough if the employee's notice reasonably informs you that the leave is for a serious health condition or birth, adoption, or foster placement.

CAUTION

There are no "magic words" for an employee to use to request FMLA leave. All the employee has to do is tell you enough information for you to determine whether the leave may be covered by the FMLA.

That means it's up to you to recognize the possibility that the leave is covered by the FMLA. For example, if you know that an employee suffers from a chronic medical condition and the employee requests leave without specifying why, you should preliminarily designate the leave as FMLA leave. Your knowledge of the chronic medical condition and the leave request amount to notice under the FMLA. Likewise, if an employee's behavior shows that the employee is suffering from a serious health condition, that may be enough to put you on notice of the need for FMLA leave. Again, you should make a preliminary designation and then investigate and determine whether a permanent designation is appropriate.

LESSONS FROM THE

Real World

An employee only has to give enough information for the employer to conclude that the employee may need time off for a serious health condition.

Samuel Cavin worked as a production associate in the assembly department of Honda of America Manufacturing, Inc. Cavin had an accident while riding his motorcycle. He called Honda and told his supervisor about it and explained that he was in the hospital. Honda claimed that this wasn't enough information to notify the company that Cavin had a serious health condition covered by the FMLA, and they fired him. Cavin sued Honda for violating the FMLA.

The court ruled that Cavin had provided enough information for Honda to conclude that he had a serious health condition entitling him to FMLA leave.

Cavin v. Honda of America Manufacturing, Inc., 346 F.3d 713 (6th Cir. 2003).

When the employee asks to use accrued paid leave, such as vacation leave, the employee isn't required to tell you the possibly FMLA-qualifying reason for the leave request. As with any request for possible FMLA leave, you are entitled to find out if the type of leave falls within both your company's paid leave policy and the FMLA. If the employee doesn't give you this information, you can deny the employee's request for leave and the employee must then give you sufficient information to establish that the need for leave falls within the FMLA. Otherwise, the employee hasn't shown that he or she is entitled to FMLA-protected leave.

Employees can notify you after returning from leave that they took leave for an FMLA-qualified reason, so long as they do so within two business days after coming back to work. If, within this two-day time period, the employee fails to give you enough information to determine if the FMLA applies, then the employee can't later claim that the leave was covered by the FMLA or entitled to the law's protections.

Getting More Information From the Employee

If you need more information than the employee gives you to figure out if the FMLA applies, ask for it. Also ask for medical certification if the employee needs the leave for a serious health condition. Once you request the certification, the employee must provide medical or parental status information supporting the need for leave. We explain how to do this in Chapters 4 and 8.

If the employee fails or refuses to tell you the reason he or she needs leave, you can deny FMLA leave. After all, you won't have enough information to determine whether the leave is FMLA-qualified, and it would be unfair and inconsistent to grant FMLA leave to some employees even without proper documentation while denying it to others.

LESSONS FROM THE

Real World

An employer could deny FMLA leave when the employee seeking leave didn't provide enough information for the employer to determine whether he had a serious health condition.

Lee Brenneman worked in the pharmacy department of MedCentral Health System for 27 years. Brenneman had diabetes and needed time off because of a medical problem related to using his insulin pump. He informed MedCentral that he was "having trouble" with his insulin pump but didn't otherwise explain the problem. Brenneman then took time off.

MedCentral didn't designate his leave as FMLA leave and terminated him for unexcused absences. Brenneman sued MedCentral for violating the FMLA.

The court ruled that Brenneman's request for leave didn't adequately notify MedCentral of a serious medical condition, since his statement that he was having trouble with his insulin pump didn't give his employer enough information to indicate that he had a serious medical condition.

Brenneman v. MedCentral Health System, 366 F.3d 412 (6th Cir. 2004).

Your Company's Leave Notification Rules

Your company is also allowed to require employees requesting FMLA leave to comply with its leave notification rules, as long as the rules:

- are reasonable
- don't require more of employees seeking FMLA leave than is required of employees seeking other types of leave, and
- don't conflict with FMLA rights.

LESSONS FROM THE
Real World

An employee doesn't have to give advance notice to substitute paid vacation time for emergency FMLA leave.

Sandra Solovey worked for Wyoming Valley Health Care System—Hospital as an emergency room nurse. Solovey's father was receiving hospice care. On June 23, 2003, Solovey left work early after hearing that her father had taken a turn for the worse. Solovey returned to work briefly on June 26, then left again to be with her father. Her father died on June 28. In total, Solovey missed three full, and two partial, days of work.

Solovey and the hospital agreed that her time off qualified as FMLA leave. The hospital deemed two of the days Solovey took off to be "family ill" days and paid her for that time. However, the hospital refused to allow Solovey to use vacation time for the remainder of her time off. The collective bargaining agreement between the nurses' union and the hospital required nurses to give two weeks' notice before using vacation time; because Solovey didn't give any notice, the hospital didn't allow her to substitute vacation time for her FMLA leave.

The court ruled in favor of Solovey. The FMLA allows employees to substitute paid vacation time for unpaid FMLA leave, and it allows employees to take leave for unforeseeable reasons. Requiring Solovey to give two weeks' notice when she was unable to do so effectively deprived her of the right to substitute vacation time and so violated her rights under the FMLA.

Solovey v. Wyoming Valley Health Care System—Hospital, 396 F. Supp.2d 534 (M.D. Penn. 2005).

Examples of rules that courts have found to be reasonable include rules requiring that leave requests be made in writing and that employees use a particular form.

However, an employee's failure to follow your company's leave notification rules doesn't mean that you can deny the employee's request for FMLA leave. You can discipline the employee for failing to follow the rules, but you must allow the employee to take the leave.

LESSONS FROM THE
Real World

An employer may not deny FMLA leave because the employee failed to comply with the employer's leave request rules.

Connie George worked for Russell Stover Candies, Inc. The company had a call-in message line for absences that employees had to use if they missed work. George took time off due to complications during her pregnancy and informed her supervisor that she would be out but did not call the designated message line. When George asked her supervisor for leave, she specifically requested FMLA leave and received the company's FMLA package from her supervisor. Russell Stover terminated her for unexcused absences. George sued Russell Stover for violating the FMLA.

The court ruled that the Russell Stover could not deny George's leave based on her failure to follow its call-in rules.

George v. Russell Stover Candies, Inc., 106 Fed. Appx. 946 (6th Cir. 2004).

How Much Notice the Employee Must Give

Sometimes employees need time off for conditions or events that are foreseeable, such as a scheduled surgery or the birth of a child. Other times, the need isn't foreseeable, such as a hospitalization and treatment following a heart attack. While the FMLA allows employees to take leave in either case, it requires different amounts of notice.

Employees requesting foreseeable leave must give at least 30 days' notice of the need for leave. There are several exceptions to this rule:

- **When the need for leave isn't certain in time** (for example, where an adoption date isn't definite). In this situation, the employee must give notice as soon as "practicable" (usually within two business days after learning that he or she needs leave).

- **When there is a change in circumstances** (for example, where a medical procedure date is changed to accommodate the hospital's schedule). In this situation, the employee must give notice as soon as he or she learns of the change, in addition to the initial notice.

- **When an employee is a union member and there is a collective bargaining agreement that provides for less notice for leave.** In that case, the employee follows the rules laid out in the collective bargaining agreement.

- **When your company's applicable leave plan permits less notice than the FMLA requires.** For example, if your vacation leave plan provides for less notice than the FMLA requires and the employee is substituting paid vacation leave for FMLA leave, the employee only need give notice as the vacation policy requires.

Where the need is unforeseeable, the employee requesting leave must give you notice as soon as practicable, which typically means within one or two business days after the employee learns of the need for leave. (29 C.F.R. § 825.302.) While you can't deny an employee leave for an unforeseeable, emergency need even when he or she gives late notice, you can discipline the employee for violating company rules.

 TIP

Follow state law notice requirements. If state law allows less advance notice for family and medical leave than the FMLA requires, your company must accept notice that meets the lesser state requirement. Some states, including Alaska, California, and Hawaii, allow for "reasonable" notice of the need for leave without a specific requirement of a number of days of advance notice. Other states specifically allow shorter notice than the FMLA (for example, New Jersey law requires only 15 days' notice for family or medical leave).

"Inquiry Notice" by the Employee

As we've discussed, an employee requesting leave doesn't have tell you he or she is seeking FMLA-protected leave. Nor does the employee have to disclose the specific medical condition, diagnosis, or treatment for which leave is needed. Once an employee tells you that he or she needs time off for what may be an FMLA-qualified reason, you have to ask for more information to determine whether the FMLA actually applies. This is called "inquiry notice."

Because the burden of designating a request for time off as FMLA leave is always on the employer, it is important to listen for any indication that the leave may be FMLA leave and be ready to ask more questions if you can't tell. Any time an employee mentions illness, caretaking, or parenting a new child, you should consider whether the FMLA might be implicated.

EXAMPLE: Tony called you on Monday morning to tell you that his daughter had a fever and he had taken her to the doctor. Tony said he would need the day off and possibly further days later in the week if his daughter didn't improve. Tony called in each of the next four mornings and reported that his daughter was still ill and had to stay home from day care. Tony took those days off, as well. You preliminarily designated Tony's time off as FMLA leave and sent Tony an FMLA certification for his daughter's doctor to fill out. How did you do?

Well done. You understood inquiry notice under the FMLA. Because Tony's daughter was seen by a doctor and her illness lasted four days, you correctly concluded that she might have a serious health condition under the FMLA, and you sent Tony the necessary documentation to confirm this conclusion.

However, the employee can't be completely tight-lipped: The employee must still give you enough information to trigger an FMLA inquiry. Different courts apply different standards to measure how much information an employee must give. For example, some courts have ruled that an employee's statement that she was ill wasn't enough information to prompt her employer to inquire further. Other courts have found that an employee's reference to a condition the employer already knows about is enough notice under the FMLA for a later request for FMLA leave.

LESSONS FROM THE
Real World

An employee's statement to her employer that she needed time off because she "didn't feel good" and needed "a couple days to get better" didn't put her employer on notice that she suffered from a serious health condition.

Shortly before Jill Beaver was scheduled to return from an approved vacation to her job at RGIS Inventory Specialists, Inc., she called in and reported to her supervisor that she was ill, "she didn't feel good," and her doctor had ordered her not to fly or return to work for "a couple of days, a few days." RGIS viewed Beaver's extra time off as unauthorized and fired her. Beaver sued RGIS for terminating her while on FMLA leave.

The court sided with RGIS because Beaver hadn't provided sufficient information to alert her supervisor that the FMLA applied to her leave. Beaver's statements to her supervisor were too general for her supervisor to conclude that she might have suffered from a serious health condition.

Beaver v. RGIS Inventory Specialists, Inc., 144 Fed. Appx. 452 (6th Cir. 2005).

Because there's no hard and fast rule about whether the FMLA applies when an employee gives you very little information about the need for leave, it's best to take a cautious approach. That means designating any possibly FMLA-qualified leave request as FMLA leave subject to withdrawal if further inquiry shows that the leave isn't covered.

 TIP

When in doubt, preliminarily designate the leave as FMLA and inquire further. You can withdraw the designation if your inquiry doesn't support FMLA coverage.

How you treat an employee for purposes of other types of leave or benefits may serve as evidence that you had notice that the employee suffered from a serious health condition. After all, if you know the employee is qualified for parenting leave or disability leave, for example, you know enough to find out whether the FMLA applies.

LESSONS FROM THE

Real World

An employer had notice of an employee's serious health condition because the employer had ordered the employee to participate in an employee assistance program.

William Moorer was the administrator and CFO of Baptist Memorial Health Care System, where he had worked for 17 years. Moorer's boss smelled alcohol on Moorer's breath and noted that his performance had started to slip; he was "fidgety" at meetings; and, at one point, he was slumped in his chair. His boss ordered Moorer to attend the company's employee assistance program, which would require several weeks of leave. Moorer underwent the program and ceased drinking. Nevertheless, Baptist Memorial fired him during the leave. Moorer filed a lawsuit claiming that the company had violated the FMLA by terminating him during an FMLA leave. Baptist Memorial argued that Moorer had never requested FMLA leave.

The court ruled that Baptist Memorial could not claim that it had no notice that the leave it placed Moorer on was FMLA leave. Baptist Memorial had recognized Moorer's serious health condition of alcoholism and need for leave, because it had ordered him into treatment for the condition.

Moorer v. Baptist Memorial Health Care System, 398 F.3d 469 (6th Cir. 2005).

When a leave-seeking employee's behavior reveals that the employee might have a serious health condition, you should give the employee a preliminary FMLA designation of the leave even if the employee doesn't request it. Then carefully document all your efforts to find out if the employee needs FMLA leave.

EXAMPLE: David's supervisor and coworkers have noticed David sleeping on the job on several occasions. David has had no prior performance issues or similar episodes of sleeping on the job. After several of the sleeping incidents, David comes to you and tells you he needs to leave early as he doesn't feel well. David subsequently asks to take several days off. David hasn't mentioned the FMLA or requested leave for a serious health condition. What do you do?

Because you realize that David's recent unusual behavior may signal a serious health condition, you grant the request, ask David for more information about why he needs leave, request medical certification, and send David a preliminary FMLA designation of the leave.

SEE AN EXPERT

Consult an attorney when you make an FMLA designation based on employee behavior. It's always a bit dangerous to make assumptions based on an employee's actions. For example, you could be accused of treating the employee as if he or she has a disability—which constitutes disability discrimination under the Americans with Disabilities Act. (See Chapter 11 for more information.) Because you are making assumptions based on your observations and you're not a doctor, talking to an attorney can help you get a reality check.

Common Mistakes Regarding Giving Notice and Designating Leave—And How to Avoid Them

MISTAKE 1: Failing to designate FMLA-qualified leave taken as FMLA leave.

AVOID THIS MISTAKE BY:

- Giving each employee an FMLA designation form (use the sample form letter in Appendix C or on the CD-ROM at the back of this book) within two business days of learning of the need for leave that may fall under the FMLA. Make sure that the FMLA designation form states that the time off will reduce the employee's available FMLA leave time.

- Giving the employee a preliminary designation as soon as you learn any information that makes you believe the leave might be covered by the FMLA, even if you learn the information after leave has started. You can always withdraw the designation later, if it turns out you were wrong. If the leave is FMLA-qualified, issue a final designation.

- Designating other time off (such as vacation or sick leave) as FMLA leave when a new FMLA-covered event occurs during the leave.

- Designating leave as FMLA leave even if the employee does not request it, if the employee's behavior reveals a serious health condition.

- Designating paid leave as FMLA leave, if the reason for leave qualifies under the FMLA. Don't forget workers' compensation leave, disability leave, and parenting leaves may also be FMLA-qualified.

MISTAKE 2: Denying FMLA leave because the employee has not followed company notice rules.

AVOID THIS MISTAKE BY:

- Granting FMLA leave requests preliminarily and conducting investigations to confirm FMLA coverage.

- Rather than denying FMLA leave, delaying it for the 30-day notice period if the need for leave was truly foreseeable. (Chapter 9 explains how to do this.)

MISTAKE 3: Failing to give individualized FMLA information to employees who need FMLA leave.

AVOID THIS MISTAKE BY:

- Giving each employee requesting FMLA leave a written notice designating the leave as FMLA leave (see above) and detailing FMLA information specific to the employee's particular situation (use the DOL optional notice form, which is included in Appendix C and on the CD-ROM at the back of this book).

- Giving the employee the individualized information in a language the employee understands.

- If the employee is sensory impaired, giving the individualized information in a form that the employee can receive and understand.

- Making sure the individualized information is tailored to the employee's particular situation (for example, telling the employee that he or she can substitute paid leave or that he or she must pay health insurance premiums during leave).

- Giving a new individual notice whenever the employee will be required to follow different rules (for example, to provide a medical certification or fitness for duty report).

✓ Managers' Checklist	Giving Notice and Designating Leave

❏ I have given a written designation form letter to the employee requesting leave. The designation form letter includes:

   ❏ a statement that the leave is FMLA leave and will reduce the employee's available FMLA leave time, or

   ❏ a statement that the leave is preliminarily designated FMLA leave and will reduce the employee's available FMLA leave time, pending investigation into whether the need for leave falls under the FMLA, or

   ❏ a statement that the leave is not FMLA leave.

❏ After giving the preliminary designation, I have asked the employee requesting leave or his or her spokesperson to tell me the reason for the leave, and

   ❏ the employee has informed me that the employee needs the leave because of a serious health condition, and I have confirmed the FMLA designation in writing

   ❏ the employee has given me some information that leads me to believe that the need for leave falls under the FMLA, and I have requested additional information, including medical certification, or

   ❏ the need for leave does not fall under the FMLA, and I have withdrawn the preliminary FMLA designation in writing.

❏ Where an employee's behavior reveals the employee might have a serious health condition, I have placed the employee on FMLA leave with a preliminary designation and have conducted an inquiry into whether the employee actually has a serious health condition.

❏ I have granted an employee's request for leave and preliminarily designated the leave as FMLA leave even though the employee did not mention the FMLA, where

   ❏ the employee gave me enough information to believe that the need for leave might fall under the FMLA, or

   ❏ I have information from another source that the employee's need for leave falls under the FMLA.

❏ Where I have learned information during an employee's leave that leads me to believe it falls under the FMLA, I have given the employee a written FMLA designation.

❏ I have informed any employee requesting FMLA leave that

    ❏ he or she may use paid leave during FMLA leave (where appropriate) and informed the employee that the leave time will reduce available FMLA leave time, or

    ❏ company policy requires that paid leave be substituted and informed the employee that the leave time will reduce available FMLA leave time.

❏ I have designated workers' compensation leave as FMLA leave, where the workplace injury is a serious health condition under the FMLA.

❏ When the employee requests leave for an unforeseeable, FMLA-covered reason, I have granted the leave and designated it as FMLA leave even though the employee did not give 30-days' notice.

❏ I have made sure not to require more employee notice for FMLA leave than is required by state law.

❏ I have made sure not to require more employee notice for FMLA leave than is required by a collective bargaining agreement covering the requesting employee.

❏ I have given the employee going out on FMLA leave an individualized notice with FMLA information specific to his or her situation.

❏ I have given additional notices to the employee on leave when

    ❏ an employee has requested FMLA leave six months or more after his or her first request for leave

    ❏ the information I initially gave the employee in the individualized notice has changed, or

    ❏ the company requires a medical certification or fitness-for-duty certification prior to the employee returning to work.

Medical Certifications (Proof of Illness)

CHAPTER HIGHLIGHTS

A medical certification is a document verifying an employee's need to take leave for a serious health condition, completed by a health care provider.

To be valid, a certification must state:

• the date when the serious health condition began

• how long the condition is expected to last

• which category of serious health condition applies and medical facts relating to that conclusion, and

• that the employee is unable to perform the functions of his or her job (if the employee is taking leave for his or her own condition) or that the employee's family member needs care (if the employee is taking leave for a family member's condition).

You should request a medical certification whenever an employee takes FMLA leave for a serious health condition.

You must request a medical certification, in writing, within two business days after learning that an employee needs leave for a serious health condition.

The employee must return the certification before going on foreseeable leave; within 15 days after your request; or as soon afterwards as is reasonably possible.

Once you receive a medical certification, you may grant FMLA leave or deny it based on the information on the form. If the form is insufficient, you must tell the employee and give him or her time to correct the problem before denying leave.

If you have reason to doubt the certification, you may ask the employee to get a second opinion, at your company's expense. If the first and second opinions conflict, you may request a third opinion, again at the company's expense.

You may ask an employee to provide a recertification only after the original certification runs out or no more often than every 30 days, unless circumstances have changed significantly, you have reason to suspect the employee's reason for leave, or the employee requests an extension of leave.

Once an employee requests time off for his or her own health problem or to care for an ailing family member, you should immediately think, "FMLA." But what if you aren't sure whether or not the employee (or family member) has a serious health condition? Do you just have to take the employee's word for it that the condition is serious and provide job-protected leave?

The answer is no. An employer always has the right to ask an employee to provide a medical certification: a written statement from a health care provider giving some basic information about the employee's (or family member's) condition. And, for reasons explained below, you should request a certification whenever an employee takes leave for a serious health condition.

This chapter explains what medical certifications are, how and when to request them, when an employee must provide them, and what to do if the certification is late or incomplete—or never shows up at all. We also explain your options for challenging a medical certification by asking for a second or even a third opinion, and the rules about requesting a recertification of the same condition.

What Is a Medical Certification?

A medical certification is a written document verifying the employee's need to take leave for a serious health condition, prepared by a health care provider. (Chapter 4 explains who qualifies as a health care provider.) You can ask an employee to provide a medical certification whether the employee needs time off for his or her own condition or to care for a family member.

A medical certification is valid only if it includes at least the following information:

- the date the serious health condition began
- how long the condition is expected to last
- which category of serious health condition applies and medical facts relating to that conclusion, and

- a statement that the employee is unable to perform the functions of his or her job (if the employee is taking leave for his or her own condition) or that the employee's family member needs care (if the employee is taking leave for a family member's condition).

If the employee needs intermittent or reduced-schedule leave, the certification must also state that intermittent leave is necessary; the expected duration of the leave; and, if intermittent leave is required for planned medical treatment, the dates and duration of such treatment. Of course, intermittent leave by its very nature may include unforeseeable absences— for example, because a chronic condition flares up unexpectedly or a permanent condition (such as cancer) takes a turn for the worse. Although your company can ask for the dates of scheduled treatment, it cannot require an employee to provide a firm schedule for intermittent leave that is less predictable.

The Department of Labor has created a medical certification form, *"Certification of Health Care Provider"* (Form WH-380), which employers can use to gather this information. (You can find a blank copy of the form in Appendix C.) The form is designed to be handed to employees, who can then ask their health care providers to complete and sign it. Using this form is optional, but if you develop your own form instead, you cannot ask for more information than Form WH-380 requests.

CAUTION

State law may prohibit you from using Form WH-380. Some states have strict laws that protect the privacy of medical records. If your state's law prohibits employers from requesting certain types of medical information, you must adhere to those restrictions—even if the FMLA allows you to have that information. And, because Form WH-380 asks the health care provider to give details about the employee's or family member's serious health condition, you may not be able to use that form in certain states (California, for one). Before you adopt Form WH-380 or any other medical certification form, talk to a knowledgeable employment lawyer in your state to make sure that it doesn't violate your employees' medical privacy rights.

POLICY ALERT

You can't require more information for FMLA leave than your medical leave policy requires. If your company's sick or medical leave policies require the employee to provide less information than the FMLA requires, and the employee elects to substitute paid sick, medical, personal, vacation, or other leave for unpaid leave, you may require the employee to provide only the information required in the policy—not the more expansive information allowed by the FMLA. In other words, if the employee is using paid leave, the employee has to provide only the information required by your leave policies, even though that leave also counts against his or her FMLA entitlement.

Why You Should Always Request a Certification

Although you have the right to request a medical certification when an employee takes leave for a serious medical condition, you aren't required to. Because it's optional, some managers don't request a certification or request one only occasionally—for example, if the employee has a history of unexcused absences or the health condition isn't obvious.

The best practice, however, is to request a medical certification every time an employee wants time off for a serious medical condition, regardless of the circumstances. Don't pick and choose which employees or conditions will require a certification: Always request one. Here are three good reasons why.

Reason 1: The Condition Might Not Be Serious

Unless you ask for a medical certification, you don't know whether the employee or family member has a serious health condition. Remember, it's not your job—or right—to diagnose. Once an employee tells you that he or she needs time off for a serious health condition, you can't simply say, "You don't look that sick to me," or "I'm sure your wife will be up and around in no time." If you want proof, the only way you are legally allowed to get it is through the medical certification process.

LESSONS FROM THE

Real World

A company that didn't request a medical certification can't later dispute the employee's serious health condition.

Katherine Thorson worked in the packing and shipping department of Gemini, Inc, a company that manufactures plastic signs. The company had a policy that employees who were absent for more than 5% of their scheduled hours in a rolling 12-month period could be fired for excessive absenteeism.

Thorson left work and went to the doctor on Wednesday, February 2, complaining of stomach cramps and diarrhea. She came back to work the following Monday, February 7, with a doctor's note saying "no work" until February 7. After a few hours, she returned to the doctor with stomach pain. The doctor suspected a peptic ulcer or gallbladder disease and ordered some tests for that Friday. The following Monday, February 14, Thorson returned to work, again with a doctor's note saying "no work" until the 14th. That Friday, she was fired for excessive absences. She was eventually diagnosed with several stress-related conditions.

When Thorson sued for violation of the FMLA, Gemini argued, among other things, that Thorson didn't have a serious health condition because she was not incapacitated—in other words, she didn't really have to miss work because of her condition. The court found that Gemini wasn't entitled to contest this issue because it failed to request a medical certification at the time. Thorson's own doctor's notes said "no work"; if Gemini doubted this statement, it was entitled to request a certification. Because it didn't exercise this right, the court refused to credit evidence that another physician, whose opinion was sought months after the fact for use in the lawsuit, said there was "no obvious reason" why Thorson had to miss work.

Thorson v. Gemini, Inc., 205 F.3d 370 (8th Cir. 2000).

As a practical matter, once an employee requests leave for a serious health condition, you have only two options: grant the request outright or ask for a medical certification. If you grant the request without proof, you'll never know whether the employee or family member really had a serious health condition—you may have provided job-protected leave and continued benefits when you didn't have to. If you don't request proof and don't grant FMLA leave, you are inviting a potentially ruinous lawsuit if the employee (or family member) really does have a serious health condition.

Requesting a certification every time is the best way to make sure that you provide the leave required by the FMLA—no more and no less.

Reason 2: You Might Want to Challenge the Employee Later

If you don't ask for medical certification, some courts have held that you (and your company) can't later claim that the employee or family member didn't really have a serious health condition. This could deprive you and your company of an important argument if the employee sues for violation of the FMLA. The lesson here is use it or lose it: If you don't ask for a certification, you may have conceded this point.

Reason 3: Inconsistency Leads to Discrimination Claims

Some managers pick and choose which employees have to get certifications and which do not. A manager might ask only employees who have a history of attendance problems to get a certification or might request a certification only for ailments that are not immediately apparent.

The problem with this approach is that it can lead to discrimination claims. Any time a manager decides to treat employees differently, there is a risk that the manager will be accused of discrimination. If, for example, you ask only pregnant employees to provide a certification, you could be accused of gender discrimination. If you ask only employees who have chronic or permanent conditions—as opposed to a one-time need for surgery or time off for an injury—to provide a certification, you could be accused of disability discrimination. To avoid this problem, you should always request a certification.

EXAMPLE: Maggie, one of your employees, has bipolar disorder. She and her doctor have been experimenting with a new medication. Unfortunately, before she and her doctor figure out the correct dosage, Maggie has a manic episode and must be hospitalized briefly. Her brother calls you about the situation and says that Maggie will have to stay in the hospital for at least a couple of days, then will be released to be cared for by her family until she's able to return to work.

You usually don't require employees to submit a medical certification. In this situation, though, you think you might ask for one. "She had to be hospitalized for getting overexcited? It sounds like someone just wants some time off work. I don't grant FMLA leave for 'mental health' days, and I bet she'll come back to work pretty quickly once she knows that." Because the FMLA allows you to request a certification, you're well within your rights to make this your first, aren't you?

Not quite. Maggie might claim that your request is discriminatory, because it's based on negative stereotypes about people with mental disabilities (that they are "faking it" or could control their conditions with a little will power, for example).

Procedures and Deadlines for Medical Certifications

You and the employee both have deadlines to meet—and procedures to follow—when dealing with medical certifications.

Requesting the Certification

As soon as an employee requests leave for a serious health condition, you have to request the certification, in writing. Although the FMLA regulations allow employers to make an oral request in limited circumstances (and only if they've already made a written request within the past six months), you want written proof that you requested a certification and the date you did so. The written request must state not only that you are requesting a medical certification, but also the deadlines for providing the certification and the consequences of failing to provide it.

You may request a medical certification as part of the detailed notice you must give to an employee who has requested leave for a purpose covered by the FMLA. (See Chapter 7 for more information on this notice.) If you instead choose to give the employee a separate written request for a medical certification, you can use our form, "Request for Medical Certification." A sample of this form is below; you'll also find a copy of this form in Appendix C and on the CD-ROM at the back of this book.

S A M P L E

Request for Medical Certification

To: Sarah Beadle
From: Rayna Harmon
Date: August 23, 2007

On August 22, 2007, you informed us that you need to take leave for a serious health condition.

You must submit a medical certification of a serious health condition from your health care provider. The medical certification form is attached to this letter. Please note that you must complete a portion of the form if you are seeking leave to care for a family member.

You must return this form to us by September 7, 2007. If you fail to return this form on time, we may delay the start of your leave, or postpone the continuation of your leave, until we receive your certification. If you are unable to return the form on time due to circumstances beyond your control, please contact me right away.

Feel free to contact me if you have any questions about this requirement.

Sincerely,

Rayna Harmon
RAYNA HARMON

August 23, 2007
DATE

CAUTION

A written policy isn't enough. Many employers have policies explaining FMLA leave in their employee handbooks. (For information on what your FMLA policy should include, see Chapter 2, "If Your Company Is Covered," and Appendix B.) Typically, these policies cover medical certifications, including the information you must give the employee when you request one. If your company has this type of policy, however, it doesn't take the place of a written request and notice to the employee, made when the employee tells you that he or she needs leave. Courts have found that employers who don't make a specific written request to the employee cannot later challenge the employee's certification—or failure to provide one.

You should make your request as soon as the employee asks for leave for a serious health condition. The regulations interpreting the FMLA say that employers "should" request a certification within two business days of learning that an employee needs leave, either because the employee has requested leave or because the employee has taken leave for an unforeseeable purpose (emergency surgery, for example). The regulations give you the right to request certification later only if you "have reason to question" the duration or appropriateness of the leave. The best practice is not to rely on this language but instead to give your notice and request a certification right away, every time.

POLICY ALERT

If your policies are more generous, you must follow them. If an employee is substituting paid time off (vacation time, sick leave, or other employer-provided leave) for unpaid FMLA leave, and your policies provide more lenient procedures or deadlines for medical certifications, you must follow those policies. For example, if your policies provide that an employee may hand in a medical certification or doctor's note after returning from sick leave, you must allow the employee to follow these procedures for FMLA leave for a serious medical condition—even if the employee would have had to return the form sooner under the FMLA.

As discussed in Chapter 7, you should make a preliminary designation of the leave if you believe it is covered by the FMLA. Then, when the employee returns and gives you the medical certification, you can issue a final designation either confirming it was FMLA leave or withdrawing the preliminary designation if it wasn't. Just be sure to issue the final designation within two business days of receiving the medical certification.

Deadlines for Returning the Certification

As explained in Chapter 7, an employee who requests leave for a foreseeable reason—for example, because the employee's wife is having a baby or the employee has scheduled surgery—is usually required to give you 30 days' notice. Once you get that notice, you can request medical certification. In this situation, the employee must return the medical certification before he or she starts leave, as long as the employee has at least 15 days to get the certification. If the employee doesn't return the certification on time and doesn't have a good reason for the delay, you can postpone the start of the employee's leave until you receive a certification.

If the employee takes leave for an unforeseeable reason—such as an injury, emergency surgery, or premature birth—the employee has 15 days to provide the certification. If the employee can't meet this deadline despite reasonable, good-faith efforts to do so, the employee must return the certification as soon as is reasonably possible. If the employee doesn't, you can delay the continuation of the employee's leave.

Because the employee will already have started leave when you ask for the medical certification, you should designate the employee's time off as FMLA leave pending your receipt of the certification; if the certification shows that the employee isn't entitled to leave, you can withdraw your preliminary designation. Chapter 7 explains how to make a preliminary designation (and how to withdraw it, if necessary).

If the employee never provides you with a medical certification you properly requested, the leave is not protected by the FMLA.

LESSONS FROM THE

Real World

An oral request for a medical certification doesn't start the clock.

Ralph Cooper worked for Fulton County, Georgia, for almost 20 years. During his tenure, Cooper had a number of health problems, including depression, for which he was repeatedly absent from work. He was disciplined, suspended, and twice threatened with termination for failing to provide proper medical documentation and contact his supervisor in connection with his absences.

In June 1998, Cooper was absent for several days because he was experiencing chest pains. He was given a letter informing him that he had to provide a doctor's excuse for each day of his absence. On July 8, Cooper provided a doctor's note that accounted for his absences and said he could return to work on July 13. He returned to work as scheduled, only to go home ill several hours later. He told his supervisor he was too ill to work; she reminded him orally to provide a doctor's excuse.

On July 14, Cooper faxed his supervisor a request for leave because he was suffering from blurred vision, having extreme headaches, and passing out. His supervisor called him and again told him to provide a medical excuse. On August 4, the county delivered a letter to Cooper, advising him that he had to provide a medical excuse for his absences by August 10. Cooper got the required excuse from his doctor several days later but did not immediately deliver it. On August 10, Cooper was sent a letter stating that his employment was terminated effective August 12; Cooper then submitted his medical excuse.

Even with his lengthy history of unexcused absences and failure to comply with employer policies, Cooper won this lawsuit. Why? Because Fulton County didn't give him 15 days to return the certification. Although the county repeatedly asked him for a doctor's excuse, it did not do so in writing until August 4. Therefore, Cooper had until August 19 to return his certification. By firing him before the time limit expired, Fulton County violated Cooper's FMLA rights.

Cooper v. Fulton County, Georgia, 458 F.3d 1282 (11th Cir. 2006).

Even though you have the right to penalize an employee for missing the deadline to return a certification, that doesn't mean you should exercise it. You must act very carefully—preferably after talking to a lawyer—if you choose to enforce these rules. If an employee is clearly entitled to the FMLA's protections, some courts have been lenient about these requirements. Particularly if your actions cause the employee harm—for example, because the employee had to delay a medically necessary treatment program—you should anticipate that a court might take the employee's side.

The best practice, both to avoid legal trouble and to provide leave when your employees need it, is to work with your employees on this issue. Remind employees that you need a certification. If an employee misses a deadline, get in touch with the employee or a family member and explain how important the certification is. Put a note confirming this contact in the employee's FMLA file and be sure to include the name of the person you contacted, the date, and the substance of your discussion.

Rather than immediately taking drastic action, such as postponing or ending an employee's FMLA leave, be a little more flexible about getting the documentation you need. Although you might need to wait a little longer, this is the safest—and most humane—approach.

Medical Certifications: Deadlines and Consequences		
ACTION	**DEADLINE**	**CONSEQUENCES**
You must request the medical certification	Within two days of learning that the employee needs leave	You can request one later only if you have reason to question the duration or appropriateness of the leave
The employee must provide the completed certification	Before starting a foreseeable leave; within 15 days after you request it; or as soon as reasonably possible after that	You can delay the start of foreseeable leave; delay the continuation of unforeseeable leave; or deny FMLA leave altogether, if the employee never provides a certification

After You Receive the Certification

Once you receive a medical certification, you have several options. You may decide, based on the information provided, that the employee is entitled to FMLA leave. In that situation, you should make sure you've provided the required notices and move on to structuring the leave with the employee (see Chapters 2 and 9.)

The information you receive might lead to the opposite conclusion: that the employee is not protected by the FMLA. This is not as common, but it does happen. For example, the health care provider might check the "none of the above" space when asked to identify the patient's serious health condition, describe the condition as a minor ailment which does not incapacitate the patient, or indicate that the employee does not need time off work. In this situation, the employee has not submitted the required proof of a serious health condition and is therefore not entitled to FMLA leave. You don't have to request a second opinion; you can simply deny leave based on this information.

TIP

Tell the employee what's wrong with the form. If the information in the certification doesn't show that the employee has a serious health condition, let the employee know. That way, the employee can make sure that the doctor didn't make a mistake in completing the form, and will understand why you are denying the leave request. If the employee subsequently gives you a new form indicating that there is a serious health condition, you can always request a second opinion (see "Second Opinions," below).

Even if the form indicates a serious health condition, however, you may still have doubts. You may wonder whether the illness or ailment described on the form really qualifies as a serious health condition. You may question the employee's inability to work due to the condition. Perhaps the form is incomplete, or you simply can't read the doctor's handwriting. This section explains your options if you need or want more information after receiving a certification.

> ## Where to Keep Medical Certifications
>
> Employees have a right to privacy in their own medical information and that of their family members. Although you can request limited medical information so you can fulfill your obligations under the FMLA, you still have to maintain the confidentiality of this material by storing it in separate files (that is, not in employees' regular personnel files) and restricting access to it. For more information, see Chapter 12.

Clarifying a Certification

You may need clarification about something you read in a certification. But you are not allowed to contact an employee's health care provider directly to ask questions about the certification.

The FMLA does provide an indirect route to very limited communications, however: Your company's health care provider may, with the employee's permission, contact the employee's doctor to clarify and authenticate the certification. Your company's health care provider may not ask for additional information that goes beyond the questions in the certification form, however. If you choose to go this route, you should get the employee's consent in writing, signed and dated.

It isn't entirely clear what it means to clarify or authenticate a certification, and the regulation that governs this practice doesn't give much guidance. (29 C.F.R. § 825.307(a).) Presumably, this provision would allow an employer's health care provider to, for example, call and verify that the employee's health care provider really did complete and sign the form or ask the employee's health care provider to read his or her responses to particular questions on the form (if they are illegible).

Incomplete Certifications

If the employee returns a medical certification that is incomplete, you must tell the employee and provide a reasonable opportunity to fix the problem. For example, if the health care provider didn't fill in some of the blanks on the form, didn't sign and date it, or didn't indicate the duration of the employee's condition, you should let the employee know what the problem is and give the employee time to hand in a complete certification.

This is another situation in which the best practice is to work with the employee to get the paperwork done. Tell the employee what's wrong with the certification form, give the employee another copy of the form (if necessary), and don't take any action until the employee has had enough time to get the corrected certification back to you.

LESSONS FROM THE
Real World

An employer can't deny leave based on inadequate medical certification if it doesn't give the employee a chance to correct it.

Curtis Sims drove a bus for the Alameda-Contra Costa County Transit District (AC Transit) for 25 years. Starting April 18, 1994, he took a couple of weeks off work because of a back injury. He went to two doctors and a chiropractor during this time and was prescribed medication and physical therapy. He returned to work on May 4 and handed in three medical slips, one from each provider. Together, the doctor's slips said he was unable to work through May 1; the chiropractor's slip said he could return to work on a trial basis on May 4.

AC Transit placed Sims on a five-day, unpaid suspension following this absence. In July Sims took two days off for an illness and was fired.

Sims sued, claiming that his FMLA rights were violated when AC Transit counted his April absence against him. AC Transit argued that Sims was not protected by the FMLA because, among other things, the chiropractor did not qualify as a health care provider, and therefore the last two days of Sims' absence were not FMLA-protected. The court found that AC Transit might be right, but it didn't matter: Because AC Transit didn't tell Sims what was wrong with his certification and give him an opportunity to correct it, they couldn't deny him FMLA leave based on that deficiency.

Sims v. Alameda-Contra Costa Transit District, 2 F.Supp.2d 1253 (N.D. Cal. 1998).

Second Opinions

What if an employee returns a complete—and legible—medical certification indicating that the employee or family member has a serious health condition, but you still have doubts? For example, the certification might say that the employee has a minor ailment (such as a cold or headache) or that the employee will need to be out of work for a long time for something that doesn't sound serious. In these situations, you have two options. You can accept the certification at face value and provide FMLA-protected leave, or you can require the employee to get a second opinion: another certification, from a health care provider of your choosing.

CAUTION

You can't use the "company doctor." Although your company can choose the health care provider who provides the second opinion, you can't require the employee to see someone who is regularly employed by your company. This includes not only providers who are on the company payroll, but also providers whom your company regularly uses, unless access to health care in your company's area is extremely limited.

Your company must pay the costs of the second opinion, including the employee's or family member's reasonable travel expenses. Even though you have to foot the bill, however, you generally cannot require the employee or family member to travel beyond regular commuting distances, absent very unusual circumstances.

While the second opinion is pending, the employee is provisionally entitled to FMLA benefits. If the employee asks for a copy of the second opinion, you must generally provide it within two business days.

SEE AN EXPERT

If the second opinion contradicts the first, proceed with caution. The FMLA gives you the right to get a third opinion if the first and second certifications differ (see "Third Opinions," below). Some courts have said that you must provide FMLA benefits unless you get this tie-breaking third opinion; others have said that you can deny benefits in reliance on the second opinion (although you might, of course, face a legal challenge from the employee, claiming that the first opinion was correct and you improperly denied FMLA protections). Based on this conflict, the safest course of action is to go ahead with the third opinion; if you're considering denying FMLA benefits based on a second opinion, talk to an experienced employment attorney.

Third Opinions

If the first and second certifications contradict each other, you may ask the employee to get a third opinion, which will be binding on everyone. The provider who gives the third opinion must be mutually agreeable to the company and the employee, and both must act in good faith when choosing the provider. (Once you reach an agreement on who will provide the third opinion, put it in writing.) The employer must again pay the costs of this process, as well as travel costs. As with the second opinion, you must give the employee a copy, upon request, within two business days.

Recertifications

In some circumstances, you are allowed to ask an employee to provide a recertification of a serious health condition. This process is intended to help employers fight abuse by employees, particularly employees who take leave periodically either because of a condition that occasionally requires time off or because of a need for intermittent leave for medical appointments or other treatment.

You must give an employee at least 15 days to return the recertification form (you can use the regular certification form for this purpose). You cannot request a second or third opinion for a recertification. How often you can request a recertification depends on the type of serious health condition and the circumstances of the employee's leave.

TIP

You can ask for a new certification every year. You have the right to request an entirely new medical certification—not a recertification—once an employee takes or requests leave in a new leave year. Even if you already requested a certification or recertification, you can request a new certification upon a new leave request after the employee's 12-month leave period rolls over. Unlike a recertification, you can get a second or third opinion on this new year certification.

Pregnancy, Chronic, and Permanent or Long-Term Conditions

When an employee takes FMLA leave for pregnancy, a chronic serious health condition, or permanent or long-term incapacity (see Chapter 4 for more information on each of these categories), an employer generally may request recertification only in connection with an absence, and no more often than every 30 days. However, the employer may request more frequent recertifications in either of the following cases:

- The circumstances described in the previous certification have changed significantly (for example, the employee has suffered complications or has been absent more often or for a longer period of time than was stated on the previous certification).

- The employer receives information that casts doubt on the employee's stated reason for the absence.

EXAMPLE: Brenda suffers from migraines. She has submitted a medical certification from her doctor indicating that her migraines qualify as a chronic serious health condition. The certification also indicates that her migraines will cause her to miss several days of work each month, on average. Brenda has been taking about this much leave for the past six months.

Brenda attends an after-work "happy hour" event to send off a coworker who is leaving the company. After Brenda orders a glass of red wine, her friend John asks her, "What's going on? I've never seen you drink red wine before; I thought it triggered your migraines." Brenda says, "I know! My doctor gave me this new medication that has totally changed my life! I've been eating chocolate, drinking red wine, and doing all kinds of things I never used to be able to do, and I haven't had a migraine for two months now."

Unbeknownst to Brenda, you—her manager—were standing behind her and overheard the conversation. The next day, you ask Brenda to recertify her health condition.

Incapacity for More Than 30 Days

If the employee's original certification indicates that he or she will be incapacitated or required to care for a seriously ill family member for more than 30 days, the employer can't request a recertification until the original certification expires, unless any of the following are true:

- The employee requests an extension of leave.
- The circumstances described in the previous certification have changed significantly.
- The employer receives information that casts doubt on the employee's stated reason for the absence.

The same rules apply if an employee is on intermittent or reduced-schedule leave: The employer may not request a recertification within the minimum necessary leave period described on the original certification unless one of the three exceptions above applies.

All Other Conditions

For all other conditions, an employer may not request a recertification more often than every 30 days, unless one of the three exceptions listed under "Incapacity for More Than 30 Days" applies.

LESSONS FROM THE

Real World

Taking every Monday or Friday off might be enough to justify a recertification.

In response to a question from an employer, the Department of Labor (DOL) issued an Opinion Letter—an interpretation of the law—regarding recertifications based on suspected abuse. The employer asked whether a pattern of Friday or Monday absences might qualify as information that casts doubt on an employee's reasons for leave. The DOL agreed that it might, as long as there was no evidence of a medical reason for this pattern.

Many employers were heartened not only by this guidance, but also by the DOL's suggestion that the employer might be able to present this information directly to the health care provider in seeking a recertification. The DOL wrote, "The FMLA does not prohibit an employer from including a record of an employee's absences along with the medical certification form for the health care provider's consideration in determining the employee's likely period of future absences. . . . [nor] from asking, as part of the recertification process, whether the likely duration and frequency of the employee's incapacity due to the chronic condition is limited to Mondays and Fridays."

Opinion Letter FMLA2004-2-A (May 25, 2004).

CROSS-REFERENCE

You can request a fitness-for-duty certification when an employee returns to work. The FMLA allows you to ask an employee to provide a statement from a health care provider, indicating that the employee is medically able to perform the job, before reinstating the employee. For more information, see Chapter 10.

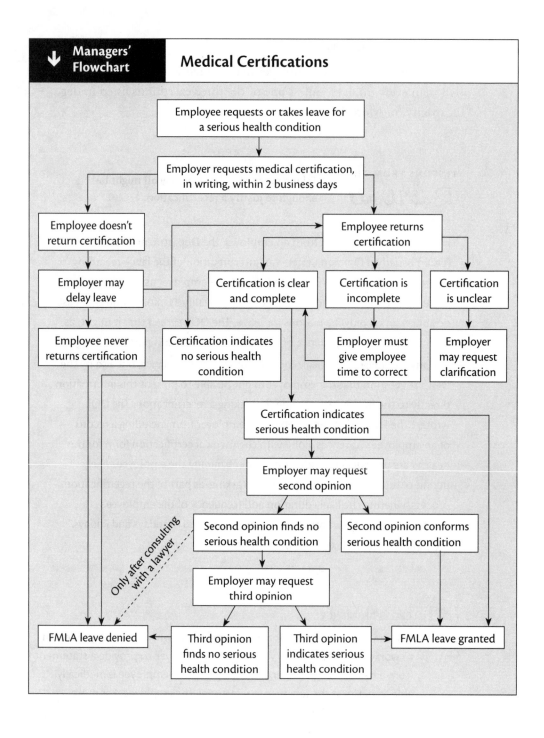

Common Mistakes Regarding Medical Certifications— And How to Avoid Them

MISTAKE 1: Denying FMLA leave inappropriately—that is, when the employee or family member really has a serious health condition.

AVOID THIS MISTAKE BY:

- Requesting a medical certification whenever an employee seeks leave for a serious health condition. Don't make a decision without getting the information you need.

- Getting a second opinion if you doubt the employee's certification. Rather than disregarding a certification confirming a serious health condition, require the employee to get a second certification from a different health care provider.

- Getting a third opinion—or talking to an attorney before taking action—if the first and second opinions conflict.

MISTAKE 2: Violating an employee's (or family member's) medical privacy rights.

AVOID THIS MISTAKE BY:

- Leaving the diagnosis to the doctors. Rather than asking an employee for details about his or her medical condition, give the employee a medical certification form and have the health care providers give you only the information to which you are entitled.

- Checking with a lawyer before choosing a medical certification form. Some states don't allow employers to request all of the information allowed by the FMLA (and by the Department of Labor's optional medical certification form, WH-380).

- Not talking directly to the employee's health care provider. Only your company's health care provider can talk to the employee's health care provider, and then only to clarify information on the form and only with the employee's permission.

- Keeping separate, confidential files of medical records. Never put medical certifications and other health-related information in employees' personnel files.

MISTAKE 3: Failing to give employees proper notice or enough time to get a medical certification.

AVOID THIS MISTAKE BY:

- Using dated written requests for medical certifications that explain what employees must provide, the deadlines for getting it back to you, and the consequences of failing to return a certification. Unless you put it in writing, you won't have proof of when you requested the certification.

- Giving employees at least 15 days to return a certification—or more time, if they have a plausible reason for missing the deadline. Don't try to shave a few days off, even for employees who are chronically absent or should already know the rules.

- Working with employees to get the certification in, rather that strictly enforcing the deadline. In the real world, courts often recognize that employees who are seriously ill or caring for a sick child or family member might reasonably need more than 15 days to return this paperwork—especially because they have to rely on health care providers, who may be busy or out of town, or simply forget to complete the form.

- Letting employees know if a certification is incomplete or doesn't support their request for FMLA leave. If you don't tell an employee what's wrong with the form, you won't be able to rely on it as a valid reason to deny the employee's leave request.

✓	Managers' Checklist	**Medical Certifications**

❏ I requested a medical certification as soon as I learned that the employee was seeking leave for a potentially serious health condition.

❏ I made the request in writing, dated and signed.

❏ The request explained the consequences of failing to return the certification on time.

❏ I gave the employee a medical certification form.

❏ I did not request any information that goes beyond what's required by the form.

❏ I worked with the employee to get a complete medical certification.

❏ If the form was not returned on time, I contacted the employee immediately to find out why and explain the importance of getting the form in.

❏ If the form was returned incomplete, I told the employee about the problem and provided an opportunity to correct it.

❏ I requested a second opinion if I had doubts about the initial medical certification.

    ❏ I did not send the employee to a health care provider who is regularly employed by my company.

    ❏ While the second opinion was pending, I provided FMLA benefits to the employee.

    ❏ I provided a copy of the second opinion to the employee, within two days after receiving his or her request.

    ❏ Before acting on a second opinion that contradicts the first, I consulted with an attorney.

    ❏ I requested recertifications as appropriate.

    ❏ I requested recertification only every 30 days or when the employee's initial certification expired, unless an exception allowed me to request one more often.

    ❏ I requested recertification whenever the employee's situation changed or I learned information that cast doubt on the employee's reasons for leave.

    ❏ I placed the medical certification(s) and any recertifications in confidential medical files, not the employee's regular personnel file.

Managing an Employee's Leave

CHAPTER HIGHLIGHTS

You may postpone the start of an employee's leave if the need for leave was foreseeable and the employee could have—but failed to—provide you with 30 days' notice.

Most employers cover an employee's workload during leave by asking coworkers to pick up the slack; other methods of handling work for an employee on leave include hiring temps, using consultants, outsourcing the work, or picking up some of the work yourself.

You must continue an employee's group health benefits while the employee is on leave.

- You may require the employee to pay his or her usual share of the premium, in one of several ways provided by the FMLA.

- If the employee is more than 30 days late in making premium payments, you may cut off insurance coverage, but only after providing written notice to the employee and at least 15 additional days to make up the payments.

You can require an employee to schedule intermittent leave so it does not unduly disrupt your company's operations, if the employee needs leave for treatment or some other foreseeable reason; the employee's health care provider must agree to any rescheduling.

You can temporarily transfer an employee on intermittent leave to another position, with equal benefits and pay, that better accommodates the need for leave

You may request periodic status reports from employees on FMLA leave regarding any changes in their planned return dates or their intent to return at all.

You may discipline or even fire an employee who is on FMLA leave, as long as your reasons for doing so are entirely unrelated to the employee's leave; before you do so, however, you should consult with a lawyer.

By the time an employee actually starts using FMLA leave, you've already done quite a bit of work. You've dealt with coverage and eligibility requirements, handled paperwork and notices, and perhaps even had to do some math to figure out how many hours the employee has worked, how much leave the employee can take, and so on. At this point, you might be thinking that most of your work is done.

There are, however, a few more things on your FMLA to-do list. You'll need to provide continued health care benefits while employees are on leave, follow the rules for employees on intermittent leave, and make sure that you'll be ready to reinstate employees upon their return.

In addition to these legal requirements, a number of practical considerations come to the forefront when employees go out on leave. How can you make sure the employee's work gets done? How often should you communicate with an employee on leave to find out how things are going and when the employee intends to return to work? What can you do to ensure a smooth transition to and from leave? And can you ever discipline—or even replace—an employee on FMLA leave? This chapter explains how to manage FMLA leave and provides practical strategies for minimizing disruptions to your company.

Scheduling Leave

When an employee requests time off, you should calendar the employee's leave. (Typically, you'll want to do this as you complete the employee's individual notice form, covered in Chapter 7.) Mark the date when the employee plans to start leave, how long the employee expects to be gone, and when the employee intends to return. If the dates are uncertain—for example, the employee doesn't know exactly when she'll have to stop working before having a baby or how long a parent will take to recuperate from surgery—make your best guess based on what the employee tells you and the information in the medical certification, if applicable.

As you calendar the employee's leave, keep in mind the basic scheduling rules set out below. Now is the time to determine, for example, whether you will postpone the start of the employee's leave or ask the employee to reschedule leave. If you decide not to allow the employee to take leave on the dates requested, you should tell the employee right away so he or she can make appropriate arrangements.

CAUTION

Raise scheduling issues in writing, with the individual notice form. If you decide to postpone or reschedule the employee's leave, let the employee know when you provide the individual notice form. That form doesn't explicitly address this subject, but it does indicate the dates when the employee requested leave. If you provide the notice form without telling the employee that you aren't granting leave for the exact dates the employee requested, the employee will be understandably confused—and will make plans based on his or her original request. The best practice is to put your scheduling decision in writing and attach it to the individual notice form, then discuss it with the employee.

Postponing the Start of Leave

As explained in Chapter 7, employees must give 30 days' advance notice if they need leave for a foreseeable reason. Examples of foreseeable leave include time off for scheduled, nonemergency surgery; for the birth or adoption of a child; or to care for a family member who has treatment scheduled well in advance. An employee who can't give 30 days' notice of foreseeable leave—for example, because the employee learned of the need for leave only a few weeks ahead of time—must give as much notice as is practicable under the circumstances. If the employee fails to give this notice, you can delay the start of the employee's leave until 30 days have passed since the employee gave notice.

CAUTION

You can delay the start of an employee's leave only if you have informed the employee of the duty to provide the notice required under the FMLA. This information should be included in your company's written FMLA policy and in workplace FMLA posters, as explained in Chapter 2.

You may not delay an employee's FMLA leave when the employee has given timely oral or written notice, even if the employee does not follow your company's particular notice rules (for example, when an employee doesn't give you a required notice form).

Of course, you shouldn't delay an employee's leave just because you can. You'll have to carefully weigh the facts to decide whether to exercise this right. The reason for caution here is simple: An employee whose leave is delayed may challenge your decision in court, especially if the employee is harmed by the delay. What's more, you will really look like the bad guy to all of your reports—and you will have poisoned your relationship with the employee who needed leave earlier (and will one day return to work).

Here are a few things to consider when deciding whether to postpone leave:

- **Why the employee needs leave.** If delaying FMLA leave could cause someone to suffer physical harm, you have strong legal and ethical reasons to be lenient. For example, if the employee or a family member requires surgery for a life-threatening condition, it's best to allow the employee to take scheduled leave, rather than insisting on a full notice period.

- **How difficult it would be for the employee to reschedule.** In some cases, an employee or family member can reschedule a medical procedure relatively easily, but other times, canceling could mean waiting months for another opportunity. Or, the employee might need leave for an event that can't be rescheduled, such as the birth of a child. The harder it is for the employee to postpone taking leave, the more likely you are to face problems if you insist on 30 days' notice.

- **Your company's needs.** If you really need 30 days' notice for business reasons—for example, because it will take that long to cover the employee's accounts or because your company's busiest season will be over by then—then it makes more sense to delay leave if the employee hasn't give sufficient notice.

- **The employee's reason for failing to give notice.** Remember, the employee has to give only as much notice as it practicable under the circumstances. If the employee had a plausible reason for not giving notice on time, it's best to grant leave without a delay.

EXAMPLE: On May 1, Cora tells you, her manager, that she needs to take several days off, starting May 10, to have surgery to remove a cancerous lump from her breast. Cora's surgeon is a renowned physician whose services are in high demand, and she only found out that she'd been scheduled (after a cancellation) on May 1, the day she notified you. Can you require Cora to delay her leave until June 1?

No. Although Cora knew that she would need time off at some point, she didn't know the exact date of her surgery until the day she gave notice. Under the FMLA, this constitutes as much notice as is practicable under the circumstances, so you cannot require her to delay her leave.

Now assume that Cora actually scheduled her surgery more than a month ago but didn't tell you about it until May 1. Should you require her to delay her leave? It's risky. Cora didn't give the required notice, but she needs surgery for a potentially life-threatening condition—and if you require her to miss her scheduled appointment, she might have to wait a long time to get a new date. Although you have the right to require her to wait for 30 days, it doesn't seem like a good idea to exercise it here. If delay could lead to serious medical problems, it's probably best not to require it.

If Cora's surgery was for something less urgent—for example, to remove her tonsils—the balance would shift. You would be well within your rights to require a full 30 days' notice. A delay wouldn't cause Cora any harm, and she has no excuse for failing to give notice as required, so you are on safer ground if you require her to delay her leave.

If you decide, after considering all the facts and circumstances, that you will insist on 30 days' notice, put your decision—including the earliest date the employee's leave can begin—in writing, attach it to the employee's individual notice form, and talk to the employee about it. Listen carefully to the employee's response; you may learn something that could change your mind. If so, simply provide a new individual notice form.

Rescheduling Leave

In addition to the 30-day notice requirement for foreseeable leave, there are a couple of additional timing issues to consider. They are:

- **One-year limit on parenting leave.** As explained in Chapter 6, new parents must conclude their parenting leave within one year after the child is born or placed with them. Review this requirement when you sit down with the employee to discuss his or her time off, to make sure the employee understands it.

- **Scheduling foreseeable treatment to avoid undue disruption.** Employees are obligated to schedule foreseeable leave for medical treatment—whether the leave will be taken intermittently or all at once—so as not to unduly disrupt the employer's operations. This means you can ask the employee to reschedule planned treatment or to work around the company's needs. However, any changes must be approved by the employee's health care provider: If the health care provider insists that treatment must begin immediately, for example, you can't make the employee wait until your company's annual reports are filed. (See "Managing Intermittent Leave," below, for more information.)

Unforeseeable Leave

As explained in Chapter 7, an employee who needs leave for an unforeseeable reason—emergency surgery or premature labor, for example—need give only as much leave as is practicable under the circumstances. If the employee has a true emergency, you might receive notice only after the employee has already missed work. How can you work out scheduling issues in this situation?

The answer depends on the circumstances. If the employee needs leave for reasons other than his or her own serious health condition—for example, because the employee's family member has been in an accident or the employee's wife has delivered a baby prematurely—you should be able to spend a few minutes on the phone with the employee. You should ask how long the employee expects the situation to last; if the employee doesn't know, tell the employee that you'll call again in a few days to check in.

If the employee is unable to talk to you personally—for example, because the employee is in a coma, recovering from surgery, or simply too weak to attend to work details—talk to a close family member. Under the FMLA, you may talk to the employee's spokesperson (typically, an adult family member) if the employee is unable to give notice personally. In this situation, you should again ask about the condition and how long it's expected to last. If the family member doesn't know, ask to be kept in the loop—and plan to call back in a few days to follow up.

CAUTION

Compassion is the order of the day. An employee who needs emergency leave is typically facing a very tough situation—often, a sudden injury or illness or a difficult birth. Although it's important to fulfill your notice obligations, don't go overboard trying to get the employee to do the same. Be sensitive to the employee's situation, and do what you can to get the information you need without being demanding or intrusive.

Covering an Employee's Duties During Leave

As a manager, you're responsible not only for administering an employee's FMLA leave properly, but also for making sure the employee's work gets done. If you're wondering how other managers do it, here's the answer: According to a nationwide survey conducted in 2000, almost all employers—98.3%, to be exact—covered the work of an employee on leave by assigning it to coworkers, at least in part; some (slightly more than 40%) also hired temporary replacements to help cover the workload. And, for the most part, coworkers were not resentful about having to take on this extra work: A whopping 85% of employees said that a coworker's use of FMLA leave had a positive or neutral impact on them.

One likely reason many employers simply divvy up the work of employees on leave is that employees tend to come back fairly quickly. The same survey showed that the median length of FMLA leave was only ten days—the equivalent of a two-week vacation.

When it's time to decide how to handle an employee's workload during his or her leave, these statistics provide some reassurance. As we all know, however, statistics give only a general picture. Every situation is different, and you'll have to consider all of the facts and circumstances when trying to figure out how to get the work done.

CROSS-REFERENCE

Sometimes you don't have to reinstate the employee. As explained in detail in Chapter 10, you don't always have to reinstate an employee. For example, if the employee is among the highest paid 10% of the company's workforce and reinstating the company would cause substantial and grievous economic injury, you don't have to reinstate the employee. And, if you don't have to return the employee to work, you have a much wider range of options for handling the employee's job duties.

Available Options

There are a number of ways to get an employee's work done while he or she is on leave. In some cases, you'll be able to use just one of these strategies; other situations might call for a combination of approaches. Here are some commonly used options:

- **Rely on coworkers.** This strategy makes good sense, especially if all your employees do similar work: The coworkers already know exactly how to do the job. Your role is to figure out what changes might need to be made (if any) to allow the employee's coworkers to take on extra work, or how to divide the work amongst several employees. In some instances, you might even handle some higher-level work—such as supervising employees or handling key transactions or relationships—yourself.

EXAMPLE: Jody is a customer service representative in a call center staffed by 12 employees. All of them do the same job: answering phone calls from customers who have questions about the company's products, processing orders and returns on a same-day basis, and contacting customers who have purchased the company's products to assess their satisfaction with the experience.

When Jody takes three weeks of FMLA leave, her manager, Leticia, realizes that it will take too long for a temporary replacement to learn the ropes: By the time a temp gets up to speed, Jody will be back at work. Instead, Leticia decides to ask Jody's coworkers to handle her calls. To make sure the workload doesn't get overwhelming, Leticia makes answering and returning customer calls the top priority but allows orders and returns to be put off until the following day, if necessary. And, Leticia asks two of the company's summer interns to take over the customer satisfaction surveys until Jody returns from leave. By making these minor adjustments, Leticia ensures that her short-handed team will still be able to get its work done.

- **Hire a temporary replacement.** Whenever coworkers won't be able to take on the employee's job duties—maybe they're too busy or don't have the necessary skills—it's time to look outside the company. Just make sure that any temp you hire understands that the job is for a very limited time; otherwise, you might be faced with a legal claim when the time comes to let the temp go.

- **Hire a consultant.** If you need to replace someone who does highly creative or technical projects, consider hiring an outside consultant: an independent contractor who specializes in particular types of work. If the work is specialized and really can't wait, it might be worth the expense to hire a pro for specific tasks like rolling out a new computer system or designing new company branding or collateral.

- **Outsource the work.** It sometimes makes sense to hire an outside company to do an employee's work—for example, if no one in-house has the skills but an outside agency offers the same service.

EXAMPLE: Sanjiv works in the bookkeeping department and spends a week each month processing payroll. The rest of his time he collects accounts receivable. Sanjiv plans to take ten weeks of FMLA leave when his daughter is born. Although his coworkers can pick up his accounts receivable work, only his manager, Brenda, knows how to do the payroll. Unfortunately, Brenda will be preparing the company for an audit while Sanjiv is out and won't have any time to devote to handling the payroll.

Brenda decides to use an outside payroll service while Sanjiv is out. It costs significantly less than hiring a replacement or training another employee to do the payroll. And, Brenda knows that the outside service knows how to handle deductions, withholdings, and other wage adjustments, which assures her that the company won't run afoul of wage and hour or tax laws while Sanjiv is out.

No matter which option(s) you choose, you'll probably have to undo any changes when the employee returns to work, because you are required to reinstate the employee when his or her leave is over. (Chapter 12 explains these requirements in detail.) This is why it's important that you explain to the people who will do the employee's job, whether they are the employee's coworkers or outside temps or contractors, that the situation is temporary. You don't want replacements believing they've received a promotion or landed a permanent position with your company.

Talk to the Employee

Before you decide how to handle an employee's workload during leave, you should talk to the employee about it, if possible. Of course, if the employee takes leave for a medical emergency, you may not get this opportunity. You'll have to patch something together quickly until you get a chance to speak with employee and figure out how long he or she will be gone.

The employee is your best source of information about exactly what he or she does every day, which job duties are top priorities, which coworkers might be able to step in and handle certain tasks, and so on. The employee also has a vested interest in making sure his or her work is handled properly during leave. After all, nobody wants to return from leave to find a pile of unfinished work, strained relationships with customers or clients, missed deadlines, and other problems. Employees who take pride in their work and value their place in the company will be eager to collaborate with you on a strategy for a smooth transition from work to leave and back again.

But you also have to proceed with caution when talking to an employee about handling his or her work. The FMLA prohibits you from interfering with an employee's right to take leave, and that includes discouraging the employee from using the FMLA. If you pressure the employee not to take leave, imply that the employee's opportunities to advance might suffer if the employee takes leave, or require the employee to work when he or she is on leave, for example, you could run into legal trouble.

EXAMPLE: Luisa is a salesperson for a company that produces office supplies. She handles some of the company's largest accounts. Luisa is planning to take a full 12 weeks of FMLA leave when she has a baby. You meet with her to talk about handling her workload. You start the conversation like this: "You know, Luisa, our back-to-school business in August and September is huge, and you're planning to be out until September. If you could come back a few weeks early, we wouldn't have to assign your accounts to someone else. Of course, you can take a longer leave if you want, but I can't guarantee that you'll get those accounts back if we have to move them."

Oops! You've basically said that you will punish Luisa for taking the full leave to which she's entitled. Here's a better way to start the discussion: "Congratulations, Luisa! I'm so excited for you. As you know, you'll be out during the biggest sales period of the year, so I want to get your ideas about how we should handle your accounts while you're gone, especially Office Club and Binders 'n' More. I really want to work with you to figure out how we can keep these customers happy—and keep our sales high—even though you won't be here. Do you think it makes sense to hire a temporary replacement, or can the other salespeople pick up the slack?"

Your conversation with the employee will depend on the facts, including what the employee does, how long the employee will be out, whether the employee supervises others, and so on. Here are some pointers that will help you in your conversation:

- **Always start by acknowledging the employee's situation.** Congratulate or offer sympathy to the employee as appropriate. Rushing straight into a discussion of work details appears insensitive to the employee's needs, and your conversation may be strained as a result.

- **Briefly state the facts.** Review what you know about the employee's job and leave, to make sure you've got the details right. For example, you might say, "I'd like to get your feedback on how to cover your work while you're out—and make sure your transition to leave and back to work is a smooth one. I understand you'll be out for five weeks and that you have one major project milestone due during that time. Is that right?"

- **Learn the priorities.** Ask what the employee has on his or her plate, focusing particularly on projects, deadlines, meetings, and deliverables that need to be handled while the employee is out. For example: "What are the most important things that we need to take care of while you're gone? What can wait until you return?"

- **Discuss options.** Ask whether the employee has any ideas or concerns about job coverage, such as which coworkers might be able to pick up the work, whether to hire a temp, or whether some matters would best be handled by you or another higher-up at the company. You might say, "When Jane took parental leave, I called on her two major accounts and the rest of the team divvied up the others. Do you think that approach will work for your leave—and are there any accounts that you think I should cover?"

- **Ask what to say.** Find out how the employee would like you to position his or her absence with third parties (vendors, clients, customers, and so on) and coworkers. Some employees want others to know what's going on, while others prefer to keep things private, and you should respect the employee's wishes. For example: "I'll tell the outside auditors that you'll be on leave for four weeks. I know some of your coworkers already know about your father's condition; would you prefer that I announce that you'll be taking leave to help care for him, or would you rather I simply say that you'll be out?"

- **Recap your strategy.** After you've talked through the options and developed a plan, review it with the employee. If either of you will have to gather more information before you can make a final decision, schedule another brief conversation. For example, you might say, "I'm going to ask Mark about his workload, and you're going to try to reschedule the in-house trainings until after you return from leave. Let's meet again on Thursday to see where we are. If everything works out, we'll plan to have Mark and Stacey cover your IT calls, and I'll free up some of their time by bringing in a part-time temp to handle the departmental paperwork."

Handle Logistics

After you've developed a plan to cover the employee's work, it's time to put it in place. If you'll need to hire a temp or consultant, make the necessary arrangements. If coworkers will be taking on part of the load, talk with them and find out if they'll need additional resources or help to handle the additional work. Give the employee's outside contacts—such as clients, suppliers, and so on—a little information about the employee's leave, including the name of someone else to call if they have any questions or concerns.

Continuing Employee Benefits During Leave

While an employee is on FMLA leave, you must continue the employee's coverage under your company's group health plan, just as if the employee had been working continuously. If the employee usually has to contribute towards the premium, you may continue to require that contribution, but your company must continue to pay its share of the premium as well. Whether you have to provide other types of benefits during leave depends on your company's policies.

The employee is entitled to continue the same type of coverage and benefit levels as before the leave. For example, if the employee's family was covered, then the continuation must include family coverage. However, any changes to the benefits plan, new plans, premium increases, and so on still apply to the employee. And, employees on leave have the same right to change their coverage as they would have had if they were employed. So an employee on leave during an open enrollment period has the same right to change coverage as employees who are actually working during that period.

Employees do not have to continue their benefits during FMLA leave if they don't want to, perhaps because the premium is significant and the employee won't necessarily require benefits during leave because he or she has benefits from a different source. However, because you must restore the employee's benefits when you reinstate the employee—and you must do so immediately, without any waiting period, physical examination, or other requalification procedure—you might have to continue the benefits and seek reimbursement later from the employee. (Chapter 10 covers benefits restoration when an employee returns to work.)

What Is a Group Health Plan?

A group health plan is any plan of, or contributed to by, an employer to pro-vide health care to employees, former employees, and their families, includ-ing self-insured plans, vision plans, dental coverage, and other health care plans, whether they are components of a single health care plan or adminis-tered separately.

A group health plan does not include an insurance program providing health coverage under which employees purchase individual policies from insurers if all of the following are true:

- The employer makes no contribution.

- Employee participation is voluntary.

- The employer's role doesn't go beyond allowing the insurer to publicize its plan to employees, collecting premiums through payroll deductions, and sending them to the insurer.

- The employer doesn't receive any compensation or other benefit from the program, other than reasonable payment for the cost of collecting and remitting premiums.

- The employee's premium does not increase if the employment relationship ends.

Cafeteria Plans

Some companies provide benefits through a cafeteria plan: a benefit program through which employees choose from a menu of benefits, such as health coverage, life insurance, disability insurance, and so on. Employees are allotted a certain number of dollars or "points" to spend on the options; if they choose not to spend the entire amount, they can typically receive the remainder as compensation.

Employers must continue making cafeteria plan payments towards group health insurance premiums (including dental and vision benefits) while an employee is on FMLA leave. If other benefits—such as life insurance or child care coverage—are paid through a cafeteria plan, the employer must continue the portion of the payment that goes towards these benefits only if it does so for employees on other types of unpaid leave. (See "Other Types of Benefits," below, for more information.)

Flexible Spending Accounts

A flexible spending account (FSA) allows employees to set aside pretax income for medical expenses not paid by health insurance (such as copayments, premiums, and expenses that are outside of the employer's plan) or for dependent care expenses. The employee determines how much to set aside each year (typically, by payroll deductions), within limits set by law.

FSAs are funded entirely by employees, so there aren't any employer contributions to be continued during FMLA leave. Employees on leave must be given three options for dealing with their FSAs:

- continue making payments as if they were still working
- continue their participation in the plan but stop making payments during leave, or
- stop participating in the plan while on leave.

If the employee either stops making payments or pulls out of the plan altogether during FMLA leave, the employee has a choice upon reinstatement: return to the previous coverage level or choose a prorated coverage amount that doesn't include payments for the time spent on leave.

EXAMPLE: David has an FSA and decides to commit $1,200 to it for the year. His employer sets aside $50 from David's twice-monthly paychecks and deposits it in his FSA. David is out for two months—July and August—on FMLA leave. He decides to continue his coverage but suspend his payments during that time.

When he returns, David would have to make higher payments to set aside a total of $1,200. Because he missed $200 worth of payments while on leave and there are eight pay periods left in the year, he would have to have an additional $25 set aside each pay period, for a total pretax contribution of $75, if he wanted to set aside the whole $1,200. Alternatively, he could continue setting aside $50 per paycheck and reduce his total coverage for the year to $1,000.

Multiemployer Health Plans

A multiemployer health plan is a special type of health insurance coverage unique to unionized companies. At least two employers contribute to a multiemployer plan, which is maintained pursuant to one or more collective bargaining agreement(s) between unions and employers.

Employers who contribute to these plans must follow the same benefits continuation rules as other employers—for example, they cannot charge the employee a higher premium to continue benefits than the employee would have had to pay if working, or provide less coverage. However, there are a couple of different rules for multiemployer plans, set forth at 29 C.F.R. § 825.211:

- If the plan contains special provisions for maintaining coverage during FMLA leave (for example, through pooled contributions from all employers subject to the plan), the employer may follow those provisions, rather than continuing to contribute the same amount as would have been due if the employee were continuously working.

- Employees who receive health care coverage through a multiemployer plan cannot be required to use "banked" hours during FMLA leave. Typically, an employee banks hours when he or she works more hours than are necessary to maintain eligibility for health care coverage; the employee can then use these banked hours to stay eligible, even when the employee's hours drop below the minimum threshold for eligibility. This provision relieves employees of the obligation to use banked hours to maintain eligibility during periods of FMLA leave.

Other Types of Benefits

For all other types of benefits, your company must only follow its usual policies for employees on unpaid leave. If your policies do not provide for other benefits to continue or accrue during unpaid leave, you do not have to continue them or allow them to accrue during FMLA leave. For example, if your company typically does not allow paid vacation leave to accrue while an employee is on unpaid leave, you do not have to allow it to accrue while the employee is on FMLA leave. The same is true of seniority and benefits based on seniority.

CAUTION

Paid leave is treated differently. If an employee uses paid time off for FMLA leave, you must follow your company's policies for paid leave. For example, if you allow employees to continue to accrue seniority or sick and vacation leave while using paid time off, you must also allow them to accrue these benefits while using paid time off for FMLA leave.

You have no legal obligation to continue other insurance benefits—such as life or disability insurance—while an employee is on FMLA leave unless you continue these benefits for other types of unpaid leave. But as a practical matter, you may be required to continue these benefits to make sure you'll be able to restore the employee's benefits upon reinstatement. As you'll learn in Chapter 10, you must give a returning employee the same benefits, at the same levels, that the employee had before taking leave, and you cannot require the employee to requalify for benefits. If your programs would require an employee who drops coverage and then picks it up again to requalify, you might have to keep the employee enrolled to avoid violating the FMLA. (If so, you can seek reimbursement for the employee's share of the premiums when the employee returns to work—see Chapter 10.)

Premium Payments

The FMLA provides several ways to collect the employee's share of the premium for group health coverage. If the employee substitutes paid leave for FMLA leave, the employee's share must be collected as it ordinarily would for any other type of paid leave (typically, through payroll deductions). If the employee uses unpaid FMLA leave, the employer may collect the premium in any of the following ways:

- The employee makes the payment at the same time it would ordinarily be due through payroll deduction—in other words, the employee would have to pay the premium every payday.

- The employee makes the payment at the same time it would be due if the employee were receiving continuing coverage through COBRA.

- The employee pays the premium in advance to a cafeteria plan (at the employee's option).

- The employee pays according to the same rules that apply to other employees on unpaid leave, as long as those rules don't require the employee to pay the premium before leave starts or require the employee to pay more than he or she would have to pay if employed.

- The employee pays in any manner agreed to by employer and employee. For example, you might agree that the employee can prepay the premiums by having a larger amount deducted each pay period prior to taking foreseeable leave.

Whichever method you choose, you must give the employee advance written notice of how and when the payment must be made. You can provide this notice as part of the employee's individual notice, covered in Chapter 7.

If the employee's premium payment is more than 30 days late, you may terminate the employee's coverage. However, you must send the employee written notice of your intent to do so. The letter must state that the payment has not been received and that the employee's coverage will terminate if payment is not received by a certain date; this date must be at least 15 days after you send the letter.

 POLICY ALERT

The date the employee's coverage officially terminates depends, in part, on your policies for other types of unpaid leave. If your company has an established policy that allows it to terminate coverage retroactively to the date of the missed payment, it may do so. If it does not have this type of policy, it may terminate coverage effective 30 days after the missed payment.

Here is a sample letter telling an employee that health insurance coverage will terminate unless payment is received; you'll find a blank form in Appendix C.

Notice of Termination of Group Health Coverage

March 28, 2008
Corinne West
123 Main Street
San Francisco, CA 94910

Dear Corinne,

As I informed you by written notice when you first requested FMLA leave, you are required to pay your share of the premium for group health insurance. We agreed that you would pay these amounts by getting a check to me, in the amount of $36.45, on the 1st and 15th of every month. I have attached a copy of the written notice explaining this requirement, for your reference.

You submitted a check on February 15 and March 1. However, I did not receive a check from you on March 15. I am writing to inform you that we are going to terminate your health insurance coverage if we do not receive your March 15 payment by April 14, 2008.

Please take care of this right away. If you have any questions, feel free to call me at 415-555-1212.

Sincerely,

Jim Ramey
HR Director

Although you have the legal right to terminate coverage for a late payment, you also have a legal obligation to restore the employee's health benefits when he or she returns to work—and you cannot require the employee to reapply, take a physical exam, or otherwise requalify for benefits. This obligation applies even if you terminate coverage because the employee doesn't pay the premium. As a practical matter, this means you may have to continue the employee's coverage in order to reinstate benefits as the FMLA requires, even if this means you have to pay the employee's share of the premium. If you find yourself in this situation, you can require the employee to reimburse you for his or her share once the employee returns to work; Chapter 10 explains how.

Managing Intermittent Leave

Intermittent or reduced-schedule leave poses some unique managerial challenges. You and the employee might not know how long the employee's need for leave will last, when the employee will have to take time off, or even whether the employee will show up for work the next day. The can present some challenges when you're trying to make sure that the work gets done.

Scheduling

Employees who need intermittent or reduced-schedule leave must try to schedule leave in a way that does not disrupt your company's operations. If the employee knows he or she will need intermittent or reduced-schedule leave, the employee should give you a proposed schedule of leave and try to arrange to take time off in a way that accommodates the company's needs. Of course, this will be easier when the employee needs leave for treatment rather than for episodic flare-ups of a serious health condition.

This doesn't mean that the company has the right to veto an employee's leave schedule, however. The employee's health care provider will ultimately decide whether treatment or leave can be rescheduled or not. If the health care provider won't approve a change, you may not insist on it.

EXAMPLE: Marcos needs weekly physical therapy for neck injuries from a car accident. Marcos tells you that he needs to be out for two hours every week for at least twelve weeks. You and Marcos agree that he will try to schedule the therapy for the late afternoon, when plenty of his coworkers will be available to handle his workload.

When Marcos calls to schedule his treatment, he learns that there are no available late afternoon slots for a couple of months. Marcos's doctor says that he must begin physical therapy immediately or risk permanent damage. In this situation, can you insist that Marcos wait for an afternoon appointment?

No. Marcos's doctor has the last word, and treatment must start immediately. You should work with Marcos to figure out which of the available time slots would be least disruptive for the company.

LESSONS FROM THE

Real World

An employee must try to reschedule foreseeable intermittent leave that would result in understaffing.

Scott Kaylor was a CT technician at Fannin Regional Hospital. During his employment at the hospital, Kaylor saw his doctor regularly for treatment for a degenerative back disease.

On December 27, 1994, Kaylor was hospitalized for a flare-up of his back injury. He spent three weeks on FMLA leave, then returned to work. On January 31, Kaylor told his supervisor that he had an appointment with his doctor on February 3. This appointment was one of his regular treatments and had been scheduled before he was hospitalized. Kaylor's supervisor told him he could not take the day off because it would leave them short-staffed and asked him to reschedule the treatment.

After hearing from other employees that Kaylor planned to call in sick on February 3, his supervisor asked him whether he intended to show up. He said that he would come to work. On the 3rd, however, he called in sick, claiming to have a stomach virus. But he still went to his doctor's appointment for back treatment. The doctor said that Kaylor could have gone to work that day, and the doctor's notes didn't mentioned a stomach virus.

Kaylor was fired for abuse of sick leave. Kaylor sued, claiming that he had a legal right to take intermittent FMLA leave on February 3 and could not have be fired for doing so. The court disagreed, finding that Kaylor had an obligation to make reasonable efforts to reschedule his leave after his supervisor told him that it would cause staffing problems. Because he didn't follow the rules for intermittent leave, Kaylor wasn't protected by the FMLA.

Kaylor v. Fannin Regional Hospital, 946 F.Supp. 988 (N.D. Ga. 1996).

When an employee needs leave for an episodic problem, such as migraines, asthma, or any other condition that comes on suddenly or waxes and wanes in intensity, it can be very difficult to manage the employee's time off. After all, the employee typically can't predict when the condition will necessitate time off work. If the condition is unpredictable, you cannot insist that the employee take leave only according to a set schedule: As long as the employee is otherwise entitled to leave and has (or is caring for someone who has) a serious health condition, the employee has the right to take unscheduled time off if it's medically necessary.

EXAMPLE: Caroline suffers from Crohn's disease, a chronic condition that causes inflammation of the intestines. On occasion, the disease flares up and she has severe abdominal pain and vomiting that makes it impossible for her to work. If she qualifies otherwise for FMLA leave, Caroline is likely entitled to take intermittent leave when her condition incapacitates her, even if she can't give any notice or "schedule" this time off.

Transfers

If an employee has a foreseeable need for reduced-schedule or intermittent leave, you may transfer the employee to another position that better accommodates the employee's leave schedule or change the employee's original position to better accommodate the employee's need for leave, as long as the employee still receives the same pay and benefits. If transferred to an alternative position, the employee must be qualified for the position.

The alternative position need not have the same job duties as the employee's original position. However, the company cannot transfer the employee to a lesser position that could discourage the employee (or others) from taking leave. For example, a change that dramatically increases the employee's commute or moves the employee from the day shift to the night shift violates the FMLA. If the alternative position is a clear and obvious demotion, it probably won't fly.

EXAMPLE: Roger is a human resources manager for a large hotel chain. He reports to the company's headquarters but travels two or three days each week to conduct trainings for employees in other cities. Roger's doctor certifies that he will need to spend four hours per day caring for his son during a ten-week cancer treatment regimen.

The company needs to continue its trainings during Roger's leave, and Roger can no longer travel. The company would be within its rights to transfer Roger to a different position with the same pay and benefits. For example, it might require Roger to handle compensation and benefits issues, to coach other representatives so they can handle the out-of-town trainings, or to help the company revise its nationwide hiring standards, if Roger is qualified to do those tasks. However, if the company tried to transfer Roger to work at the front desk of one of its hotels or process reservations in a call center, that would violate the FMLA.

Once the employee's leave ends, you must return the employee to his or her original position.

Tips to Prevent Abuse

Some managers worry that employees who qualify for intermittent leave will abuse that right to take time off whenever they want—and that the company just has to sit back and take it. This isn't quite right, however. Although employees have a right to take intermittent leave if it's medically necessary, this doesn't mean that they are free to use that time off for any purpose. If you think an employee might be abusing intermittent leave—for example, by taking unscheduled intermittent leave only on Fridays or calling in sick whenever a major deadline is looming—here are a few things you can do:

- **Check the medical certification.** As explained in Chapter 8, you should always get a medical certification for serious health conditions. On the form, the employee's doctor must indicate how long the employee's need for intermittent leave is expected to last; the frequency and duration of episodes of incapacity due to chronic conditions; and the number, duration, dates, and estimated recovery time of any scheduled treatment. If the employee's time off doesn't jibe with these predictions, you can seek recertification. (Chapter 8 explains how.)

- **Get a new certification if the employee's reason for leave changes.** For example, if an employee takes time off every week for scheduled treatment for an injury, then claims to need additional time off for another condition, require a certification of the new condition. This will help you pin down exactly what the employee needs and why.

- **Let the doctor review the employee's schedule.** The Department of Labor has said that employers may attach a copy of the employee's attendance records to the medical certification form so the health care provider may consider it in determining the employee's likely future absences. A doctor who sees that an employee is gaming the system—by taking only Fridays off, for example—may be willing to place some limits on the certification.

- **Require employees to adhere to a schedule for foreseeable intermittent leave.** If an employee needs intermittent leave only for scheduled treatment (not for a condition that might worsen suddenly), you can ask the employee to stick to the schedule. Of course, the employee's doctor might have to cancel every once in a while, but if the employee seems to be taking a lot of unscheduled time off, you should ask the employee what's going on—and seek recertification.

- **Require employees to talk to a manager for every absence.** One of the toughest challenges that arises from intermittent leave is properly recording and designating the time off. It's especially difficult if an employee takes a lot of unscheduled time off in small increments. This is why it's a good idea to require employees using intermittent leave to call in and let a manager know why they're taking time off; the manager can then record the leave as FMLA leave or pass the message on to the person responsible for managing FMLA in your organization. If the employee is unable to call in ahead of time for health reasons, make sure the employee provides notice as soon as possible.

Some companies have adopted fairly aggressive policies to combat abuse of sick leave by employees. When these policies are applied to employees who are using FMLA leave, however, they can create legal problems. If these rules conflict with the FMLA or have the effect of discouraging employees from taking FMLA leave, they might violate the law. Here are a few examples:

- Requiring employees to call in 30 minutes before their shift starts violates the FMLA, because the FMLA requires only as much notice as is practicable under the circumstances. *Mora v. Chem-Tronics, Inc.,* 16 F.Supp.2d 1192 (S.D. Cal. 1998).

- Requiring employees to call in within three days of an absence or be fired for job abandonment does not violate the FMLA, because the employee was able to call in during that time and should have done so. *Lewis v. Holsum of Fort Wayne, Inc.,* 278 F.3d 706 (7th Cir. 2002).

- Requiring an employee on sick leave to call a "sick control hotline" whenever the employee leaves home does not violate the FMLA, because it doesn't conflict with the law or diminish its protections. *Callison v. City of Philadelphia*, 128 Fed. Appx. 897 (3rd Cir. 2005).

As you can see, the rules on this subject aren't entirely clear. If your company's usual notice, certification, and reporting requirements for using paid sick leave go beyond the FMLA's requirements, you should probably talk to a lawyer before enforcing them against an employee who is using FMLA leave.

Requesting Status Reports

The FMLA gives employers the right to require employees on leave to provide periodic reports on their status and intent to return to work. (29 C.F.R. § 309.) This rule serves a couple of purposes: First and foremost, it helps employers manage the employee's workload and plan for a smooth reinstatement. As explained in Chapter 10, employers must reinstate employees immediately upon their return from leave, as long as employees provide at least two days' notice of their intent to return. Knowing when the employee plans to return to work date helps employers prepare for the transition.

Requiring status reports also gives employers notice if the employee won't return to work. If the employee tells the employer, unequivocally, that he or she will not return to work, the employer can replace the employee permanently or make any other necessary changes. If the employee voluntarily chooses not to return—for example, to stay home with a healthy baby—then the employer can also discontinue the employee's health benefits and seek reimbursement for any premiums already paid. (These rules are explained in Chapter 10.)

If you require status reports, tell employees what you expect. Your request must be reasonable, considering the facts and circumstances of the employee's leave. If you ask for reports too frequently or request too much detail, especially of an employee who is struggling with a serious health condition, you could run into legal trouble. The Department of Labor has said that employers who take advantage of this limited right to communicate with employees on leave by making disruptive or burdensome requests could violate the law. At some point, an employer who is too persistent could appear to be punishing the employee for taking leave or trying to bully the employee to either return to work or forfeit his or her health benefits.

How often you should request a status report depends on how long the employee will be on leave and how definite the employee's return to work date is. If the employee will be on leave for 12 weeks and has a scheduled return-to-work date, you might ask for a status report once a month, then check in with the employee a week or two before his or her leave runs out, to make sure that the employee is still planning to come back as scheduled. If the employee doesn't know how long he or she will have to be off, you might reasonably request more frequent status reports. And for a shorter leave, you might simply ask the employee to check in a week before returning, to make sure everything is still going according to plan.

You should ask for two pieces of information in the status report: whether the employee still intends to return to work and, if so, when. Don't try to use a status report requirement to get medical information—that's governed by the recertification process explained in Chapter 8.

You can request that employees make status reports orally or in writing. Of course, it will be much easier for an employee to pick up the phone than to write a letter. If you allow oral status reports, however, you must document any changes to the employee's leave dates or intent to return to work. If the employee calls and tells you that he or she is no longer planning to come back, for example, you should put that in writing immediately. The best practice is to also send a confirming letter to the employee right away, to make sure you got it right.

 TIP

You might need to talk about reasonable accommodations. If an employee who is out for his or her own serious health condition expresses concerns about being able to do the job after returning from FMLA leave, consider the possibility that the employee might have a disability as defined by the Americans with Disabilities Act (ADA). If so, your company has a duty to begin a conversation about whether and how you can make it possible for the employee to perform the job by providing a reasonable accommodation. It's best to start talking about possible accommodations as soon as you learn that the employee might have a disability, to give you time to make any necessary adjustments before the employee is ready to return. See Chapter 11 for more on the ADA.

Disciplining or Firing an Employee During Leave

You may fire or discipline an employee who is on FMLA leave, as long as your reasons for firing are entirely unrelated to the employee's use of the FMLA. This is easier said than done, because it might be hard to prove that the employee's FMLA leave played no part in your decision. This is particularly true if you are disciplining or firing the employee for poor attendance. Even if you consider only absences that were not covered by the FMLA, chances are good that the employee will claim to have been punished for taking legally protected leave.

The best practice is to make absolutely sure that you'll be able to prove that you had independent reasons for acting. You'll be on safest legal ground if you initiated discipline or termination proceedings before you knew that the employee might need FMLA leave. That way, the employee will have a tough time showing any relationship between the leave and your decision. If you are imposing discipline for excessive absenteeism, you must be very sure that you aren't counting any protected absences against the employee.

Even if you have entirely legitimate reasons for disciplining or firing an employee, you might find yourself on the wrong end of a lawsuit if you take action as soon as the employee asks for FMLA leave. Perceptions matter—to the employee, the lawyer(s) whom the employee consults about filing a lawsuit, and the judge and jury. If you act right after the employee requests leave, it's probably going to look like you acted because of the request, even if that's not the case. Although you might eventually win in court (if the jury believes your side of the story), you and your company will spend a lot of time and money getting to that victory. You should consult with a lawyer whenever you are considering disciplining or firing an employee who has requested or taken FMLA leave.

LESSONS FROM THE

Real World

An employee can be fired for problems discovered during FMLA leave.

Candis Smith worked as an Administrative Secretary at the Memorial Foundation of Allen Hospital. She was responsible for sending a receipt and thank-you card to hospital donors. In December 1998, Robert Justis, the Executive Director of the Foundation, told Smith that he had received complaints from donors whose had not been acknowledged for their contributions. Smith told him that she would try to send out acknowledgments as soon as possible.

Smith took FMLA leave starting January 1, 1999, to adopt a child from Romania. She left a stack of donor receipts that had to be sent out and wrote a note asking another employee to type thank-you cards and mail them, along with the receipts, to donors. One week into Smith's leave, another employee found another pile of donor receipts in Smith's work area. There were approximately 400 receipts, for donations totaling more than $350,000, going back a couple of months. One of the receipts was for a gift of $136,000, from one of the donors who had complained about not receiving a receipt.

Justis and Richard Seidler, the CEO of the hospital, decided to terminate Smith's employment immediately. On January 14, when she returned from Romania, they called her in for a meeting and fired her for failing to send out the receipts.

Smith sued, claiming that she was fired illegally for taking FMLA leave. As evidence, she pointed out that she was fired just two weeks after starting her leave and that she was fired for problems that came to light only because she took leave. The court didn't buy these arguments. Instead, the court noted that Smith was fired shortly after she started her leave because the Foundation didn't know how serious the problem was until it discovered the unsent receipts, which put the Foundation in a difficult position with its donors. In light of these facts, the timing of the decision did not demonstrate that Smith was fired for taking leave.

Smith v. Allen Health Systems, Inc., 302 F.3d 827 (8th Cir. 2002).

Common Mistakes Regarding Managing Leave —And How to Avoid Them

MISTAKE 1: Requiring employees to give more notice than the FMLA requires.

AVOID THIS MISTAKE BY:

- Not requiring an employee to give more notice than is practicable under the circumstances.

- Delaying the start of an employee's leave only if you have the right—and a good reason—to do so. If the employee could have given 30 days' notice, delaying the employee's leave won't harm the employee, and your company really needs the employee at work in the next 30 days, consider asserting your rights.

- Applying company policies only if they don't conflict with the FMLA, especially for using sick and vacation leave. For example, you cannot require an employee to follow your usual advance notice requirements if the employee's need for leave is unforeseeable. (See Chapter 7 for more information.)

MISTAKE 2: Overloading coworkers when an employee takes FMLA leave.

AVOID THIS MISTAKE BY:

- Planning ahead if you know an employee will need leave (to have a baby, for example). Talk to the employee and coworkers ahead of time about your plans for getting the work done.

- Cross-training your reports. It will be much easier for employees to cover each other's work if they already know how to do it.

- Getting extra help, if necessary. You might need to bring in a temp or consultant to help you get the work done, especially when an employee takes an extended leave.

- Taking on important tasks yourself. It doesn't help your company to have inexperienced folks handling major clients or projects. Make time in your schedule to handle these key tasks.

MISTAKE 3: Mismanaging intermittent leave.

AVOID THIS MISTAKE BY:

- Seeking recertification of the employee's condition, if necessary. If an employee is taking leave beyond what the medical certification anticipated, ask for another one.

- Making sure that every qualified absence is designated as FMLA leave. An employee who takes a lot of intermittent leave may also take time off for other reasons—such as vacation or minor illnesses. You need to know which absences count as FMLA leave, so ask these employees to talk to you or another manager every time they need time off.

- Requiring employees to stick to their treatment schedules. If an employee needs intermittent leave for scheduled treatment, the certification should state when that treatment will be. You can ask the employee to reschedule, with the doctor's approval, to avoid undue disruption to the company's operations.

- Transferring the employee, if necessary. You are entitled to transfer the employee temporarily to a position that better accommodates his or her need for intermittent leave. Just make sure that the transfer isn't a demotion in disguise.

MISTAKE 4: Firing or disciplining an employee for taking FMLA leave—or appearing to do so.

AVOID THIS MISTAKE BY:

- Consulting with a lawyer—every time. Because it's so easy to get in trouble here, you should always talk to a lawyer to make sure that you've made the right decision before taking action.

- Making sure you have a very compelling reason to fire the employee. Even if your company is an at-will employer (as most are), this isn't the time to exercise your right to fire without a very good reason.

- Firing only if you can prove that you would have taken the same action if the employee hadn't taken leave. This means, for example, being able to document that termination proceedings were in the works before the employee requested leave or that you discovered truly egregious problems that warrant immediate firing.

- Not counting FMLA leave against an employee with an attendance problem. You can't consider FMLA leave when deciding whether an employee has missed so much work that termination is warranted.

✓ Managers' Checklist	Managing FMLA Leave

Scheduling

❑ I calendared the start and end dates of the employee's leave, if I know them.

❑ If the employee did not give 30 days' notice of foreseeable leave, I considered whether to require the employee to delay the start of his or her leave.

❑ If I didn't let the employee take leave on the date requested because the employee didn't provide enough notice, I put that decision in writing and gave it to the employee.

❑ If the employee is taking parenting leave, I made sure the employee's leave will be complete within one year of the child's arrival.

❑ If the employee's foreseeable leave will cause undue disruption to the company's operations, I asked the employee to try to reschedule (subject to the approval of his or her health care provider).

❑ If the employee had to take unforeseeable leave, I made initial contact with the employee or a family member to gather information and made plans to follow up in a few days.

Handling the Employee's Work

❑ If the employee was available, I talked to the employee and came up with a plan to cover his or her job duties during leave.

❑ If the employee's coworkers will pick up some extra work, I made any changes necessary to ensure that they will not be stretched too thin.

❑ I determined which, if any, of the employee's responsibilities I will handle and made the necessary arrangements to do so.

❑ If we will bring on temporary help, I made the necessary arrangements to hire a temp.

❏ If we will be using an outside consultant or company, I took any steps necessary to start the process.

❏ I informed everyone who needs to know about these arrangements, such as my manager, the employee's coworkers, vendors, clients, and so on.

Benefits

❏ I made arrangements to continue the employee's group health benefits—including medical, dental, and vision coverage—during FMLA leave.

❏ I applied any benefits changes to the employee, just as if he or she were not on leave.

❏ If the employee chose not to continue benefits, I made sure that we can reinstate those benefits immediately, without any requalification requirements, when the employee returns to work; if not, I continued the employee's benefits, arranged to pay the employee's share of the premium, and sought reimbursement from the employee after his or her return to work.

❏ I collected the employee's share of the premium as permitted by the FMLA and provided written notice, in advance, of how and when to make these payments.

❏ Before terminating the employee's coverage for failing to pay the premiums, I sent the employee written notice, including the following information:

  ❏ The employee's payment hasn't been received.

  ❏ The company intends to terminate the employee's coverage if payment isn't received by a specified date, at least 15 days after the date I sent the letter.

❏ Before terminating the employee's coverage for failing to pay the premiums, I made sure we could reinstate the employee's coverage without any requalification requirements.

❏ For other benefits, I followed my company's usual policies for employees on unpaid leave.

❏ Before discontinuing any life, disability, or other insurance benefits, I made sure that we could reinstate the employee's coverage without any requalification requirements; if not, I continued the employee's coverage, arranged to pay the employee's share of the premium, and sought reimbursement from the employee after his or her return to work.

Reinstatement

CHAPTER HIGHLIGHTS

An employee returning from FMLA leave is entitled to reinstatement to his or her former position or an equivalent position, unless an exception applies.

An equivalent position must be virtually identical to the employee's former position in pay, benefits, job duties, worksite, shift, schedule, and other job terms and conditions.

The employee must be reinstated immediately upon returning from leave, as long as the employee gave at least two work days, advance notice of return.

You may require a returning employee to provide a fitness-for-duty certification from a health care provider if your company:

- has a consistently applied policy or practice of requiring certifications from similarly situated employees, and

- has an important, job-related reason for requesting the certification.

When you reinstate an employee, you must also restore the employee's pay and benefits, including any automatic raises that occurred during leave.

Employees are entitled to the same insurance coverage benefits and may not be required to take a physical, wait for open enrollment, or otherwise requalify for coverage.

You may not deny an employee an attendance, safety, or other bonus that depends on an absence of problems (rather than quantity or quality of performance) solely because the employee took FMLA leave.

You may not be required to reinstate an employee under the FMLA if any of the following are true:

- The employee cannot perform the essential duties of the position (however, the Americans with Disabilities Act may require your company to make a reasonable accommodation).

- The employee's job was eliminated through company restructuring or layoffs, and the employee would have lost the job if he or she hadn't taken leave.

- The employee was fired for reasons unrelated to taking FMLA leave (such as poor performance or misconduct).

- The employee was hired for a limited term or project, which has ended.

- The employee obtained FMLA leave fraudulently (for example, by submitting a forged or altered medical certification).

- The employee stated an unequivocal intent not to return to work.

- The employee is a key employee (among the highest-paid 10% of employees within 75 miles) and reinstatement would cause substantial and grievous economic injury to your company.

If an employee chooses not to return to work following FMLA leave, you may recoup your company's share of the premium spent to continue the employee's health care coverage, as well as amounts you paid to cover the employee's share of premiums to continue other benefits.

The FMLA provides employees with job-protected leave, and that includes the legal right to be reinstated to the same or an equivalent position once leave ends, unless an exception applies. The right to reinstatement gives meaning to the right to take leave: It ensures that employees will have jobs to return to once their time off is through.

This chapter will help you manage an employee's return to work. It covers every aspect of reinstatement, including what position you must restore the employee to, deadlines for reinstatement, how to handle employee benefits when an employee returns to work, and exceptional circumstances when you might not be legally required to reinstate an employee. It also explains your company's rights if an employee cannot—or decides not to—return to work after using up his or her allotment of FMLA leave.

The Basic Reinstatement Right

An employee must be reinstated to his or her former position or an equivalent position upon returning from FMLA leave. Although there are a few situations when an employee's right to reinstatement might be limited (see "When Reinstatement Might Not Be Required," below), these cases are the exception rather than the rule. The employee is entitled to be reinstated even if your company made changes to accommodate the employee's absence—for example, by replacing the employee or restructuring his or her job.

What Is an Equivalent Position?

Although you are legally required to reinstate an employee returning from FMLA leave, that doesn't mean the employee has a right to be put back in exactly the same position he or she held before taking time off. Employers may reinstate the employee to his or her former position or to an equivalent position. In practice, however, this doesn't give employers much leeway: The equivalent position must be "virtually identical," in every important respect, to the employee's former position. (29 C.F.R. § 825.215.)

TIP

If the employee's position has changed substantially due to company restructuring, different rules apply. See "When Reinstatement Might Not Be Required," below, to find out what your obligations are.

An equivalent position is one with equivalent pay, benefits, and other terms and conditions of employment to the employee's former job. Here are some of the things courts will look at when determining whether a position is equivalent to the employee's old job:

- **Pay.** An employee is entitled to receive his or her former salary or hourly compensation, as well as any opportunities to earn extra money (through overtime, a shift differential, or bonuses based on performance, for example) that were previously available. (For more information, including how to handle bonuses and raises, see "Restoring Pay and Benefits," below.)

- **Benefits.** The equivalent position must offer the same benefits, at the same levels, as the employee's previous job. (For more information, see "Restoring Pay and Benefits," below.)

- **Job duties and responsibilities.** An employee is entitled to "substantially similar" job duties and responsibilities. Minor alterations (such as a change in the employee's reporting structure or job title) are allowed, but make sure the employee's new position is just as desirable—and has the same status in the company—as the employee's former position. If the new position looks like a demotion, the company could find itself in legal trouble.

- **Shift and schedule.** Ordinarily, an employee is entitled to be returned to the same shift and to the same or an equivalent schedule.

- **Worksite.** An employee must be reinstated to the same worksite or one that is geographically proximate to the employee's old worksite. A job at a different worksite is not an equivalent position if it significantly increases the employee's commute in time, distance, or both.

LESSONS FROM THE

Real World

Taking away an employee's obligation to travel for work does not violate the FMLA's right to reinstatement.

Phyllis Smith was the Assistant Supervisor of School Accounts for the East Baton Rouge Parish School Board. She assisted school principals and staff with bookkeeping, which included travel to the parish's schools to provide bookkeeping training and support to school officials.

Smith took parental leave under the FMLA. When she returned to work, her job description was revised. She no longer traveled to assist school officials onsite; instead, she audited the schools' books from a central office location. Smith agreed that her pay was the same and that her job duties were largely similar. However, she filed a lawsuit claiming that her new job was not equivalent to her old position because of the elimination of her travel responsibilities.

The court disagreed. It found that she was doing essentially the same work for the same pay before and after she took time off. The court also decided that eliminating travel from her job duties was only a minimal, intangible change—not a significant enough difference to support a lawsuit.

Smith v. East Baton Rouge Parish School Board, 453 F.3d 650 (5th Cir. 2006).

The FMLA doesn't prevent you from giving an employee returning from leave a promotion or some other benefit, as long as the employee wants it. Similarly, if the employee asks to be restored to a different position, you can grant the request. For example, if an employee returning from FMLA leave is planning to move soon and requests a transfer to a different facility, you may grant the request without running afoul of the law. If the employee feels pressured or coerced to take a different position, however, that violates the FMLA.

EXAMPLE: Charlotte works as a sales associate in the junior's section of a large department store. She receives a base salary plus commissions based on her sales. She takes FMLA leave to care for her husband while he undergoes treatment for leukemia. When she returns, her boss, David, tells her that he would like to promote her to a position in the home furnishings department. David explains that she'll receive the same base salary, plus the opportunity to earn much more in commissions, because furniture is more expensive than junior clothing and accessories.

Charlotte thanks David but tells him she wants to return to the junior's department. She explains that she enjoys keeping up with fashions and trends and feels her sales record is driven by her interest in this market. She doesn't think she'd do very well selling furniture.

David responds, "You know, Charlotte, opportunities for advancement don't come along here very often. I'm telling you that we need you in home furnishings. You're free to say 'No, I'll only work where I want to, not where the company needs me,' but I can't guarantee that there will be other opportunities down the road for someone who displays this kind of attitude." Charlotte decides that she'd better accept the move.

Did David violate the FMLA? You bet. Although the company is free to restore Charlotte to a different position if she voluntarily agrees, it isn't free to pressure her or threaten her job opportunities if she doesn't accept the new position. Here, Charlotte wasn't free to make a voluntary decision: She was told that refusing the new position would affect her future opportunities. This violates her legal right to reinstatement.

Deadlines for Reinstatement

An employee is entitled to immediate reinstatement once he or she reports for duty. In some situations, you'll know well in advance exactly when an employee will return to work. For example, if you and the employee agreed that the employee would take six weeks of leave, and the employee's time off goes as expected, the employee will simply report back once his or her leave is over.

EXAMPLE: Barbara is pregnant and requests time off. She decides to take the full 12 weeks of leave all at once. Her first day off work is Monday, June 1. She takes three weeks of leave for a serious health condition (pregnancy and childbirth), and the remaining nine weeks as parental leave. She returns to work on Monday, August 24. Her employer is legally obligated to reinstate her to her former position (or an equivalent one) that same day.

Sometimes, however, an employee's return to work is delayed or accelerated. Typically, this happens when the employee's or family member's serious health condition takes an unexpected turn. Even in this situation, you must reinstate the employee immediately upon his or her return to work. However, the employee must give you notice, at least two work days ahead of time, of the date he or she plans to come back. If the employee just shows up unexpectedly at work, and you are unable to reinstate the employee immediately, consider that your notice—and reinstate the employee within two work days.

EXAMPLE: Calvin requests FMLA leave to care for his father, who has to have hip replacement surgery. Because the doctor predicts recovery will take a couple months, Calvin requests eight weeks of FMLA leave. Instead, Calvin's father recovers in five weeks. Calvin lets his manager know that he will return to work right away. If the company can reinstate Calvin immediately, it should. If not, then Calvin is entitled to reinstatement within two work days.

TIP

Ask the employee to keep you in the loop. You have the right to ask for periodic updates on the employee's plans to return to work—and you should use it. Chapter 9 explains how.

LESSONS FROM THE

Real World

A company must reinstate an employee within two days or face the consequences.

Lori Hoge worked at a Honda production plant. Honda assigned her to a "door line" position, which accommodated work restrictions she had because of a back injury.

On May 11, 2000, Hoge began taking FMLA leave for a planned abdominal surgery. She reported for work on June 27. She said this was the agreed-upon date for her return to work; Honda said that it didn't expect her to return until sometime in July.

When Hoge reported for work, Honda told her it did not have an available position that accommodated her work restrictions because of changes to its manufacturing process. On July 31, 2000, she was reinstated on a part-time basis to a position on the engine line, and she didn't receive a full-time position until September 18.

Hoge sued Honda for failing to reinstate her when she was ready to return to work. Honda argued that it was entitled to take a "reasonable" amount of time to find an appropriate job, both because it didn't know when Hoge was returning to work and because her former position had changed.

The court sided with Hoge. The FMLA says employees are entitled to reinstatement upon their return to work, not within a reasonable time after they return. If Honda didn't know that Hoge was returning to work on June 27, it was entitled to take two days—the amount of notice Hoge should have given—to reinstate her to an equivalent, full-time position. Because Honda took several months to fully reinstate Hoge, it lost the case.

Hoge v. Honda of America, 384 F.3d 238 (6th Cir. 2004).

Fitness-for-Duty Certifications

If an employee takes leave for his or her own serious health condition, you may require the employee to provide a fitness-for-duty certification: a signed statement from a health care provider indicating that the employee is able to return to work. However, you may require this certification only if you meet the following requirements:

- **Your company must have a consistently applied practice or policy of requiring employees to provide a fitness-for-duty statement.** The company need not require every employee to provide a fitness-for-duty certification, but it must require all similarly situated employees (that is, employees in that position and/or with that serious health condition) to provide one. (29 C.F.R. § 310.) For example, a company might require all employees in positions that require manual labor to provide such a certification following time off for an injury of any kind.

POLICY ALERT

Include fitness-for-duty certification requirements in your written policies. If your company has a uniform policy or practice of requiring certifications from similarly situated employees, it must include this information in its employee handbook or any other written material it provides to employees about the FMLA. See Chapter 11 and Appendix B for more information on company policies that affect your rights or obligations under the FMLA.

- **The certification must be job related and consistent with business necessity.** This language, taken from the ADA, simply means that the company must have an important business reason for requiring the certification.

EXAMPLE: Maurice works in a warehouse, lifting and loading heavy packages. After taking FMLA leave to have surgery and recuperate from a broken ankle, Maurice is ready to return to work. The company asks him to provide a fitness-for-duty certification, in keeping with its policies. This would be job related and consistent with business necessity, because the company could reasonably believe that Maurice's injury might affect his ability to do the job.

Now assume that Maurice works as a fulfillment clerk in the same warehouse. His job is to process orders made at the company's website, prepare packing labels and invoices, and handle customer questions and complaints about deliveries. He performs all of his job duties sitting in front of a computer at his desk. Even if Maurice's ankle is still bothering him when he returns to work, it's hard to see how that would affect his ability to do his job. It's probably not a good idea to ask Maurice to provide a fitness-for-duty certification, because the company doesn't really need to know these details.

Contents of the Certification

A fitness-for-duty certification is simply a written statement, signed by the employee's health care provider (see Chapter 4 for information on who qualifies as a health care provider), that the employee is able to resume work following an FMLA leave. The employer may request certification only for the serious health condition that necessitated FMLA leave, not for any other illness or impairment.

If the employer has questions about the employee's fitness-for-duty certification, a health care provider working for the employer may contact the employee's health care provider for clarification, with the employee's permission. However, the employer's health care provider may request clarification only on the employee's ability to work, and only regarding the serious health condition for which the employee took leave. The employer may not request a second or third opinion on a fitness-for-duty certification, as it can for a medical certification. (See Chapter 8 for more on medical certifications.)

Notice and Deadlines

If you require fitness-for-duty certifications from employees returning from leave, you should include that requirement in the individual notice you give to each employee who requests leave. (See Chapter 7 for more information on this notice.) If the employee's condition changes to one for which a fitness-for-duty certification is required under your company's policies, you should request such a certification, in writing, when you learn of the change. We've included a sample letter requesting such a certification below; you can adapt it to meet your situation following the guidelines in "Drafting Your Letter," below. Typically, you won't need to write this type of letter; instead, you will include this information in the individual notice you provide to employees who request leave, as noted above.

You may postpone an employee's return to work until you receive the fitness-for-duty certification. (29 C.F.R. § 825.310.) Though you may clarify the employee's certification by having your health care provider contact the employee's health care provider, you may not delay the employee's reinstatement until you learn the outcome.

SAMPLE

Letter to Employee Requesting Fitness-for-Duty Certification

Karen Randall
5541 Stanwick Way
Yuba City, CA 95991

Dear Karen,

I was sorry to hear about your recent diagnosis. I hope you feel better soon.

As we discussed on the phone yesterday, the notice I gave you when you requested leave indicated that you would not need to supply a return-to-work form from your doctor. I made this decision based on what I knew at the time, which was that you needed time off to recover from an infection. Because your doctor has now diagnosed the underlying cause as rheumatoid arthritis, company policy requires a return-to-work form. As explained in the employee handbook, we require any employee to supply this form when returning to work following medical leave for anything other than a temporary illness.

I've attached a copy of the form; as you can see, you must fill in a few lines, then your doctor must certify that you are ready to work. You must return this form before returning to work; otherwise, we will have to delay your return until we receive the form.

Please let me know if you have any questions, and accept my best wishes for a speedy recovery.

Sincerely,

Stephanie Anderson
Director, Human Resources

Drafting Your Letter

Because the contents of your letter requesting a fitness-for-duty certification will depend on the employee's condition and your company's policies, we can't give you a fill-in-the-blank form. Consider including the following:

- **Sympathy.** You'll be writing this letter only if the employee has a serious health condition, which may have worsened unexpectedly. Acknowledge this unfortunate fact by wishing the employee a speedy recovery or otherwise expressing a little sympathy.

- **Certification requirement.** Explain what's required so the employee understands that his or her health care provider needs to be involved.

- **Consequences of failing to provide the certification.** Tell the employee that he or she cannot be reinstated until you receive the certification. Otherwise, the employee might assume that this can be handled after returning to work.

- **Policy information.** Let the employee know why you are requesting a certification. Explain the company policy that requires it for any employee in particular circumstances, and cite to the employee handbook or other relevant policies, if possible.

- **The form.** Don't forget to attach a copy of the fitness-for-duty certification form. If your company doesn't already have a form, you can use the sample form in Appendix C.

Restoring Pay and Benefits

When you reinstate an employee, you must also restore the employee's pay and benefits. The requirements for restoring benefits depend on the type of benefit and your company's policies.

Pay

Whether you reinstate an employee to his or her former position or to an equivalent one, you must restore all components of the employee's pay including base wage or salary, plus the same opportunities to earn bonuses, a shift differential, overtime, commissions, and other extra compensation that he or she enjoyed before taking leave.

TIP

You can restart an exempt employee's pay midweek. An exempt employee (who is paid on a salary basis and is not entitled to earn overtime) is usually entitled to a full salary for any week in which he or she does any work. FMLA leave is an exception to this rule. If an exempt employee returns to work midweek, you can pay a prorated share of the employee's weekly salary. For example, an employee who returns to work on Wednesday morning is entitled to 3/5 of his or her usual weekly salary. (29 C.F.R. § 541.602.)

Raises

A returning employee is also entitled to any automatic raises that took place while the employee was out on leave. So if your company provides an annual cost-of-living raise to all employees, you must provide that same raise to an employee returning from FMLA leave.

If the raise is not automatic but is instead based on the employee's performance or seniority, the rules depend on your company' policies and practices. Generally, you must treat employees on FMLA leave just as your company treats employees who take unpaid leave for any other reason. If unpaid leave doesn't count towards an employee's seniority for purposes of awarding seniority-based raises, for example, then you don't have to count FMLA leave towards an employee's seniority.

CAUTION

Employees substituting paid time off are not on "unpaid" leave. As explained in Chapter 7, in certain circumstances an employee (either voluntarily or per company requirements) substitutes accrued paid time off for unpaid FMLA leave. If an employee is using paid time off for FMLA leave, you must treat that employee just like any other employee who is taking paid time off. Often, this means that at least certain benefits (for example, vacation or sick days) continue to accrue.

Bonuses

Your employees may be eligible to earn bonuses for certain behavior or actions, like productivity, attendance, performance, safety, or customer service. Whether an employee who takes FMLA leave is eligible for these bonuses depends on the nature of the bonus. Safety and attendance bonuses are typically based on an "absence of occurrences," in the language of the FMLA regulation, because the employee earns the bonus by not being absent or not having any safety violations or accidents. Because these are not based on performance, the employee returning from FMLA leave is still eligible for this bonus.

EXAMPLE: FunCo offers its employees an incentive for perfect attendance. Employees who have no absences for an entire year receive $1,500. Kara has no absences until November, when she takes two weeks of FMLA leave to care for her son while he recovers from mononucleosis. Kara then returns to work and has no more absences for the rest of the year. She is entitled to receive the year-end attendance bonus, despite her absence for FMLA leave.

Bonuses that depend on the employee's performance are treated differently. Because an employee who is on leave cannot perform during that time, the employee may not be eligible for these types of bonuses. The company simply has to treat these employees the same way that it treats employees who take time off for other reasons.

EXAMPLE: FunCo also offers productivity bonuses to its in-house sales staff. Employees who sell at least $10,000 worth of products in a month receive $100; employees who sell at least $15,000 worth of products receive $200. Kara works in the sales department and often earns a bonus. During November, however, her sales were only $6,000, because she took two weeks of FMLA leave to care for her son. The company does not have to pay her a productivity bonus for that month.

LESSONS FROM THE

Real World

An employer may prorate a production bonus to account for FMLA leave.

Robert Sommer worked as a financial administrator for The Vanguard Group. Sommer took eight weeks of FMLA leave, from December 7, 2000 to February 4, 2001.

Vanguard had a partnership plan that paid employees an annual bonus based on company performance that year. Each employee's bonus factored in the employee's position, how long the employee had worked for the company, and how many hours the employee worked during the year. Employees who worked fewer than 1,950 hours during the year would receive a prorated bonus; hours spent on unpaid leave didn't count as hours worked.

Vanguard gave Sommer a prorated partnership plan bonus for 2001 because his FMLA leave brought his total hours worked for the year below the 1,950-hour threshold. Sommer received $1,788.23 less than he would have gotten had he worked the requisite number of hours.

Sommer sued Vanguard, arguing that it unfairly penalized him for taking FMLA leave by reducing his bonus. He claimed that the bonus was based on an "absence of occurrences" because it depended only on showing up for work. But the court disagreed with Sommer's argument. It found that the partnership plan bonuses were productivity bonuses and that hours worked provided the basis for measuring productivity. Because the bonus was performance-based, the company could legally provide a lesser bonus to recognize the time he was out on FMLA leave.

Sommer v. Vanguard Group, 461 F.3d 397 (3rd Cir. 2006).

Benefits

You must restore an employee's benefits, at the same levels, when the employee returns from leave, subject to any changes in benefit levels that took place while the employee was on leave and affected the whole work force. For example, if a company offers life insurance to its employees and increases the benefit from $30,000 to $35,000 while an employee is on leave, that employee is also entitled to the increased benefit amount.

The specific rules for restoring benefits depend on the type of benefit.

Insurance Coverage

An employee is entitled to restored insurance benefits, including life insurance, disability insurance, health benefits, and so on. As explained in Chapter 9, you must continue the employee's health insurance coverage while he or she is on leave, though you may also require the employee to pay any portion of the premium for which he or she is usually responsible. While your company can cut off an employee's health care benefits if the employee is more than 30 days late paying his or her share of the premium, those benefits must be restored, at the same level, when the employee returns from leave. An employee who chooses not to continue benefits during leave is also entitled to restoration.

Employees may not be required to requalify for benefits, wait for an "open enrollment" period, undergo a physical examination, be subjected to new preexisting conditions limitations or exclusions, or go without benefits during a waiting period. This is true even if the employee's coverage lapsed while he or she was on leave. To comply with this rule, your company may have to keep an employee enrolled in certain benefit programs while he or she is on leave. In this situation, you may recover the employee's share of the premium for this coverage from the employee after he or she returns to work.

If there are changes to a benefit plan while the employee is on leave, these changes apply to the employee as well. If, for example, premiums increase, coverage changes, or a new benefit becomes available, the employee is entitled to be treated as if he or she had been working continuously.

If a benefit is available only to employees who work a minimum number of hours each year, hours spent on FMLA leave do not count as hours worked. This means that, as a practical matter, an employee may be ineligible to receive certain benefits because the employee took FMLA leave.

Retirement Benefits

Just like other benefits, retirement benefits must be restored at the same level when an employee returns from leave. A few special rules apply to these benefits:

- FMLA leave cannot be treated as a "break in service" for purposes of pensions and other retirement benefit plans.

- If a retirement benefit requires an employee to be employed on a particular date to be credited with a year of service for vesting, contributions, or participating in the plan, an employee who is on FMLA leave is considered to be employed during that time.

- FMLA leave does not have to be counted as time in service or hours worked for purposes of vesting, accrual of benefits, or eligibility.

EXAMPLE: Hal began working at Jefferson's Tool and Die on January 1, 2006. The company allows an employee who has worked at least one year and was employed as of January 1 to participate in the 401(k) plan for the coming year. When Hal becomes eligible, he contributes monthly. The company matches his contributions up to $3,000 a year. Hal is always fully vested in his own contributions to the account; the company's contributions vest over three years, one-third each year.

Hal takes FMLA leave for all of December 2007 and January 2008 to bond with his new daughter. While Hal is on FMLA leave, his 401(k) account must be treated as if he is still working. The company may not close his account or otherwise treat his time off as a break in service. The company must also treat him as if he were employed on January 1 for purposes of participating in the program for the coming year. However, Hal's time off does not have to be counted towards the three-year vesting period. In other words, Hal might have to wait an additional two months to vest employer contributions that had already been made when he took leave.

Other Benefits

Many companies allow employees to accrue certain benefits, such as sick leave, vacation days, or other paid time off. Employees on FMLA leave are entitled to earn these benefits only if employees on other types of unpaid leave are. However, an employer may not take away benefits the employee has earned: If the employee had accrued time off before taking FMLA leave and did not substitute that time for FMLA leave, the employee is entitled to have that accrued leave available upon returning from FMLA leave.

The same rules apply to seniority. The company does not have to count FMLA leave towards an employee's seniority unless it counts other types of unpaid leave. However, the employee is entitled to the same seniority upon reinstatement that he or she had when starting leave.

When Reinstatement Might Not Be Required

There are several circumstances in which an employee might not be entitled to reinstatement after taking FMLA leave:

- The employee would have lost the job even if he or she hadn't taken FMLA leave.
- The employee can't perform an essential function of the job.
- The employee takes FMLA leave fraudulently.
- The employee fits within the "key employee" exception, which gives employers the right to deny reinstatement to certain highly paid employees, if returning them to work would cause substantial harm to the company.

Employee Would Have Lost the Job Regardless of Leave

An employee has no greater right to reinstatement than he or she would have had if not for taking leave. If the employee would have lost the job even if still employed, the FMLA does not guarantee reinstatement.

Restructuring and Layoffs

If the employee's job has been eliminated, the employee is not entitled to reinstatement. For example, let's say the company outsourced the work of the employee's department or closed the facility where the employee worked. In this situation, the employee would have lost his or her job whether the employee took FMLA leave or not, and the employee has no right to be reinstated.

However, this rule applies only if the restructuring is unrelated to the employee's leave. Changes made to accommodate the employee's leave—such as hiring a temporary replacement or shifting some job responsibilities around—don't relieve the company of its obligation to reinstate the employee. And, if the company made structural changes because it wanted to avoid reinstating an employee who took leave, that would violate the FMLA's prohibition against discriminating against employees for taking FMLA leave.

EXAMPLE 1: Alexander takes FMLA leave to bond with his newborn son. While on leave, his company implements layoffs. Fifty of the least senior employees in the company lose their jobs, and Alexander is one of them. Alexander has no right to reinstatement.

EXAMPLE 2: Now assume that Alexander's company didn't have major layoffs. Alexander's manager, Maya, is upset about his leave. Maya doesn't think Alexander should use a full 12 weeks of FMLA leave—after all, his wife doesn't work, and she can stay home with the baby. Maya decides to eliminate Alexander's position so she doesn't have to reinstate him. She has already redistributed his work while he is on leave; she figures she'll just wait a while, then hire someone—under a new job title—to pick up the slack.

Maya's actions violate the FMLA. The only reason Alexander has no job to return to is because Maya wanted to punish him for exercising his legal right to take FMLA leave. What's more, Maya's sexist reasoning could leave her company open to a discrimination lawsuit.

Termination for Cause

As explained in Chapter 9, you may fire an employee who is on FMLA leave only, for reasons entirely unrelated to the employee's use of the FMLA. If you have sufficient, independent grounds to terminate employment, you do not have to reinstate the employee. In this situation, as when the employee's job is eliminated in a layoff or restructuring, the employee would have lost the job whether or not he or she took FMLA leave. (For more on firing or disciplining an employee who is on leave, see Chapter 9.)

CAUTION

Don't rely on the right to fire at will. Most employees work at will, which means that they can be fired at any time, for any reason that isn't illegal. But you should not exercise this right when firing an employee on FMLA leave. To successfully defend against an employee lawsuit (an all-too-common scenario when an employee is fired while on leave), you'll have to prove that your reasons for firing the employee were not related to the employee's use of the FMLA. As a practical matter, this means you must have a different reason for firing the employee, one that is compelling enough to convince a jury that your actions were justified.

You may also discipline an employee who takes FMLA leave—again, only if it is for independent reasons. If your discipline will make the employee's position less than equivalent (for example, the employee will be demoted, will have more onerous reporting requirements, or will lose some independence and job perks), that's okay—even though it would normally violate reinstatement requirements.

SEE AN EXPERT

Get some legal advice before firing or disciplining an employee on leave. As explained in Chapter 9, even though you believe you have entirely independent and sound reasons for firing an employee on FMLA leave, chances are very good that the employee will see things differently. This is the most likely source of an FMLA lawsuit, so it's a good idea to talk to a lawyer before you take any action.

Temporary Employment

If the employee was hired for a set period of time only (for example, for two years), and that time runs out while the employee is on leave, the employee isn't entitled to reinstatement. Similarly, if the employee was hired to work on a discrete project and that project is completed while the employee is on leave, the employee isn't entitled to reinstatement. In both of these situations, employment would have been terminated even if the employee hadn't taken leave. In effect, the employee has no job to return to because the work or employment term is complete.

Employee Announces Intent Not to Return

If an employee states that he or she will not return from leave (in other words, the employee quits), your company is no longer obligated to continue the employee's health benefits or reinstate the employee. However, the employee must give clear and unequivocal notice of the intent not to return to work. If, for example, the employee says, "I'm afraid I might not be able to come back" or "I'm not sure we can afford to pay for day care," that's not good enough.

When you hear that an employee won't be returning from work, you should confirm it in writing. See "Requesting Status Reports," in Chapter 9, for more information.

Employee Cannot Perform an Essential Job Function

An employee who can't perform the job's essential functions once his or her leave runs out has no right to reinstatement under the FMLA. The FMLA provides only for reinstatement to the same or a similar position: It doesn't require an employer to provide a different position that the employee might be able to do. Therefore, if the employee can no longer do the job—even if that inability is due to the serious health condition for which the employee took leave—there is no right to job restoration under the FMLA.

> ### You Must Allow the Employee to Requalify for the Position
>
> Sometimes, an employee is physically able to do the job but is no longer qualified for the position as a result of taking leave. For example, the employee may have been unable to complete a necessary course, fulfill a certification requirement, or meet a service standard (such as a minimum number of hours in training). In these situations, you must give the employee a reasonable opportunity to fulfill any necessary qualifications after returning to work.

That's not the end of the story, however. If the employee has a disability as defined by the Americans with Disabilities Act (ADA), your company may be obligated to provide a reasonable accommodation: a change to the workplace or job that will allow the employee to do the essential functions of the position. In this situation, you would no longer have a reinstatement obligation under the FMLA, but you might have a legal duty to return the employee to a modified position under the ADA. Chapter 11 explains the ADA in more detail.

You might also have an obligation to give the employee more time off. Extended leave might qualify as a reasonable accommodation under the ADA, if it allows the employee to do the job upon return. If the employee is receiving workers' compensation, state law might also require you to hold the employee's job for a longer period of time. Although the employee has no further rights under the FMLA—and, therefore, has no valid legal claim against your company for failure to reinstate—the employee might still have rights under these other laws. See Chapter 11 for more information.

Fraud

If an employee obtains FMLA leave through fraud, the company is not obligated to reinstate the employee. This sometimes occurs when the employee submits false documents (such as a fake or altered medical certification) to get FMLA leave. In some cases, companies find out about the fraud only accidentally, when another employee happens to see the leave-taking employee engaged in activities that seem incompatible with the reason for leave.

Dealing With Employee Moonlighting

Some managers assume that an employee who works another job while on FMLA leave is committing fraud against the company. After all, if the employee has the time and ability to work, he or she should be working at your company, not taking leave. Right?

Not necessarily. According to FMLA regulations, employees may moonlight while on FMLA leave unless your company has a policy prohibiting all employees, on any kind of leave, from working another job. An employee's ability to work a different job doesn't necessarily prove that the employee took leave fraudulently—and you can't deny reinstatement on that basis alone unless you have a uniformly applied policy against moonlighting.

POLICY ALERT

Prohibit moonlighting by employees on leave. You can avoid having employees continue their health benefits—and perhaps even receive paid time off, if they substitute paid leave for FMLA leave—while working for another company by adopting a strict policy that prohibits moonlighting while on leave. See Appendix B for more information on policies that affect FMLA rights and obligations.

Key Employees

Your company has a legal right to deny reinstatement to certain highly paid employees (called "key employees") if returning them to work would cause the company substantial and grievous economic injury.

Who Is a Key Employee

A key employee is a salaried employee who is among the highest-paid 10% of the company's employees within 75 miles of the employee's worksite. Here's what these terms mean:

- **Salaried employee.** The definition of a salaried employee comes from the Fair Labor Standards Act (FLSA). A salaried employee earns the same amount each week, regardless of how many hours the employee works or the quality or quantity of work performed. To be salaried, the employee must earn at least $455 per week.

- **Highest-paid 10%.** To find out whether an employee is in the highest-paid 10% of the workforce, divide the employee's year-to-date compensation by the total number of weeks worked in the year, including any weeks during which the employee took paid leave. You must include wages, premium pay, incentive pay, and bonuses. You don't have to include any amount that will be determined only in the future (such as the value of company stock options awarded during the year).

- **Company employees within 75 miles of the employee's worksite.** In determining which employees work within 75 miles, you should use the same rules used to determine an employee's eligibility for FMLA leave, explained in Chapter 3. Count all employees, whether they are eligible for FMLA leave or not.

You must determine whether someone is a key employee as of the date he or she requested leave.

Initial Notice to Key Employee

If you believe that you might deny reinstatement to a key employee, you must notify the employee, in writing, that he or she qualifies as a key employee and might not be reinstated if the company determines that reinstatement will cause the company substantial and grievous economic injury. Typically, you must give this notice when the employee requests leave or starts leave, whichever is sooner. If you need some time to determine whether the employee is a key employee, you must give this notice as soon as is practicable. If you don't, you must reinstate the employee—no matter what damage it causes your company.

The individual notice form described in Chapter 7 includes a box to check indicating that the employee is a key employee.

Notice of Determination of Substantial and Grievous Economic Injury

In addition to the above requirements, you can deny reinstatement to an employee only if reinstatement would cause your company substantial and grievous economic injury. And you must provide another written notice to the employee if you determine that such injury will result from reinstatement.

The FMLA and its regulations don't provide much guidance on what constitutes a substantial and grievous economic injury—and, perhaps because few employers rely on this exception to deny reinstatement, there have been very few court cases on the issue. A few things are clear:

- The injury must stem from reinstatement, not from the employee's absence.
- You don't have to show that the whole company will go under.
- You must show more than minor inconvenience or "undue hardship," as defined by the Americans with Disabilities Act.

Once you determine that substantial and grievous injury will result from reinstating the employee, you must tell the employee in writing. This second notice must include all of the following:

- a determination that reinstating the employee will cause substantial and grievous economic injury to the company
- the reasons for that determination
- a statement that the company may not deny FMLA leave to the employee
- a statement that the company intends to deny reinstatement to the employee once his or her FMLA leave is finished, and
- if the employee is already on leave, a deadline for the employee to return to work to avoid being denied reinstatement. You must give the employee a reasonable amount of time to return, considering the circumstances.

If you have already determined, when you give the employee his or her initial notice, that reinstating the employee will cause substantial and grievous economic injury, you can use that notice form to provide this information.

However, you will have to add more details than the form allows space for, so you'll have to attach an additional document. We have included a sample "Notice to Key Employee of Substantial and Grievous Economic Injury" below; you'll find a blank copy in Appendix C.

S A M P L E

Notice to Key Employee of Substantial and Grievous Economic Injury

To: Carlos Sandoval

As indicated by written notice dated <u>February 22, 2008</u>, you are a key employee of this company. This means that you can be denied reinstatement following FMLA leave if such reinstatement would cause substantial and grievous economic injury to the company.

We have determined that reinstating you would cause substantial and grievous economic injury to the company, because <u>we have been unable to find a temporary replacement who is qualified to take over your responsibilities as Chief Financial Officer. To complete all of our annual financial filings by the end of March, we will have to hire a permanent replacement and commit substantial resources to bringing that person up to speed quickly. The company cannot afford to pay both you and your replacement to do this work, and we have no alternative positions available.</u>

We cannot deny you the right to take FMLA leave, or discontinue your health benefits, based on this determination. However, we intend to deny you reinstatement once your leave is finished.

If you wish to avoid these consequences, you must return to work no later than <u>March 1, 2008. This is the latest possible date that will enable us to operate without hiring a replacement and give you enough time to complete the annual reports.</u> If you do not return to work by <u>March 1, 2008</u>, we intend to replace you and deny you reinstatement.

Please contact me immediately if you have any questions.

Sincerely,

Carol Singh

Director of Human Resources

Dated:

Even if you determine that you intend to deny reinstatement, you must continue the employee's health benefits while the employee is on FMLA leave. The employee's FMLA rights continue unless and until the employee gives unequivocal notice that he or she doesn't intend to return to work or you actually deny the employee reinstatement at the conclusion of his or her FMLA leave. Also, you may not recover your company's share of health care premiums paid while the key employee was on leave.

Handling a Key Employee's Request for Reinstatement

Even if you notify a key employee that he or she will be denied reinstatement and the employee doesn't return to work, the employee still has a right to request reinstatement after using FMLA leave. If the employee makes this request, you must redetermine, based on the facts available to you at that time, whether reinstatement would cause substantial and grievous economic injury.

If you conclude that such injury would result from reinstating the employee, you must notify the employee of this conclusion in writing. (You can modify the sample form above for this purpose.) If you reach a different conclusion—that is, you decide that the company won't suffer such an injury—then you must reinstate the employee according to the usual rules.

EXAMPLE: Let's consider Carlos, the employee who received the sample notice of substantial and grievous economic injury, above. When Carol sent this notice, she had determined that reinstatement would cause such an injury. If Carlos doesn't return to work by the deadline Carol imposed, but instead requests reinstatement when his leave ends, Carol must again determine whether reinstating him would injure the company.

If the company already hired a permanent replacement and paying both Carlos and the replacement would significantly harm the company's finances, Carol could justifiably conclude that she doesn't have to reinstate Carlos. On the other hand, if Carol were unable to find a replacement, and the company received extensions on its filing deadlines, reinstating Carlos might not cause such an injury—in fact, it might be exactly what the company needs. In this situation, Carol may not refuse to reinstate Carlos. Instead, she must reinstate him according to the rules explained in "The Basic Reinstatement Right," above.

When Employees Don't Return From Leave

When an employee is unable to—or decides not to—come back to work after taking FMLA leave, your company might be able to recover at least some of the money it spent to continue the employee's benefits.

When You Can Seek Reimbursement for Benefits

The company has a right to reimbursement only if the employee chose not to return to work. The purpose of this rule is to avoid heaping more problems on employees who are already losing their jobs due to circumstances out of their control.

You cannot recover any money spent on benefits continuation if the employee can't return due to:

- **The continuation of the serious health condition for which the employee took leave.** This applies whether the employee is too ill to return to work or the employee's family member continues to require care after the employee's FMLA leave ends.

- **Other circumstances beyond the employee's control.** This exception applies if an employee cannot return to work for other reasons, such as: the employee needs time off to care for new child with a serious health condition; the employee's spouse is transferred to a location more than 75 miles away from the employee's worksite; the employee is needed to care for a relative who has a serious health condition but doesn't qualify as a family member under the FMLA; the employee is not reinstated due to the "key employee" exception (see above); or the employee is laid off while on leave. This exception doesn't apply if the employee chooses to stay home with a new child who is healthy or to stay with a parent who no longer has a serious health condition.

TIP

Request a medical certification for continuing health conditions. If an employee can't return to work because of a continuing serious health condition, you are legally entitled to ask the employee to provide a medical certification. Like regular medical certifications, it's a good idea to request this form whenever an employee claims that a serious health condition prevents his or her return to work; otherwise, you might be giving up your right to reimbursement unnecessarily. The employee must return the form within 30 days after you request it. If the employee doesn't return the form on time, or the form indicates that the employee or family member no longer has a serious health condition, you may seek reimbursement.

You can't seek reimbursement if an employee returns to work. An employee who comes back for at least 30 days has returned to work, even if the employee later quits. Similarly, an employee who goes directly from FMLA leave to retirement or retires within 30 days after reinstatement is considered to have returned to work.

What Your Company Can Recover

If the employee doesn't return to work and neither of the exceptions described above applies, your company may recover the following amounts:

- **Health insurance costs.** The company may seek reimbursement for its share of the premium of the employee's health benefits. If the employee failed to pay his or her own share while on leave, the company may seek reimbursement for that as well. Self-insured employers can recover what the employee would have had to pay to continue health insurance benefits under the Consolidated Omnibus Budget Reconciliation Act (COBRA), which allows employees to continue their health insurance benefits for a period of time, at their own expense, after leaving a job. Although employers are allowed to charge employees an additional 2% under COBRA to cover the administrative expenses of continuing benefits, you cannot recover this additional amount under the FMLA.

CAUTION

Your company can't recover its own premiums if the employee is on paid leave. As explained in Chapter 7, sometimes employees may—voluntarily or by company requirement—substitute accrued paid leave, such as sick or vacation time, for FMLA leave. If an employee does this and does not return to work, your company may not recover its share of the premium for health benefits while the employee was on paid leave.

- **The employee's share of premiums for other benefits.** If you continue any other benefits while an employee is on leave, like life or disability insurance, you may seek reimbursement of the employee's share of the premium only—not for your company's share. (As explained above, your company might choose to do this to make sure that it will be able to reinstate these benefits when the employee returns).

How to Seek Reimbursement

The best way to start is simply to ask the employee to repay the money. If that doesn't work, your company can collect the employee's debt through deductions from amounts still owed to the employee (such as commissions, unpaid wages, or unpaid accrued vacation time), if allowed by law, or in the worst case, through a lawsuit. However, your company's right to seek reimbursement does not give it the right to cut the employee off entirely. For example, your company is still obligated to pay any claims the employee incurred while on FMLA leave (if it is self-insured) or to provide continuing coverage under COBRA.

 CAUTION

Some states don't allow deductions from amounts owed to the employee. Talk to a lawyer before you start deducting the cost of providing benefits from compensation your company owes the employee.

State law may require you to get an employee's written consent before taking a deduction to repay money the employee owes the company. If your company operates in a state that imposes this type of requirement, get the employee's written consent *before* the employee starts FMLA leave. Include a deduction authorization form in your standard FMLA paperwork, and ask the employee to sign it. Experience shows that it's much easier to get this type of consent up front, before the employee owes you any money.

Common Mistakes Regarding Reinstatement— And How to Avoid Them

MISTAKE 1: Failing to reinstate employees on time.

AVOID THIS MISTAKE BY:

- Checking in with employees who are on leave. Ask employees to update you periodically on their plans to return to work. (Chapter 9 explains how.)

- Keeping track of employees on leave. Remember, you'll have to save an equivalent spot somewhere for returning employees—and you can't wait until they're ready to come back to start looking for one.

MISTAKE 2: Mishandling benefits when an employee returns.

AVOID THIS MISTAKE BY:

- Not requiring employees to requalify, reapply, or wait to restart their benefits. Remember, you can't require returning employees to do anything in order to get their benefits back.

- Maintaining employee benefits during leave, if necessary to ensure immediate reinstatement. Even if the employee chooses not to continue disability or life insurance while on leave, you may have to so you can reinstate it.

- Seeking reimbursement when legally entitled to it. If you continued benefits that were not legally required, you can recoup the employee's share of the premium once the employee returns from leave.

MISTAKE 3: Mishandling reinstatement of key employees.

AVOID THIS MISTAKE BY:

- Properly identifying key employees in the first place. If more than 10% of your workforce are key employees, you didn't get it right.

- Providing all necessary notices. If you're going to refuse to reinstate a key employee, you have to provide two written notices—and perhaps a third, if the employee requests reinstatement.

- Allowing leave and continuing benefits. You can't simply fire a key employee who requests FMLA leave. While a key employee is on leave, he or she is still employed by your company—and you have to allow leave (including substitution of leave) and continue the employee's health insurance coverage.

Managers' Checklist

Reinstating an Employee

If the Employee Was Reinstated

❏ I reinstated the employee to the position he or she held prior to taking leave or to an equivalent position.

    ❏ The position has the same base pay, and the same opportunities to earn extra pay, as the former position.

    ❏ The position offers the same benefits, at the same levels, that the employee used to receive.

    ❏ The position has the same or substantially similar job duties as the employee's former job.

    ❏ The position has the same or a substantially similar shift or schedule as the employee worked before taking leave.

    ❏ The position is at the same worksite, or one that is geographically proximate to, where the employee worked before taking leave.

❏ I reinstated the employee immediately upon his or her return from leave or within two working days of receiving notice of intent to return to work from the employee.

❏ I restored the employee's pay, including base pay, opportunities to earn extra pay, and any across-the-board raises (such as cost-of-living increases) that became effective during the employee's leave.

❏ I did not count the employee's FMLA leave time against him or her when determining eligibility for bonuses based on an absence of negative occurrences, such as attendance or safety bonuses.

❏ I restored the employee's benefits, including any across-the-board changes that took effect during the employee's leave.

❏ I did not require the employee to requalify for benefits, take a physical exam, wait a certain period of time, or do anything else to receive benefits.

❏ I did not count the employee's FMLA leave as a break in service for purposes of our pension plan.

❏ I counted the employee as "employed" while on leave if our pension plan requires employees to be employed on a particular date for purposes of contributions, eligibility, or vesting.

❏ I restored the employee's seniority-based benefits.

❏ If our company's policies allow employees to accrue seniority-based benefits while on unpaid leave, I added these accrued benefits to the employee's total.

❏ I required the employee to provide a fitness-for-duty certification, but only if:

❏ I gave the employee notice that a certification would be required.

❏ Company policy requires it for all similarly situated employees.

❏ It was job-related and consistent with business necessity.

If the Employee Was Not Reinstated:

❏ I did not reinstate the employee because one of the following occurred:

❏ The employee was unable to perform an essential function of the position.

❏ I researched our company's obligations under the Americans with Disabilities Act and/or workers' compensation law.

❏ The employee's position was eliminated, for reasons unrelated to his or her FMLA leave.

❏ The employee was fired for reasons unrelated to his or her FMLA leave.

  ❏ If the employee was fired for attendance problems, I made sure that the employee's FMLA leave was not counted against him or her.

  ❏ I talked to a lawyer to make sure that we are on legally safe ground in taking this action.

❏ The employee's job or work was temporary and has been completed.

❏ The employee committed fraud in obtaining FMLA leave.

  ❏ If the employee was not reinstated because he or she worked another job while on FMLA leave, I made sure our company policies prohibit moonlighting.

❏ The employee gave unequivocal notice that he or she did not intend to return from FMLA leave.

❏ The employee is a key employee, and reinstating him or her would cause our company substantial and grievous economic injury.

  ❏ The employee is among the highest-paid 10% of employees within a 75-mile radius.

  ❏ I notified the employee, when he or she requested leave or shortly thereafter, of this key employee status.

  ❏ I notified the employee when the company determined that reinstatement would cause substantial and grievous economic injury and gave the employee a reasonable time frame to return to work.

  ❏ If the employee requested reinstatement, I reevaluated whether reinstating him or her would cause substantial and grievous economic injury and notified the employee of my conclusions.

✓ Managers' Checklist	If an Employee Doesn't Return From Leave

❑ I determined why the employee did not come back to work.

❑ If the employee did not return to work because of the continuation of a serious health condition, I

    ❑ asked the employee to provide a medical certification, and

    ❑ did not seek reimbursement for premiums the company paid to continue the employee's health insurance.

❑ I did not seek reimbursement for health insurance premiums if the employee could not return to work for reasons beyond the employee's control.

❑ If the employee's failure to return from work was voluntary, I determined what amount (if any) we can recover from the employee for what we spent on benefit premiums while the employee was on leave.

    ❑ I included in this amount our company's share of the premium for health insurance continuation during the employee's leave.

    ❑ If the employee did not pay his or her share of the premium for health insurance, I included any part of the employee's share that we paid during the employee's leave.

    ❑ If we continued any other insurance benefits (such as life or disability coverage), I included any amounts we paid towards the employee's share of the premium during the employee's leave.

    ❑ I did not include the company's share of the premium for any other insurance benefits.

❑ Regardless of whether or not we are entitled to seek reimbursement from the employee, I offered the employee continued health care coverage under COBRA and, if we are self-insured, paid any claims the employee incurred while on FMLA leave.

❑ Before seeking reimbursement via withholding from money we still owe the employee, I made sure that this is allowed by state law.

How Other Laws Affect FMLA Leave

CHAPTER HIGHLIGHTS

An employee covered by the FMLA and other employment laws is entitled to every protection of every applicable law. If the laws call for different approaches to the same situation, you must apply whichever law is more beneficial to the employee.

An employee who has a serious health condition under the FMLA may also have a disability under the Americans with Disabilities Act (ADA).

- Only qualified employees with disabilities—those who can perform the essential functions of the job, with or without a reasonable accommodation—are protected by the ADA.

- Employers must provide reasonable accommodations to allow employees with disabilities to do their jobs. This may include more time off than the FMLA requires, changes to the job, or a transfer to another position.

An employee who does not return to work at the end of FMLA leave may be entitled to continuing health benefits pursuant to the Consolidated Omnibus Budget Reconciliation Act (COBRA).

Title VII prohibits employers from discriminating based on race, color, national origin, religion, or sex (including pregnancy) in any aspect of employment, including providing leave.

Time an employee spends on leave to serve in the armed forces counts as time worked when determining the employee's eligibility for FMLA leave.

State laws also give employees the right to take time off for a variety of reasons, including family and medical leave, adoption, and pregnancy.

- Some of these laws cover smaller employers, have more lenient eligibility requirements for employees, allow longer periods of leave, allow leave to care for a broader range of family members, or allow leave for different purposes from the FMLA.

- If an employee takes leave that is covered by both the FMLA and a state law, that leave counts against the employee's entitlement pursuant to both laws—and the employee need comply only with whichever law's notice and certification requirements are more lenient.

- If an employee takes leave that is covered by the FMLA or the state law but not both, the employee may be entitled to more than 12 weeks of total leave.

An employee whose serious medical condition comes from a workplace injury or illness is probably also entitled to workers' compensation benefits; an employee who is out on leave for a workers' comp injury or illness almost always has a serious health condition covered by the FMLA.

- An employee who is on FMLA leave does not have to accept a "light duty" position; however, an employee who rejects such a position may no longer be entitled to workers' comp benefits.

- Most state workers' compensation laws do not require employers to hold an employee's job for the duration of his or her workers' comp leave; this might come into play if an employee uses up his or her FMLA leave and still needs time off.

The FMLA is not the only law that might protect an employee who needs time off for family or medical reasons. Depending on the employee's condition and/or situation, other federal laws may also apply—for example, to protect the employee from disability discrimination or provide continued health insurance. And that's not all: state laws that provide for family and medical leave, pregnancy disability leave, workers' compensation, or temporary disability insurance might also come into play.

Sometimes, these laws cover the same territory as the FMLA. How do you know which to follow? The basic rule when employment laws overlap is this: The employee is entitled to every benefit available under every law that applies. If the FMLA and another law both cover the employee's situation, the employee is entitled to the protections of both laws. If both laws apply and provide different rights, the employee is entitled to the protections that are most beneficial in the circumstances.

This chapter explains how to apply this rule when more than one law protects an employee who takes family and medical leave. This is a topic that many managers dread—and it can be a bit daunting. But, understanding the purpose and requirements of each law will help you figure out what to do.

TIP

Consider each law separately. The easiest way to make sure you meet all of your legal obligations when laws overlap is to think of each law as a separate protection. Run through the laws that might apply, think about what each requires or prohibits, then make sure you offer or provide those protections to the employee. Trying to combine all of your legal obligations into one grand "to-do" list will only confuse you—and you risk forgetting something one of the laws requires. You can use the chart at the end of this chapter to figure out which laws apply.

Federal Laws

A handful of federal laws other than the FMLA might protect an employee who takes family or medical leave. These laws, which are covered in detail below, include:

- the Americans with Disabilities Act (ADA), which protects disabled employees from discrimination and requires employers to make reasonable accommodations to allow employees with disabilities to do their jobs
- the Consolidated Omnibus Budget Reconciliation Act (COBRA), which requires employers to provide continued health insurance to employees and former employees
- Title VII of the Civil Rights Act, which prohibits discrimination on the basis of race, national origin, sex (including pregnancy), and religion, and
- the Uniformed Services Employment and Reemployment Rights Act (USERRA), which requires employers to provide certain rights and benefits to employees who take military leave.

Americans with Disabilities Act (ADA)

If an employee's serious health condition under the FMLA also qualifies as a disability under the ADA, both laws apply. Here, we explain some basic ADA concepts and how the ADA and FMLA might overlap.

TIP

The ADA and FMLA have different purposes. Although the ADA and FMLA both are intended (in part, at least) to help employees with physical or mental ailments, they have different goals—and remembering this avoids confusion. The goal of the ADA is to bring qualified workers with disabilities into the workforce—and keep them there—by requiring employers to make reasonable changes to allow them to do their jobs. The goal of the FMLA's medical leave provision, on the other hand, is to allow workers who are unable to do their jobs to take time off.

ADA Basics

The Americans with Disabilities Act (ADA) prohibits employers from discriminating against employees with disabilities who can perform the job's essential functions with or without a reasonable accommodation. An employee has a disability for purposes of the ADA if the employee:

- has a long-term physical or mental impairment that substantially limits a major life activity, such as the ability to walk, talk, see, hear, breathe, reason, work, or take care of oneself (short-term or temporary impairments—such as pregnancy—are not covered)

- has a history of such an impairment (for example, the employee suffered cancer or depression in the past), or

- is perceived by the employer as having a disability. This sometimes comes up when an employee has an obvious impairment (such as a limp or speech impediment) that is not actually disabling.

Employers are required to make reasonable accommodations to allow employees with disabilities to do their jobs. A reasonable accommodation is assistance (technological or otherwise) or a change to the workplace or job that allows the employee to perform its essential functions—the job's most fundamental tasks. Examples include providing voice-recognition software for an employee with carpal tunnel syndrome; altering the height of a desk for an employee in a wheelchair; providing a distraction-free environment for an employee with attention deficit disorder; or allowing a diabetic employee to take more frequent breaks to eat and drink, take medication, or test blood sugar levels.

Under the ADA, an employer does not have to provide a reasonable accommodation if doing so would create an undue hardship. Whether an accommodation creates an undue hardship depends on a number of factors, including:

- the nature and cost of the accommodation

- the size and financial resources of the business and the facility where the employee works

- the structure of the business, and

- the effect the accommodation would have on the business.

An accommodation that would be extremely costly (for example, adapting technical equipment that would eat up months' worth of company profits) or would change the character of the business (for example, installing bright lighting in a previously dimly lit, romantic restaurant) could create an undue hardship.

Rules for Handling Medical Records

Under the FMLA, employee medical records must be handled confidentially, kept in secured files, and released only to limited people in limited circumstances. These rules also apply to medical records covered by the ADA. You can find a description of these rules in Chapter 12.

Overlap Between the FMLA and the ADA

The FMLA and the ADA overlap only if an employee has both a serious health condition under the FMLA and a disability under the ADA. Although many ailments—such as cancer, multiple sclerosis, HIV/AIDS, stroke, and diabetes—likely qualify under both laws, some do not. For example, an employee who is pregnant, has a broken bone, or has suffered a temporary serious injury is covered by the FMLA but not the ADA. An employee who is blind or hard of hearing and can perform the job's essential functions with an accommodation has a disability but perhaps not a serious health condition.

An employee who is protected by both the FMLA and the ADA is entitled to the rights provided by both laws: up to 12 weeks of job-protected leave with benefits continuation under the FMLA, and a reasonable accommodation to enable the employee to perform the job's essential functions under the ADA. If the laws allow different rights in the same situation, the employee is entitled to whichever provides the greater benefit.

EXAMPLE: Sam uses a wheelchair due to a back injury that left him paralyzed from the waist down. He needs to have surgery related to his condition and expects to be out of work for two months. Because you know Sam has a disability, you consider whether he is entitled to two months off as a reasonable accommodation. Sam's job is to maintain, update, and troubleshoot the company's website. No one else knows how to do this work and, because the website is relatively new, it requires a lot of work to keep it running smoothly. You decide that it would be an undue hardship to give Sam two months off, and you tell him that the company will have to replace him.

Although you might have been right under the ADA, you were wrong under the FMLA. Sam's disability almost certainly qualifies as a serious health condition, for which he is entitled to FMLA leave (assuming he is otherwise eligible). The FMLA doesn't include an undue hardship defense: An eligible employee can't be denied leave because it would place too much of a burden on the company (unless the employee qualifies as a "key employee," as explained in Chapter 10). You must give Sam his time off and figure out some way to get the work done in his absence.

There are several situations in which the FMLA and ADA are most likely to overlap: when an employee requests a modified schedule, when an employee requests (or an employer proposes) modified job duties, and when an employee is unable to return to work after FMLA leave.

 TIP

Count disability leave as FMLA leave. If an employee is covered by both the ADA and the FMLA, make sure you count any time off the employee takes due to his or her disability as FMLA leave, too.

Schedule Changes

An employee can take FMLA leave intermittently or on a reduced schedule, and this might also be a reasonable accommodation for an employee's disability under the ADA. If the employee is protected by both laws, the FMLA provides the greater benefit, because employees are entitled to job protection and benefits continuation during intermittent or reduced-schedule leave. And even if an employer transfers an employee to a different position that better accommodates the need for leave, that position must have the same pay and benefits of the employee's original position. The ADA allows a transfer as a reasonable accommodation but doesn't give the employee the right to the same pay and benefits, nor to benefits continuation.

EXAMPLE: Najeet is scheduled to begin a ten-week round of chemotherapy and radiation treatment for cancer and needs time off work. She asks to work 20 hours a week for the duration of her treatment. You tell Najeet that you are happy to grant her request as a reasonable accommodation for her disability but remind her that the company provides health benefits only to employees who work at least 30 hours a week. You offer her COBRA coverage, for which she would have to pay the entire premium, until she is able to once again meet the minimum hours requirement.

Uh oh! In this situation, the FMLA provides a greater benefit—and Najeet is entitled to its protections. She can take the time off she needs for treatment with continued health insurance benefits, regardless of the company's policy on eligibility for coverage. Under the FMLA, Najeet has to pay only her usual share of the premium (if any), not the whole thing.

Job Modifications

The FMLA does not entitle an employee to a different job or to any changes in his or her current job. Instead, the FMLA provides for reinstatement, once leave is over, to the same or an equivalent position—a position that is "virtually identical" to the employee's former position. In contrast, the ADA may entitle an employee to job modifications or even to a different position in the company as a reasonable accommodation. Here are a couple of ways this issue might play out when an employee has both a disability and a serious health condition:

- **The employee asks for changes to the job.** You must consider whether the requested changes constitute a reasonable accommodation and whether providing them would be an undue hardship. If the accommodation won't work, you must work with the employee to come up with a different accommodation. If you and the employee conclude that time off might reasonably accommodate the employee's disability, your obligations under the FMLA kick in.

EXAMPLE: Carmen is a dispatcher for a delivery company. She works from 6 a.m. until noon. When she arrives, she reviews the schedule to see which deliveries must be made that day, assigns deliveries to drivers, and arranges for the items to be loaded on the trucks. By about 10 a.m., all of the trucks have left the warehouse. Carmen spends the rest of her day processing paperwork from the morning deliveries.

Carmen is diagnosed with depression, for which her doctor prescribes her medication that makes her groggy and disoriented in the morning. Carmen asks if she can change her schedule to arrive at work at 10 a.m. and work until 4 p.m. The FMLA doesn't apply, because she isn't asking for time off. You consider it as a request for a reasonable accommodation, and you deny it as an undue hardship. The essential duties of Carmen's job require her to be there in the early morning. There wouldn't be anything for her to do later in the day. You research whether there are other positions in the company that Carmen might be suited for, but there are no positions for which she is qualified.

You and Carmen talk through some alternatives, none of which will work. Carmen says, "My doctor said that this side effect might go away after I've been taking the drug for a month or so. Some of his other patients have had that happen." You ask Carmen whether she wants to take some time off work and see whether she feels well enough in the morning to resume her job. You explain her right to leave under the FMLA, and she decides to use it.

- **You offer a light-duty position.** If an employee requests time off for a serious health condition/disability, some employers respond by offering a light-duty position—often, one that doesn't require lifting or other physically strenuous activities. If the employee wants to keep working and accepts the position, that's fine. If, however, the employee is covered by the FMLA, he or she does not have to take the position—and you must inform the employee of his or her FMLA rights. The employee can choose to take FMLA leave rather than working a light-duty assignment, as long as the employee is eligible.

Reinstatement

Once an employee's FMLA-protected leave runs out, the company must reinstate the employee to the same or an equivalent position. If the employee is not able to return to work or perform the essential duties of his or her position, the company's FMLA obligations end. However, if the employee is also covered by the ADA, the company must provide a reasonable accommodation, unless it creates an undue hardship. This means that the company might have to provide additional leave, make changes to the employee's position to allow the employee to do the job, or even transfer the employee to a different position. And, the ADA requires the company to return the employee to the same job with a reasonable accommodation—not an equivalent one—unless doing so would be an undue hardship. Therefore, if an employee's leave qualifies under both laws, you might not be able to reinstate the employee to an equivalent position.

Leave as a Reasonable Accommodation

Here are some things courts have considered when deciding whether leave constitutes a reasonable accommodation:

- **The nature of the job.** If regular attendance is an essential function of the job (as it often is), some courts have found that an employee who needs a significant amount of time off is not a qualified employee with a disability and isn't protected by the ADA nor entitled to a reasonable accommodation.

- **How much leave the employee needs.** While many courts have found that an employer is not required to provide open-ended leave, courts are more likely to see a finite period of leave as a reasonable accommodation. If an employee will be able to return to work after two additional weeks of leave (beyond the 12 weeks allowed by the FMLA) for physical therapy following surgery, for example, a court is more likely to find that the employee is entitled to this time off.

- **How much time off the employer provides in other circumstances.** If an employer grants extended leaves for other purposes, it will be hard pressed to claim that allowing leave to an employee with a disability is an undue hardship.

Ultimately, the undue hardship test will determine whether you must grant an employee's request for time off under the ADA. Before you decide to deny this type of request, talk to an employment lawyer to find out how courts in your area look at these cases—and to make sure you've considered all of the angles before making your decision.

LESSONS FROM THE

Real World

When an employee's depression causes poor attendance, she isn't protected by the ADA but might be entitled to FMLA leave.

Theresa Spangler worked in the Demand Services Department of the Federal Home Loan Bank of Des Moines. After she was diagnosed with dysthemia (a form of depression), she began having attendance problems. Over the years, she took two leaves of absence for treatment and missed days of work due to her depression.

After being warned, being put on probation, and facing customer complaints about her absences, Spangler was eventually fired for excessive absenteeism when she called in and saying she would be out for "depression, again." She sued the bank for violating the ADA and the FMLA.

The court found that Spangler had no claim under the ADA, because she could not prove that she could perform the job's essential functions with or without accommodation. One of Spangler's job duties was to make sure member banks had adequate daily cash, and the court found that regular attendance was therefore an essential function of her job.

The court also found, however, that Spangler might have a valid FMLA claim. Unlike the ADA, which protects employees who can do the job but might need an accommodation, the FMLA protects employees who cannot perform the job's essential functions, at least for a limited time. When Spangler called in and said she would miss work for depression, the company should have treated it as a request for FMLA leave.

Spangler v. Federal Home Loan Bank of Des Moines, 278 F.3d 847 (8th Cir. 2002).

RESOURCE

For more information on the ADA. The Equal Employment Opportunity Commission, the federal agency that administers the ADA, has a number of helpful resources available on its website, including a fact sheet on how the ADA interacts with the FMLA. You can find these resources at www. eeoc.gov. An excellent resource on reasonable accommodations is the Job Accommodation Network (JAN), at www.jan.wvu.edu.

Consolidated Omnibus Budget Reconciliation Act (COBRA)

COBRA allows employees, former employees, and their families to receive continuing coverage under an employer's group health plan even after experiencing a "qualifying event"—an event that would end coverage under ordinary circumstances, such as a layoff or reduction in hours. Employees and their families typically have to pay for this continued coverage, but they pay the employer-negotiated group rate, which is often less expensive than an individual rate. This right to continued coverage lasts for 18 to 36 months, depending on the type of qualifying event.

Often, COBRA and the FMLA don't overlap at all. Taking FMLA leave doesn't count as a qualifying event under COBRA, because employers are legally obligated to continue the employee's group health benefits during leave (as explained in Chapter 9). In a few situations, however, an employee who takes FMLA leave might be entitled to COBRA protection:

- **The employee can't return to work after FMLA leave.** If an employee is unable to come back to work when FMLA leave runs out, the employee is entitled to continued health care coverage under COBRA. The qualifying event occurs on the last day of the employee's FMLA leave. Similarly, if an employee passes away while on FMLA leave, and the employee's family is covered by your company's group health plan, the employee's death is the qualifying event that entitles his or her family members to the protections of COBRA.

- **The employee chooses not to return to work.** As explained in Chapter 10, an employer's obligation to provide continued health benefits ends if the employee provides unequivocal notice of his or her intent not to return to work. The qualifying event in this situation occurs on the date the employee gives such notice.

- **The employee returns to work in a schedule or position that is not entitled to benefits.** Many companies provide group health benefits only to certain employees—typically, those that work a minimum number of hours per week. If an employee takes FMLA leave and chooses to return to a part-time position, the employee might no longer be entitled to benefits. The qualifying event here occurs on the last day of the employee's leave.

These rules apply even if the employee failed to pay his or her portion of the premium while on leave or the employee refused coverage during FMLA leave. Neither situation deprives the employee of the right to coverage, so neither counts as a qualifying event under COBRA.

RESOURCE

Need more information on COBRA? You can find detailed information on COBRA's requirements, including the paperwork and notices your company must provide to an employee who is entitled to continuing coverage, in *The Essential Guide to Federal Employment Laws*, by Lisa Guerin and Amy DelPo (Nolo).

Title VII of the Civil Rights Act

Title VII prohibits employment discrimination on the basis of race, color, religion, sex (including pregnancy), and national origin. Title VII applies to every aspect of the employment relationship, including hiring, compensation, benefits, and termination. It also prohibits harassment on the basis of any of the characteristics listed above.

There are a few ways Title VII might overlap with the FMLA. Because Title VII prohibits employers from discriminating in the provision of benefits, an employer might violate Title VII by administering requests for FMLA leave in a discriminatory way. For example, if you routinely allow white employees to take foreseeable leave on short notice while requiring nonwhite employees to provide 30 days' notice, that would violate Title VII. In this type of situation, the employer is using the FMLA as a vehicle for discrimination.

Overlap may also occur when an employee takes FMLA leave for pregnancy and childbirth. Courts have interpreted Title VII's prohibition on pregnancy discrimination to require employers to treat pregnant employees just as they treat other workers who are temporarily disabled by other conditions. This means that you cannot treat employees who take FMLA leave for pregnancy any differently from other employees who use the FMLA, and you might have to provide time off to a pregnant employee who isn't eligible for FMLA leave (because, for example, she hasn't worked enough hours in the past year) if you provide such time off to employees with other types of short-term disabilities.

Parenting and caretaking leave are another potential source of overlap. This issue typically arises when a male employee wants to take parental leave or leave to care for a seriously ill family member. Even in this day and age, some employers still expect women to be the primary parents and caretakers. However, denying a man FMLA leave based on these expectations not only violates the FMLA; it's also gender discrimination, prohibited by Title VII.

EXAMPLE: Connor is an employee at your company. He and his wife, who does volunteer work for a local nonprofit, have a young son who has leukemia. Connor asks to work a reduced schedule while his son undergoes treatment that is expected to leave him fatigued, ill, and unable to care for himself. You respond: "Connor, I'm so sorry to hear about your son, but isn't your wife available to take care of him? We could really use you around here, and if she puts her volunteer work on hold, your family won't lose part of your salary. I'm sure he'll want his mother at a time like this."

Oops. It's not an employer's right to tell employees how to manage their private lives—including which parent should be the primary caretaker, whose job is more important to the family, and so on. If you denied FMLA leave to Connor because you think his wife should take care of their son, your company might well be facing a lawsuit for violating both the FMLA and Title VII's prohibition on sex discrimination.

Uniformed Services Employment and Reemployment Rights Act (USERRA)

USERRA provides a number of employment-related rights to employees who take time off to serve in the armed forces. Such employees may not be discriminated against based on their service; are entitled to reinstatement and benefits restoration upon returning from leaves of up to five years; and may not be fired, except for cause, for up to a year after they return from service.

TIP

Some states have similar laws. Many states have laws prohibiting discrimination or providing employment-related rights to individuals serving in the armed forces or state militias. These laws can overlap with the FMLA the same way Title VII and USERRA do—and their protections could be even broader. To find out more about the laws in your state, talk to an experienced lawyer.

USERRA and the FMLA overlap only when determining an employee's eligibility for FMLA leave. As explained in Chapter 3, an employee must have worked for the employer for at least one year, and at least 1,250 hours during the previous year, to qualify for FMLA leave. You must count time the employee spends on leave for military service as time worked when determining eligibility for FMLA leave. When calculating the employee's hours, you can use the employee's schedule prior to taking military leave.

EXAMPLE 1: For eight months, George, a member of the Army Reserve, works full time (40 hours a week) in your company's IT department. He is called for service and takes six months of military leave, then returns to work. After he has been back for a month, George requests FMLA leave to care for his seriously ill wife. Is he eligible for leave?

Yes. You must count the eight months George spent on leave as hours worked. This means that George has "worked" 15 months for your company, and 2,080 hours (40 hours a week times 52 weeks) in the last year. He is eligible for FMLA leave.

EXAMPLE 2: Now assume that George works a part-time schedule, 20 hours per week. Is he still eligible for FMLA leave?

No. Although George still gets credit for 15 months of work for your company, he hasn't "worked" enough hours in the last year. You must credit George with an entire year of work at his previous schedule—20 hours per week. That means George gets credit for only 1,040 hours (20 hours a week times 52 weeks), which falls short of the threshold for FMLA coverage.

State Laws

In addition to the federal laws described above, there are state laws that might overlap with the FMLA as well. This section describes the types of state laws that might come into play as you administer the FMLA:

- state family and medical leave laws
- workers' compensation statutes, and
- temporary disability or family leave insurance programs.

State Family and Medical Leave Laws

A number of states have adopted their own laws that allow employees to take time off for family and/or medical reasons. These laws fall into a handful of categories:

- comprehensive family and medical leave laws similar to the FMLA that may provide additional protections or apply to more employees
- pregnancy disability leave laws, which allow female employees to take time off for conditions related to pregnancy and childbirth
- adoption leave laws, which generally require employers to make the same parental leave available to adoptive parents that they make available to biological parents
- small necessities laws, which provide time off for employees to attend a child's school conferences or other activities or to take a relative to routine medical and dental visits, and

- domestic violence leave laws, which require employers to allow employees to take leave to seek medical care, attend legal or therapy appointments, or otherwise deal with domestic violence issues.

CAUTION

Your state may require you to offer other types of leave. In this section (and in Appendix A), we discuss only those state laws that might overlap with, or provide leave similar to, the FMLA. We do not cover the many other types of leave laws states have adopted, such as laws requiring leave for voting, military service, jury duty, or donating blood or bone marrow. To find out more about your state's leave laws beyond the realm of family and medical leave, contact your state labor department. (You'll find contact information in Appendix A.)

Each of these categories is explained more fully below. Appendix A provides detailed information on each state's family and medical leave laws, including which employers are covered, what types of leave are eligible, and so on.

TIP

Remember to designate FMLA leave. If any time an employee takes off pursuant to a state law also qualifies as FMLA leave, designate it as such and provide the required notices (explained in Chapter 7). If you don't, the employee may be entitled to additional leave.

Comprehensive Family and Medical Leave Laws

About a dozen states currently have laws that require employers to provide family and medical leave. These laws are quite similar to the FMLA, in that they typically provide a certain number of weeks of parenting, caretaking, or medical leave to eligible employees. However, these laws differ from the FMLA in the following important ways:

- **Some apply to smaller employers.** For example, Vermont employers must provide parental leave if they have at least ten employees, and leave to care for a seriously ill family member if they have at least fifteen employees. In these states, smaller employers may be covered only by the state law, not the FMLA.

- **Some cover more family members.** In California, for example, an employee may take leave to care for a domestic partner with a serious health condition. When an employee takes leave to care for a family member that is not covered by the FMLA, it doesn't count as FMLA leave. This means, for example, that an employee in California could take 12 weeks (the state law maximum) of family leave to care for a seriously ill domestic partner and still have 12 weeks of FMLA leave left to use.

- **Some may allow longer periods of leave.** In Connecticut, for example, employees are entitled to 16 weeks of family and medical leave in a two-year period. If an employee needs 16 weeks at once, this provides more leave than the FMLA requires.

Whether leave taken pursuant to one of these state laws counts as FMLA leave depends on whether both laws apply. When an employee takes leave for a reason that's covered by state law but not by the FMLA (for example, to care for a grandparent, in Hawaii), the FMLA doesn't apply—and the employee's leave doesn't use up any of his or her FMLA entitlement. If, however, the employee's leave is covered by both laws (for example, that Hawaiian employee takes leave to care for a parent), the time counts against both the employee's FMLA and state leave entitlements.

If your company does business in a state with a comprehensive family and medical leave statute, keep these tips in mind:

- **Start by figuring out which laws apply.** If the employee's leave is covered only by your state's law, you don't have to deal with the FMLA at all, and vice versa.

- **If both laws apply, the leaves run concurrently.** Even if your state's law provides leave in situations not covered by the FMLA, the employee can't take that leave after using up his or her leave entitlement.

EXAMPLE: Oregon's family and medical leave law allows eligible employees to take up to 12 weeks of leave per year for various reasons, including caring for a family member with a serious health condition. The definition of "family member" includes a parent-in-law. If an employee in Oregon took 12 weeks of leave to care for a child with a serious health condition, that leave would use up both the employee's FMLA and state leave entitlements, and no leave would be available for the rest of the year.

If, on the other hand, the employee first took 12 weeks of leave to care for his or her mother-in-law, that leave would count against the state leave entitlement only. The employee would still have 12 weeks of FMLA leave to use.

- **If both laws apply, you must allow the employee to comply with whichever notice and certification requirements are less strict.** For example, if a state's law requires only two weeks' notice of foreseeable leave to care for a family member with a serious health condition, the employer cannot require more, even if the employee's leave is also covered by the FMLA (which normally requires 30 days' notice). The same is true of medical certification requirements and fitness-for-duty certification requirements. In California, for example, employers cannot request recertifications. If an employee's leave is covered by both California law and the FMLA, the employer can't ask for a recertification.

- **If only one law applies, the employee will be able to "stack" leave.** If an employee's time off counts only under one law and not the other, the employee will still have leave available. This means that the employee could take significantly more than 12 weeks of leave in a 12-month period, if the employee is eligible.

Pregnancy Disability Leave

Some states require employers to provide time off for pregnancy disability: the length of time when a woman is temporarily disabled by pregnancy and childbirth. Typically, these laws don't provide for a set amount of time off per year or per pregnancy. Instead, they require employers to provide either a "reasonable" amount of leave or leave for the period of disability, often with a maximum time limit. For example, Louisiana requires employers to allow a "reasonable period" of leave for pregnancy disability; the statute goes on to say that this period shouldn't exceed six weeks for a normal childbirth but might be as long as four months, depending on the circumstances.

Because pregnancy is a serious health condition under the FMLA, leave an employee takes under a state pregnancy disability leave law typically runs concurrently with FMLA leave. If your state's law provides for more than 12 weeks of pregnancy disability leave, the first 12 weeks will use up the employee's FMLA allotment. Although the employee may be entitled to take more time off, the employee won't necessarily be entitled to continued health insurance if the state law doesn't require it.

Adoption Leave Laws

A handful of states require employers to offer the same leave to adoptive parents as to biological parents. Generally, these laws don't require an employer to offer parental leave. However, those employers that choose to offer some form of parental leave must make it equally available to adoptive parents. A couple of these states set an age limit: For example, New York employers that provide parental leave must allow adoptive parents to use it, but only if they are adopting a child who is no older than preschool age or, if disabled, no older than 18.

The FMLA provides leave for adoption, so any time an employee takes off pursuant to one of these state laws would also count as FMLA leave (and you should designate it as such).

Small Necessities Laws

Some states require employers to allow time off for various family needs, such as attending school functions, taking a child to routine dental or medical appointments, or helping with eldercare. These laws have come to be known as "small necessities" laws, to recognize needs that don't take up much time but are important to employees. Here are a few examples:

- In Illinois, employees can take up to eight hours off in any school year—not to exceed four hours in a single day—to attend a child's school conferences or classroom activities, if those activities can't be scheduled during nonwork hours.

- In Washington, D.C., employees can take up to 24 hours off per year to attend a child's school-related events, including parent-teacher association meetings, student performances, teacher conferences, and sporting events—as long as the parent actually participates and is not just a spectator.

- In Vermont, employees can take a total of 24 hours of leave per year for school activities; to attend or accompany a child, parent, spouse, or parent-in-law to routine medical or dental appointments or other appointments for professional services; or to respond to a medical emergency involving the employee's child, parent, spouse, or parent-in-law.

Many of these laws apply to situations not covered by the FMLA (such as school conferences or routine doctor's appointments). In this situation, the leave provided by a small necessities law would be in addition to FMLA leave, and the two laws wouldn't overlap. However, there are limited situations in which the FMLA might also apply. For example, if your company does business in Vermont, and a parent takes small necessities leave to respond to a child's medical emergency, that might also qualify as FMLA leave (depending on whether the child has a serious health condition).

Domestic Violence Leave Laws

Some states allow employees to take time off for issues relating to domestic violence. In Colorado, for example, employees can take up to three days of leave to seek a restraining order, obtain medical care or counseling, relocate, or seek legal assistance. These laws may apply to employees who need to help a family member—such as a child—who has been a victim of domestic violence, as well.

Whether leave taken under one of these statutes qualifies as FMLA leave depends on whether the employee has a serious health condition or is caring for a family member with a serious health condition. An employee who takes time off to appear in court to testify against her abuser might not qualify for FMLA leave; an employee who is hospitalized following a violent incident probably does. When an employee takes domestic violence leave, you should find out whether a serious health condition is present—and, if so, designate the leave accordingly.

Putting It All Together

Now that we've reviewed the most common types of state laws that provide leave for family and medical reasons, it's time to see how they might work together—along with the FMLA—when an employee needs time off. Here are a few examples that will help you see how the process works.

EXAMPLE 1: Joan works for a company in California. She and her domestic partner, Betty, are expecting a baby in a couple of months; Joan is carrying the baby. Joan's doctor puts her on bed rest for the last four weeks of her pregnancy. Joan also wants to take some parental leave after the baby is born. What are her leave rights?

Under California law, Joan can take up to four months of pregnancy disability leave, taken concurrently with her 12 weeks of FMLA leave. However, she gets an additional 12 weeks of leave under the California Family Rights Act (CFRA), which doesn't cover pregnancy disability. If Joan is disabled for the last four weeks of her pregnancy and another four weeks after the baby is born, she has used up eight weeks of FMLA leave. However, she is still entitled to 12 weeks of CFRA leave, which she can use for any purpose covered by that law—including parental leave. This means Joan can take 24 weeks off in one block and still be entitled to job reinstatement (12 weeks of FMLA and pregnancy disability leave, plus 12 more weeks of CFRA leave). In fact, if she is disabled by pregnancy and childbirth for the full four months, she can take seven months of job-protected leave before returning to work (4 months of pregnancy disability leave, the first 12 weeks of which are also FMLA leave, plus 12 more weeks of CFRA leave).

During the eight weeks when she is covered only by the FMLA and California's pregnancy disability leave statute, Joan's employer can require her to comply with the FMLA's notice and certification requirements. Once the CFRA kicks in, however, her employer can require her to comply only with its more lenient notice and certification requirements—even during the four weeks when she is also covered by the FMLA.

EXAMPLE 2: Carla works for a company in Hawaii. Carla's boyfriend batters her son, who is hospitalized for his injuries. Under Hawaii law, Carla is entitled to up to 30 days of unpaid leave per year to deal with domestic violence issues. Hawaii also has a comprehensive family and medical leave law, which allows employees to take up to four weeks off per year to care for a family member with a serious health condition. What are Carla's leave rights?

If Carla takes three weeks off to care for her son, that time counts against her state family and medical leave entitlement, her FMLA entitlement, and her domestic violence leave entitlement. If, after her leave is over, Carla needs an additional week off to relocate her family and seek a restraining order against her boyfriend, that leave is not protected by either the FMLA or Hawaii's leave law. However, it is protected by the state's domestic leave law, which allows time off for these purposes. Carla is still entitled to one week of state leave and nine weeks of FMLA leave in the same 12-month period, but her domestic violence leave is used up.

EXAMPLE 3: David, a single father of three children, works for a company in Vermont. Vermont law allows him to take up to 24 hours of leave per year to participate in a child's school activities, take family members to routine medical or dental appointments, or respond to a family member's medical emergency. Vermont also has a comprehensive family and medical leave law that provides up to 12 weeks of leave in a year for the same reasons covered by the FMLA. What are David's leave rights?

If David uses his 24 hours of leave to attend parent-teacher conferences and take his children to regular medical and dental checkups, he still has 12 weeks of FMLA leave and state family and medical leave left to use. Because school activities and routine appointments are not covered by those laws, this time off doesn't count against his state or federal family and medical leave entitlement.

EXAMPLE 4: Maek works for a company in Rhode Island. He has cerebral palsy and needs time off work occasionally for reasons related to his condition. Rhode Island law allows employees to take up to 13 weeks off every two calendar years for family and medical reasons, including the employee's own serious health condition. What are Maek's leave rights?

If Maek needs 13 weeks off in one year, the first 12 weeks use up his FMLA entitlement for that year; the final week is covered under state law only. Maek is not entitled to any additional state leave for the rest of that year or the following calendar year. However, Maek does have an additional 12 weeks of FMLA leave to use in the following year (when that leave year starts depends on how the company calculates its 12-month FMLA period; see Chapter 6).

Workers' Compensation

Most employers in most states are required to carry workers' compensation insurance (workers' comp), which provides reimbursement for medical bills and partial wage replacement to employees who are unable to work due to a work-related injury or illness. Typically, state law provides that an employee's injury or illness is covered by workers' comp if it is related to work, whether it occurs at the workplace during normal work hours; while the employee is traveling for business; or while the employee is attending a required work function, such as a company picnic or team-building event.

If an employee's serious health condition is due to a work-related injury or illness, both the FMLA and workers' comp might apply. In this situation, the employee would be entitled to up to 12 weeks of unpaid, job-protected leave under the FMLA, and to partial wage replacement, reimbursement for medical bills, and perhaps some retraining or occupational therapy under workers' comp.

Workers' Comp Medical Inquiries

As explained in Chapter 8, employers have very limited rights to request medical information under the FMLA. The employer may require the employee to submit a medical certification from a health care provider, giving some basic facts about the serious health condition that necessitates leave. However, the employer may not request additional information or contact the health care provider directly. Although the employer can, with the employee's consent, have its own health care provider contact the employee's health care provider, this is only for the limited purpose of clarifying and authenticating the information on the medical certification form.

The workers' compensation statutes of most states allow quite a bit more contact between employers and health care providers. If an employee is on FMLA leave for a workers' comp injury, and the state's workers' comp law allows direct contact between the employer and the employee's health care provider, the FMLA doesn't prohibit that contact. In other words, the employer can still communicate with the health care provider in any way the workers' comp statute allows.

TIP

An employee who is out on workers' comp leave probably has a serious health condition under the FMLA. Under the laws of many states, an employee becomes entitled to temporary disability benefits under workers' comp only after being out of work for a specified waiting period (typically, at least three days). And, an employee seeking workers' comp benefits must be seen by a doctor. This adds up to incapacity of more than three days with continuing treatment by a health care provider—a serious health condition. The upshot for managers is this: Whenever an employee is out of work and receiving workers' comp benefits, you should designate that time as FMLA leave.

Workers' comp is, of course, a very detailed and complicated system, which varies greatly from state to state. Our purpose here is not to explain your obligations under workers' comp law, but to highlight the areas where your obligations under the FMLA and workers' comp are most likely to overlap: light-duty assignments and reinstatement.

Light Duty

Under the FMLA, an employee with a serious health condition is entitled to leave until he or she is once again able to do the original job or one that is nearly identical to it, up to 12 weeks. The employee doesn't have to come back early to a different position or "light duty" if he or she is capable of lesser tasks or responsibilities.

Workers' comp is different. If the company offers a light-duty position that the employee is medically able to perform, the employee typically has to accept that position or lose his or her benefits under workers' comp. If the employee is also covered by the FMLA, the employee remains entitled to up to 12 weeks of job-protected leave—but could lose the workers' comp benefits if the employee chooses not to take the light-duty position.

If an employee decides to accept a light-duty position while on FMLA leave, the employee is entitled to 12 weeks of total time out of his or her original position—the time the employee spends out of work entirely plus the time the employee spends in the light-duty position. While the employee works in the light-duty position, the FMLA is protecting his or her original job, up to the 12-week time limit.

Reinstatement

Unlike the FMLA, workers' comp laws often don't place a time limit on how long an employee may be off before returning to work. But most don't give an employee the right to be reinstated, either. Although employers may not fire or discipline employees for making a worker's comp claim, most states do not explicitly prohibit an employer from firing an employee who is out with a workers' comp injury—for example, because the employer has to fill the position and cannot wait any longer for the employee to recuperate. (Some states do require reinstatement, however—check with a lawyer to find out how your state deals with this issue.)

An employee who is out with a workers' comp injury that is also a serious health condition under the FMLA is still entitled to only 12 weeks of job-protected leave. The fact that the employee has a workers' comp injury does not extend this protection. If the employee is unable to return to work after 12 weeks, the laws of most states allow the employer to terminate employment—unless the employee has a disability that requires reasonable accommodation (see "Americans with Disabilities Act (ADA)," above).

CAUTION

Talk to a lawyer before you fire someone with a workers' comp claim. Although the laws of your state may allow you to fire someone who is out on workers' comp leave (after the employee's FMLA leave entitlement has run out), that doesn't mean it's a good idea. Whenever you fire an employee who has exercised a legal right, you risk a retaliation lawsuit. Before you fire someone who is using workers' comp, consult with an experienced employment attorney.

State Disability Insurance Programs

A handful of states (California, Hawaii, New Jersey, New York, and Rhode Island) have temporary disability insurance programs that provide partial wage replacement (typically funded by payroll deductions) to workers who are temporarily unable to do their jobs. California's program also provides partial wage replacement for up to six weeks' leave for parenting or to care for a seriously ill family member.

An employee who has a serious health condition (or, in California, takes parental or caretaking leave) may be entitled to payment from one of these programs, depending on the state's eligibility requirements. However, these laws do not give employees any substantive rights—for example, to a particular amount of time off or to job protection. Instead, they provide some pay to employees who are otherwise entitled to time off, whether pursuant to the FMLA or some other law.

Although you may have some administrative duties, these benefits are really between the employees and the state. Your job is mostly to let employees know that the program exists and perhaps to provide the necessary forms. It's the employee's responsibility to file those forms with the state and handle things from there. Of course, when an employee takes time off for a temporary disability, you should investigate whether the leave qualifies as FMLA leave and, if so, designate it as such.

Common Mistakes Regarding Other Laws and Benefits—And How to Avoid Them

MISTAKE 1: Confusing the ADA's requirements with the FMLA's.

AVOID THIS MISTAKE BY:

- Figuring out which law applies. An employee with a serious health condition doesn't always have a disability, and vice versa. If only one law applies, you don't have to apply the other.

- Applying the most beneficial provisions to each situation. If both laws apply, the employee is entitled to the maximum protections available—and this may depend on what the employee wants. If, for example, an employee qualifies for FMLA leave but wants to work with a reasonable accommodation, you must provide the accommodation. Conversely, if the employee could work with a reasonable accommodation but wants to take FMLA leave, you must provide leave.

- Remembering that undue hardship doesn't apply to the FMLA. This is a common source of confusion: Although the ADA doesn't require an employer to provide a reasonable accommodation to help an employee perform the essential functions of his or her job if it poses an undue hardship, no such defense applies to FMLA leave. The employer has to provide the leave, no matter how difficult it might be. (The employer might not have to reinstate "key employees" if that would cause grievous economic harm to the company, however—see Chapter 10).

- Considering additional time off or job modifications for employees who can't return to their old jobs. Although the FMLA entitles an employee to return to his or her former position after using up leave, the ADA might entitle the employee to additional protections, such as more leave or changes to the job, as a reasonable accommodation for the disability. If it appears that an employee won't be able to return to work after completing FMLA leave, it's time to start thinking about reasonable accommodations.

MISTAKE 2: Forgetting to designate leave taken concurrently under the FMLA and other statutes as FMLA leave.

AVOID THIS MISTAKE BY:

- Always considering the FMLA when an employee takes time off for his or her own illness or injury. Some companies outsource their workers' compensation claims handling, then neglect to designate this time off as FMLA leave. Or, if an employee has had an obvious disability (for example, having to use a wheelchair) from his or her first day of work, you might be so accustomed to allowing the ADA to guide your actions that you forget to consider the FMLA when the employee needs leave.

- Thinking "FMLA" when an employee uses state temporary disability insurance programs. Any time for which the employee is reimbursed by one of these programs (in the states that have them) is almost always FMLA leave.

- Designating parenting leave—whether taken pursuant to state law, company policy, or otherwise—as FMLA leave. Parenting leave is FMLA leave, plain and simple.

MISTAKE 3: Getting confused as to whether state leave laws apply.

AVOID THIS MISTAKE BY:

- Learning the coverage and eligibility requirements of your state's leave laws. Your first step is always to figure out which laws apply—and many states have different standards than the FMLA. Whenever you're faced with a leave situation, start by determining which laws cover your company, the employee, and the reason for leave.

- Counting leave only against the law that covers it. Sounds simple enough, but many managers have mistakenly counted state leave against an employee's FMLA entitlement when the reason for leave isn't covered by the FMLA. For example, if your state allows employees to take time off to care for grandparents, domestic partners, or in-laws, that time off cannot count against the employee's FMLA leave entitlement, because the FMLA doesn't apply to leave for those reasons.

- Applying the more lenient notice and certification requirements when state law and the FMLA apply. This is a tough one, because it means you have to apply different standards in different situations. But the employee cannot be required to comply with the stricter standards of one law (typically the FMLA) if the other applicable law is less strict.

- Paying careful attention to record keeping. If your company is subject to both the FMLA and a state leave law, you must designate leave under every law that applies and keep careful track of the employee's leave usage under each law. If an employee's leave is covered by one law and not the other, for example, you'll have to keep records of that fact so you and the employee know how much leave is still available for what purposes.

Do Other Laws Apply?

Americans with Disabilities Act (ADA)

Applies if:

- Employer has at least 15 employees.
- Employee has a disability: a physical or mental impairment that substantially limits one or more major life activities.
- Employee can perform the job's essential functions, with or without a reasonable accommodation.

Overlaps with the FMLA if:

- Employee has a serious health condition that also qualifies as a disability.

If the ADA and the FMLA both apply:

- Employee may be entitled to a reasonable accommodation instead of, or upon returning from, leave.
- Employee is entitled to take FMLA leave, if eligible, rather than accept a reasonable accommodation "light duty" position.
- Employee may be entitled to more leave than the FMLA requires as a reasonable accommodation.

Consolidated Omnibus Budget Reconciliation Act (COBRA)

Applies if:

- Employer has at least 20 employees.
- Employee receives benefits from employer's group health plan.
- Employee has a qualifying event that would otherwise end health coverage.

Overlaps with the FMLA if:

- Employee does not return from FMLA leave for any reason.
- Employee returns from FMLA leave to a position that does not offer health benefits.

If COBRA and the FMLA both apply:

- Employee (and/or employee's dependents, if covered by employer's group health plan) may receive continued benefits for 18 to 36 months, but must pay the entire premium.

Title VII

Applies if:

- Employer has at least 15 employees.

Overlaps with the FMLA if:

- Employer makes FMLA decisions on the basis of race, religion, or other protected characteristics.
- Employer treats men and women differently in administering the FMLA.
- Employer treats pregnancy leave different than other types of FMLA leave.

Do Other Laws Apply?, continued

Uniformed Services Employment and Reemployment Rights Act (USERRA)

Applies if:

• Employee needs or takes leave to serve in the armed forces.

If USERRA and the FMLA both apply:

• Time the employee spends on leave protected by USERRA counts as months and hours worked for the employer, for purposes of calculating employee's eligibility for FMLA leave.

State Family and Medical Leave Laws

Apply if:

• Employer meets the coverage requirements of the state law: Some apply to smaller employers than the FMLA.

• Employee meets the eligibility requirements of the state law: Some require less time in-service for eligibility.

• Employee is taking leave for a reason covered by the state law: Some allow leave for a wider variety of family members or for different conditions from the FMLA.

Overlap with the FMLA if:

• Employer is covered by both laws, employee is eligible for leave under both laws, and employee is taking leave for a reason covered by both laws.

If a state family and medical leave law and the FMLA both apply:

• Time the employee takes off counts against the employee's leave entitlement under both laws.

• The employee need comply only with whichever notice and certification requirements are less strict: the state law's or the FMLA's.

State Workers' Compensation Laws

Apply if:

• Employer is required to carry workers' compensation coverage (almost all are).

• Employee suffers a work-related injury or illness.

Overlap with the FMLA if:

• Employee's serious health condition is also a work-related injury or illness.

If a state worker's compensation law and the FMLA both apply:

• Employee may not be required to accept a light-duty position; however, employee's workers' compensation benefits may cease if the employee chooses not to work light duty.

• If employee accepts a light-duty position, the employee's right to reinstatement under the FMLA continues for 12 weeks total: the time the employee spends on leave plus the time the employee spends in the light-duty position.

• Employee who cannot return from work after FMLA leave may still have some reinstatement rights under the state workers' compensation law.

Do Other Laws Apply?, continued

State Temporary Disability Insurance Programs

Apply if:

- Employee works in California, Hawaii, New Jersey, New York, or Rhode Island.
- Employer is covered by the program, and employee is eligible for benefits from the program.
- Employee is temporarily unable to work or, in California, takes leave for parenting or to care for a seriously ill family member.

Overlap with the FMLA if:

- Employee's temporary disability is also a serious health condition under the FMLA.
- Employee in California is taking parenting leave or leave to care for a seriously ill family member that is also covered by the FMLA.

If a state temporary disability insurance program and the FMLA both apply:

- Time for which the employee is on leave and receiving compensation from the insurance program counts against the employee's FMLA leave entitlement.
- Employee may not be able to substitute paid leave, and employer may not be able to require employee to substitute paid leave, for time during which the employee is receiving compensation from the state program.

Record Keeping Requirements

CHAPTER HIGHLIGHTS

Keep all FMLA documents and forms organized and readily accessible, for at least three years.

Keeping accurate, organized records will help you:

- track employee hours for FMLA-eligibility determinations

- track employee leave time taken and available

- remember the dates that employees will return to work after leave

- remember when to give a six-month notice to an employee requesting leave (see Chapter 7)

- show others (including the U.S. Department of Labor) that you have complied with the FMLA

- justify FMLA designations or other decisions, and

- protect confidential medical records.

The three types of records you need to keep under the FMLA are:

- company-wide FMLA data

- individual employee FMLA records, and

- confidential medical records.

B y now, you probably realize that you have to handle a lot of paper under the FMLA, what with notices, forms, and so on. While it may seem like a lot to keep track of, you need to keep accurate records calculating employee FMLA eligibility, leave taken, and available leave time, as well as the documents that employees taking FMLA leave have to give you. Keeping all of these documents together in an organized, easily retrievable way will make your job much easier as you try to administer employee FMLA leaves and will help you stay out of legal trouble, too.

In this chapter, we tell you what documents you need and give you some suggestions about the best way to keep them. Good document control will help you keep track of employee leave time and ensure that you meet all your obligations under the FMLA. It will also make it easier to respond if an employee ever challenges leave decisions or if a governmental agency conducts an investigation, as you will be able to quickly pull all of the documents that show that you followed the law.

Why You Should Keep Records

If your company is covered by the FMLA, the law requires it to "make, keep, and preserve" detailed records of FMLA leaves taken by its employees, including copies of all notices given to employees taking leave. (29 U.S.C. § 2616(b).) Good organization of records is not just the law—it is also a good business practice. Thorough, accurate records help you keep track of how much leave each employee has taken or is eligible for, return dates for employees on leave, and other important pieces of information.

Keeping accurate records will also help you avoid or fight legal battles. You may have to show certain of these documents to the employee, his or her spokesperson, or even to the U.S. Department of Labor (DOL) if the agency decides to examine your company's FMLA practices. And, if any employee challenges your company's FMLA practices, you may have to gather certain of these documents to show that you provided adequate notices, denied leave based on adequate documentation, or treated the employee consistently with company policy and past practice. By putting all such records in separate files for each employee, you will be able to pull the exact document you need in any of these situations.

While the FMLA doesn't insist on a particular form or order for keeping the records, whatever form they are in must be clear and identifiable by date or pay period. They must be kept for at least three years and readily available for inspection, copying, and transcription by the DOL upon request. (29 CFR § 825.500(b).) Records your company keeps on its computer system have to be available for transcription or copying upon request by the DOL.

TIP

Do a regular check up. Keeping orderly FMLA records doesn't do you much good if the information in them is out of date or otherwise inaccurate. Be sure to periodically update the records so that they reflect employee leave taken, any changes in employee hours or FMLA status, or any other new data. One way to build the practice of updating the files into your personnel procedures is to review and update the files at the time of six-month or annual employee reviews.

Keeping Track of Company Workforce FMLA Data

If your company is covered by the FMLA, but none of its employees are eligible for FMLA leave (because, for example, none of them has worked for your company for 12 months), you only need to keep basic payroll data, including:

- payroll records showing that your company is covered by the FMLA
- documents describing employee benefits (whether kept in written or electronic form), and
- documents describing your company's paid and unpaid leave policies (whether kept in written or electronic form).

Keep all of these company workforce records together for easy review, if needed. These records can be kept in you company's usual human resources area. The manager in charge of FMLA compliance should be tasked with control, updating, and maintenance of these records.

Individual Employee Records

If your company has employees who are eligible for FMLA leave, you also need to keep records relating to those employees. These records include:

- basic payroll and identifying data for each employee, including:
  - name and address
  - occupation
  - rate of pay and terms of compensation
  - daily and weekly hours worked per pay period
  - additions to or deductions from wages
  - total compensation paid
- charts showing the dates FMLA leave is taken by each eligible employee (for example, from time records or requests for leave)
- charts of FMLA leave time available to each employee
- preliminary FMLA designations issued to each employee when seeking leave
- final FMLA designations issued to each employee when seeking leave
- for FMLA leave of less than a full day, records of the hours of leave taken
- copies of notices of FMLA leave given by each employee, if in writing
- copies of all general and individualized notices given by your company to each employee taking FMLA leave
- records confirming a family relationship, for employees who take leave for parenting or caring for a family member
- records of premium payments of employee benefits
- subsequent notices issued to each employee who requests FMLA leave six months after a first FMLA leave
- subsequent notices issued to any employee on leave informing the employee of a change in FMLA information
- status reports received from employees on leave
- records of any dispute between an eligible employee and your company regarding designation of leave as FMLA leave, including:

- any written statement of the reasons for designation from either your company or the employee

- any written statements of the reasons for the disagreement from either your company or the employee

• initial notice to a key employee that he or she might not be reinstated

• final notice to a key employee that reinstatement is denied

• notes, memos, letters, emails, or other documents that refer to the reason for any decision to grant or deny FMLA leave, including designation decisions, and

• confirmation that an employee has elected not to return from leave.

These records should be organized by employee but kept in a file separate and apart from the employee's regular personnel file. Each employee's FMLA file can be kept with his or her personnel file. The manager in charge of FMLA compliance should oversee the control, updating, and maintenance of these files, with the assistance of each employee's immediate supervisor.

If your company is a joint employer with another company (see Chapter 2), your record-keeping duties depend upon whether your company is the primary or secondary employer. As a primary employer, you have to keep all of the records listed above. As a secondary employer, you have to keep only the basic payroll data listed above.

If your company isn't required to keep overtime or minimum wage records for its FMLA-eligible employees, you don't have to keep records of actual hours worked, provided that both of the following are true:

• Your company treats any employee employed for at least 12 months as eligible for FMLA leave.

• Your company reaches written agreement with any employee taking intermittent or reduced-schedule leave as to the employee's normal schedule or average hours worked each week.

TIP

For the sake of accuracy and convenience, your company should keep records of hours worked by all employees. This will make it easier for you to track employee FMLA eligibility, intermittent and reduced-schedule leave taken, and FMLA leave available.

Medical Records

When an employee requests FMLA leave for the employee's own or a family member's serious medical condition, the employee has to give you certain documents containing medical information upon request. These medical records or any other documents containing medical information must be treated as confidential and kept in files separate and apart from your company's usual personnel files. Such records include:

- medical certifications
- recertifications
- medical histories of employees or their family members created for FMLA purposes
- fitness-for-duty certifications received from the employee when returning from FMLA leave, and
- second and third opinions you requested to verify a medical need for leave.

And, if the ADA also applies, you must keep the medical records in conformance with ADA confidentiality requirements. Under both the FMLA and the ADA, your company can disclose medical information only in the following circumstances:

- You can inform supervisors and managers of necessary restrictions on an employee's work or duties and any necessary accommodations.
- You can inform first aid and safety personnel if the employee's physical or medical condition might require emergency treatment.
- You must provide the information to government officials upon request.

(42 U.S.C. § 12112(d)(3); 29 CFR § 1630.14(c).)

EXAMPLE: Your employee, Cara, has disclosed to you that she is HIV-positive and needs to take intermittent leave to attend medical appointments. One of your company's managers later asks you if you have noticed that Cara seems thin and listless. You tell the manager privately that Cara is ill but "doesn't have full-blown AIDS," so you hope she will be able to get treatment for her condition. You figure that a fellow manager who has expressed concern for an employee may be told about the employee's condition, as long as it is done privately. Have you stayed inside the lines?

Unfortunately, no. Cara's diagnosis is confidential medical information. You cannot disclose confidential medical information just because a manager is genuinely concerned, unless the manager needs to know because of restrictions on the employee's ability to work or the manager is a first aid provider at the worksite and the employee's condition may require emergency care.

CAUTION

The ADA's confidentiality rule applies to employee medical records even if the employee is not disabled. All employee medical records should be treated as confidential, regardless of whether or not the employee has a disability as defined by the ADA (see Chapter 11).

The confidentiality of employee medical records is also protected by the Health Insurance Portability and Accountability Act ("HIPAA"; 42 U.S.C. § 1320d). In general, the HIPAA bars an employer from discussing an employee's medical condition with the employee's health care provider unless the employee has consented to the discussion. There are exceptions to this general rule when health care is provided to the employee at the employer's request (for example, where the health care provider is retained by the employer in connection with the employer's medical benefits for employees).

You may need to ask for certain medical information covered by the HIPAA in order to determine if a leave request is FMLA-qualified. You can ask the employee to complete an incomplete medical certification or for a second opinion from a health care provider. (See Chapter 8 for a full discussion of how you can legally verify the medical reason for the leave.)

SEE AN EXPERT

Get some record keeping help. Consult an attorney with expertise in the ADA, the HIPAA, and state medical records confidentiality laws to find out how you must handle employee medical records under these laws, as well as under the FMLA.

Review by the Department of Labor (DOL)

There's another important reason to keep accurate records of FMLA leaves: You may have to show those records to the DOL. You don't have to submit records to the DOL unless the DOL requests them. The DOL can request to examine your company's FMLA records only once in a 12-month period, except when it suspects the company may have violated the FMLA. DOL investigations occur in two circumstances:

- **Employee complaints.** Most frequently, DOL investigations are triggered by employee complaints, which the agency keeps confidential. The DOL won't tell you the name of the complaining employee, the nature of the complaint, or even if a complaint was made.

- **Industry investigations.** The DOL also selects certain types of businesses or industries to investigate because the agency believes there is a high rate of FMLA violations in the business or industry (for example, in industries that employ a high percentage of employees who don't speak English or have a lot of younger workers).

In a typical investigation, the DOL will do the following:

- **Examine the records listed above.** Even if investigating just a single complaint, the DOL may look at all your records.

- **Take notes about, make transcriptions of, and/or make photocopies of the documents reviewed.**

- **Interview certain employees.** Usually, these interviews will happen on company premises, but not always. The purpose of these interviews will be to verify the information in the records you presented and to confirm employees' particular hours.

- **Meet with your company representative,** The DOL will meet with someone with authority to make decisions and commit your company to corrective actions (for example, your FMLA compliance manager, if that person has such authority, or a company officer) if a violation is found.

Your company may (and probably should) be represented by an attorney during the investigation. And, after a finding is made, your company has the opportunity to present additional facts to the DOL for consideration. The DOL won't reveal information from your company's records to any unauthorized person.

Now You're Ready!

Congratulations! You've educated yourself on what the FMLA requires of your company and what it offers your employees. You have all of the tools you need to assess, administer, and track FMLA leave requests and time off, including forms, charts, posters, and sample policies. Now you and your employees can move forward together with the goal of keeping your workplace family-friendly, healthy, and operating smoothly.

Nice job.

Common Mistakes Regarding Record Keeping —And How to Avoid Them

MISTAKE 1: Losing track of the amount of FMLA-protected leave time an employee has available.

AVOID THIS MISTAKE BY:

- Keeping the payroll and leave records listed in this chapter organized and readily accessible.
- Consulting those records whenever an employee requests FMLA leave.
- Updating the information in the records periodically (for example, at the time of each employee's review).

MISTAKE 2: Granting (or denying) an employee's requests for intermittent leave because you have lost track of how much leave the employee has already taken and when.

AVOID THIS MISTAKE BY:

- Keeping hourly or daily payroll and leave records for employees taking intermittent or reduced-schedule leave, depending on how the leave time is taken.
- Keeping an updated intermittent or reduced-schedule leave chart for each employee taking such leave, including a running total of leave time taken and when.

MISTAKE 3: Improperly disclosing confidential employee medical information.

AVOID THIS MISTAKE BY:

- Keeping each employee's medical information in a separate file (not in the employee's personnel or FMLA file).
- Revealing medical information only when allowed by the law.

✓	Managers' Checklist	**Record Keeping**

❏ I have collected all FMLA forms and documents for the employee and have put the documents into files separate from the employee's personnel files, including:

❏ payroll records (showing FMLA eligibility or noneligibility)

❏ charts showing FMLA leave time taken and FMLA leave time available (for intermittent or reduced-schedule leave, in hours or days, depending on how the leave was taken)

❏ preliminary FMLA designation forms

❏ forms confirming or withdrawing preliminary FMLA designations

❏ individualized FMLA notices

❏ medical certifications and second and third opinions

❏ six-month notices (issued when the employee takes FMLA leave more than six months after first taking leave or when there is a change in leave information)

❏ fitness-for-duty certifications and requests for such certifications, and

❏ periodic reports of employee status while on leave.

❏ I have kept a chart showing the running total in hours or days (depending on how the leave was taken) of intermittent or reduced-schedule FMLA leave time taken by the employee taking such leave.

❏ I have kept all employee (or employee family member) medical information in separate files and

❏ I have treated these records and the information in them as confidential, barring others from gaining access to them except to supervisors and managers to provide necessary accommodations or first aid personnel if a condition might require emergency medical treatment.

Glossary

Adoption. The legal process of transferring the rights and responsibilities of a child's biological parents to persons other than the child's biological parents.

Alternative position. A position to which an eligible employee may be temporarily reassigned during a period of intermittent or reduced-schedule leave; it must have the same pay and benefits as the employee's original position.

Americans with Disabilities Act (ADA). A federal law that prohibits discrimination against qualified employees with disabilities and requires employers to make reasonable accommodations to allow such employees to do their jobs.

Cafeteria plan. A benefit program through which employees choose from a menu of benefits, such as health coverage, life insurance, disability insurance, and so on.

Chronic serious health condition. A serious health condition that requires periodic visits for treatment; continues over an extended period of time; and may cause episodic, rather than continuing, incapacity.

Consolidated Omnibus Budget Reconciliation Act (COBRA). A federal law that requires employers to provide continued coverage under a group health plan to employees and their dependents after an event that would otherwise terminate their coverage.

Continuing treatment. At least two treatments by a health care provider; nurse or physician's assistant acting under the direct supervision of a health care provider; or provider of health care services acting on the orders of, or referral by, a health care provider; or at least one treatment by a health care provider that results in a regimen of continuing treatment under the provider's supervision.

Department of Labor. The federal agency responsible for administering and enforcing the FMLA.

Designate leave. To tell the employee, in writing, that time off will be treated as FMLA leave.

Discriminate. To treat similarly situated employees differently.

Domestic partners. An unmarried couple granted certain of the rights and privileges enjoyed by married couples by the laws of the state in which they reside.

Employee with a disability. An employee who has a long-term physical or mental impairment that substantially limits a major life activity, has a history of such an impairment, or is perceived by the employer as having such an impairment.

Equivalent position. A position that is virtually identical to the position an employee held prior to taking FMLA leave, with equivalent pay, benefits, and other terms and conditions of employment to the employee's former job.

Essential job functions. The fundamental duties of a position—those things that the person holding the job absolutely must be able to do.

Exempt employee. An employee who is not entitled to extra pay for overtime hours worked under the Fair Labor Standards Act ("FLSA").

Family member. A spouse, child, or parent.

Fitness-for-duty certification. A signed statement from a health care provider indicating that an employee is able to return to work following FMLA leave.

Flexible savings account (FSA). An account into which employees may set aside pretax income for medical expenses not paid by health insurance (such as co-payments, premiums, and expenses that are outside of the employer's plan) or for dependent care expenses.

Foreseeable need for leave. A reason for taking FMLA leave that is anticipated or known in advance, such as planned medical treatment or the birth or adoption of a child.

Foster placement. The legal process of awarding the care, comfort, education, and upbringing of a child to someone other than the child's biological parents.

Full-time employee. An employee working 40 hours per week or more.

Group health plan. Any plan of, or contributed to by, an employer to provide health care to employees, former employees, and their families, including self-insured plans, vision plans, dental coverage, and other health care plans, whether they are components of a single health care plan or administered separately.

Health care provider. A medical doctor, doctor of osteopathy, podiatrist, dentist, optometrist, chiropractor (only for manual manipulation of the spine to treat a subluxation of the spine—that is, misalignment of vertebrae—identified by x-ray), clinical psychologist, nurse practitioner, nurse midwife, clinical social worker, Christian Science practitioner, or other provider from whom the employer will accept medical certification for purposes of substantiating a claim for health care benefits.

Incapacity. Inability to work, attend school, or perform other regular daily activities due to a serious health condition, treatment for the condition, or recovery from the condition.

Independent contractor. A person who contracts to perform services for another person or company but does not have the status of an employee; a freelancer or consultant.

Individualized notice. Written information a company must provide to an employee who requests or takes FMLA-qualified leave.

Inpatient care. Care that involves an overnight stay at a hospital, hospice, or residential medical care facility.

Inquiry notice. Information provided by an employee indicating that an absence might be FMLA-qualified, which creates an obligation for the employer to inquire further.

Integrated employers. Companies that have common management, interrelation between operations, centralized control of labor relations, and common ownership or financial control.

Intermittent leave. FMLA leave taken in separate blocks of time for a single qualifying reason, such as a course of treatment spread over months or flare-ups of a chronic illness.

Joint employer. A company that shares control with another company over the working conditions of the other company's employees.

Key employee. A salaried employee in the highest-paid 10% of the company's employees working within 75 miles of the employee's worksite.

Leave year. The 12-month period during which an eligible employee is entitled to 12 weeks of FMLA leave.

Light duty. Work that is less demanding (physically, mentally, or because it requires fewer hours of work) than an employee's usual position.

Medical certification. A written document verifying an employee's need to take leave for a serious health condition, prepared by a health care provider.

Moonlighting. Working for another employer while on leave.

Multiemployer health plan. A health plan established pursuant to a collective bargaining agreement, into which at least two employers make contributions.

Overtime. Hours worked over and above 40 hours in a week (or eight hours in a day, in some states) and requiring premium pay under the FLSA.

Parenting leave. Leave following birth, adoption, or foster placement, including bonding leave.

Part-time employee. An employee working fewer than 40 hours per week.

Pregnancy disability. Disability due to pregnancy, childbirth, or related conditions.

Preliminary designation. A written designation of leave as FMLA leave, pending an investigation into whether the leave actually qualifies for the FMLA's protections.

Primary employer. A joint employer that has authority to hire and fire the employee seeking leave, place the employee in a particular position, assign work to the employee, make payroll, and provide employment benefits.

Qualified employee with a disability. An employee with a disability who can perform the job's essential functions, with or without a reasonable accommodation.

Reasonable accommodation. Assistance (technological or otherwise) or change to the workplace or job that allows the employee to perform the essential functions of the job.

Recertification. A subsequent certification of an employee's serious health condition.

Reduced-schedule leave. FMLA leave taken by working fewer hours per day or fewer days per week than usual.

Regulations. Interpretations of a law written by the federal agency responsible for its enforcement and administration.

Reinstatement. Restoration of an employee to his or her original position or an equivalent position when the employee returns from leave.

Salaried employee. An employee earning the same amount each week, regardless of how many hours the employee works or the quality or quantity of work performed. To be salaried, the employee must earn at least $455 per week.

Second opinion. A second medical certification, from a health care provider of the employer's choosing.

Secondary employer. A joint employer that does not have the authority to hire and fire the employee seeking leave, place the employee in a particular position, assign work to the employee, make payroll, and provide employment benefits.

Serious health condition. An illness, injury, impairment, or physical or mental condition that involves 1) inpatient care at a hospital, hospice, or residential medical care facility; 2) incapacity for more than three calendar days with continuing treatment by a health care provider; 3) incapacity due to pregnancy or prenatal care; 4) incapacity or treatment for a chronic serious health condition; 5) permanent or long-term incapacity for a condition for which treatment may not be effective (such as a terminal illness); or 6) absence for multiple treatments for either restorative surgery following an injury or accident or a condition that would require an absence of more than three days if not treated.

Spouses. A couple married under the laws of the state in which they reside.

Status report. An employee's report to the employer, while on FMLA leave, on his or her status and intent to return to work.

Substitution of paid leave. Using accrued paid leave provided by the employer's policies during FMLA leave.

Temporary disability insurance. A state insurance program that provides partial wage replacement while an employee is unable to work due to a temporary disability, including pregnancy.

Termination. End of employment by any means other than resignation, retirement, or disability.

Third opinion. A third medical certification, from a health care provider chosen jointly by the employer and the employee, which breaks the tie when the first and second medical certifications conflict as to whether the employee has a serious health condition.

Title VII. The federal law that prohibits discrimination in employment on the basis race, color, national origin, sex (including pregnancy), and religion.

Undue hardship. A reasonable accommodation that would cause significant difficulty or expense, considering the nature and cost of the accommodation, the size and financial resources of the business and the facility where the employee works, the structure of the business, and the effect the accommodation would have on the business.

Unforeseeable need for leave. A reason for FMLA leave that is not known in advance, such as injuries caused by an accident, a sudden illness, premature birth, or another medical emergency.

Uniformed Services Employment and Reemployment Rights Act (USERRA). A federal law that provides certain job protections to members of the uniformed services, including the right to take leave for military service.

Workers' compensation. An insurance program run by the states, which provides wage replacement, reimbursement for medical bills, and other benefits to employees who suffer work-related injuries or illnesses.

Worksite. The company location where an employee works, which may include a "campus" of buildings grouped together or unconnected buildings used by a company within a reasonable geographic vicinity (for example, within the city limits).

State Laws and Departments of Labor

This appendix summarizes basic information about each state's family and medical leave laws. We have included only laws that apply to private employers; laws that apply to government employers are not listed here. If your state is not included, it currently has no applicable leave laws.

We have not included all state leave laws, only those that provide for family and medical leave. For example, we have not included state laws that require employers to give leave for military service, jury duty, or voting.

The following categories of laws are included (each is explained in more detail in Chapter 11):

- **Family and medical leave laws.** These laws provide leave similar to the FMLA, such as leave for the employee's own serious health condition, leave to care for a seriously ill family member, and parental leave.

- **Pregnancy disability leave laws.** These laws provide leave when a woman is disabled by pregnancy, childbirth, and related conditions.

- **Adoption leave laws.** These laws provide leave for adoption, generally by requiring employers who offer leave for childbirth to make the same leave available to adoptive parents.

- **Small necessities laws.** These laws provide leave for activities relating to a child's school and/or to take a child or elderly relative to routine medical and dental appointments.

- **Domestic violence leave laws.** These laws provide leave for an employee who has been, or whose family member has been, a victim of domestic violence.

We provide some basic information on each law, including which employers are covered, which employees are eligible for leave, how much leave must be provided, and for what purposes. We have not included every detail about every law—for example, what constitutes a "serious health condition" under the state's rules, what a medical certification must include, whether employers have posting or record-keeping requirements, and so on. To find out more about your state's laws, contact your state's department of labor (contact information is at the end of this appendix). If you have any questions about how the FMLA interacts with your state's laws, consult with an experienced employment lawyer.

California

Family and Medical Leave (Cal. Gov't. Code § 12945.2)

Covered Employers: Employers with at least 50 employees.

Eligible Employees: Employees who have worked for at least one year and at least 1,250 hours in the 12 months preceding leave.

Types of Leave: For the birth, adoption, or foster placement of a child; for the employee's own serious health condition; or to care for a family member with a serious health condition. Disability for pregnancy, childbirth, and related conditions is not covered. If both parents work for the same employer, they may be limited to a total of 12 weeks of leave for the birth, adoption, or foster placement of a child.

Amount of Leave: 12 weeks in a 12-month period.

Family Members: Same as FMLA, plus domestic partners and children of domestic partners.

Procedural Requirements

- **Notice:** If need for leave is foreseeable, employee must provide reasonable advance notice. This means notice 30 days in advance or as soon as is practicable.

- **Certification:** The employer may require an employee who takes leave for a serious health condition to provide a certification from a health care provider. The state has its own certification form.

- **Paid Leave:** The employee may request, or the employer may require the employee, to substitute accrued paid leave, except that accrued sick leave need not be used for any purpose not included in the employer's policy.

Pregnancy Disability Leave (Cal. Govt. Code § 12945)

Covered Employers: Employers with at least five employees.

Eligible Employees: All employees of covered employers.

Reasons for Leave: Disability relating to pregnancy, childbirth, or related conditions.

Amount of Leave: A reasonable period, not to exceed four months.

Procedural Requirements

- **Notice:** Employer may require the employee to give reasonable notice of the need and expected duration of leave.

- **Paid Leave:** Employee may use accrued vacation leave.

Small Necessities Law (Cal. Lab. Code. § 230.8)

Covered Employers: Employers with at least 25 employees.

Eligible Employees: All employees of covered employers.

Reasons for Leave: To participate in activities at the child's school or daycare.

Amount of Leave: Forty hours of unpaid leave in any 12-month period, not to exceed eight hours in a single month. If both parents work for the same employer, employer may prohibit them from using this leave at the same time.

Procedural Requirements

- **Notice:** Employee must give reasonable notice of the need for leave.

- **Certification:** Employer may require employee to provide documentation from the school or daycare.

- **Paid Leave:** Employee must use accrued vacation, personal leave, or compensatory time off, if available.

Domestic Violence Leave (Cal. Lab. Code §§ 230 & 230.1)

Covered Employers: All employers; employers with at least 25 employees must provide leave for additional reasons.

Eligible Employees: Any employee who is the victim of sexual assault or domestic violence.

Reasons for Leave

- **All Employers:** For the employee to obtain a restraining order or seek other judicial relief for the employee or his or her child.

- **Employers With 25 Employees:** For the employee to:
  - seek medical treatment

- obtain services from a rape crisis center or domestic violence shelter or program
- get counseling
- engage in safety planning and/or relocate.

Amount of Leave: None stated. The law does not create a right to leave beyond that provided in the FMLA

Procedural Requirements

- **Notice:** Employee must give reasonable advance notice, unless it isn't feasible.

- **Certification:** Employer may require employee to provide certification, which can be a court order, police report, or documentation from an advocate, health care provider, or counselor.

- **Paid Leave:** Employee may elect to substitute any type of accrued paid leave that covers the employee's reason for leave.

Temporary Disability Insurance

California has a state temporary disability insurance program, funded by withholdings from employees' paychecks. Eligible employees who are unable to work due to a temporarily disability (including pregnancy) can receive up to 55% of their wages. For more information, go to the state's website, www. edd.ca.gov/direp/diind.htm.

Paid Family Leave

California's temporary disability insurance program also funds paid family leave. Eligible employees may collect the same benefits available for a temporary disability for up to six weeks in order to care for a seriously ill parent, spouse, domestic partner, or child, or to bond with a new child. For more information, go to the state's website, www.edd.ca.gov/direp/pflind.asp.

Colorado

Domestic Violence Leave (Col. Rev. Stat. § 24-34-402.7)

Covered Employers: Employers with at least 50 employees.

Eligible Employees: Employees who have worked at least 12 months and have been the victim of domestic violence, sexual assault, domestic abuse, or stalking.

Reasons for Leave: For the employee to:

- seek medical treatment or counseling for the employee or his or her children
- seek a civil protection order
- seek new housing or make an existing home secure, or
- seek legal assistance or attend court-related proceedings.

Amount of Leave: Three days in a 12-month period.

Procedural Requirements

- **Notice:** Except in cases of imminent danger, the employee must provide advance notice as required by employer's policies.
- **Certification:** Employer may require documentation.
- **Paid Leave:** Employer may require employee to use up accrued paid leave before taking unpaid leave pursuant to this law.

Adoption Leave (Col. Rev. Stat. § 19-5-211)

Covered Employers: All employers.

Eligible Employees: All employees.

Leave Provided: Employer that provides parental leave following the birth of a biological child must make the same amount of leave available to adoptive parents. This requirement does not apply to stepparent adoptions.

Connecticut

Family and Medical Leave (Conn. Gen. Stat. §§ 31-51kk to 31-51qq)

Covered Employers: Employers with at least 75 employees, to be determined annually on October 1.

Eligible Employees: Employees who have worked for at least one year and at least 1,000 hours in the 12 months preceding leave.

Types of Leave: For the birth, adoption, or foster placement of a child; for the employee's own serious health condition; to care for a family member with a serious health condition; or for organ or bone marrow donation.

Amount of Leave: 16 weeks in any 24-month period. The 24-month period begins on the first day of an employee's leave. Spouses who work for the same employer are entitled to a total of 16 weeks for the birth, adoption, or foster placement of a child and to care for a parent with a serious health condition.

Family Members: Same as FMLA, plus parents-in-law, domestic partners, and domestic partners' children.

Procedural Requirements

- **Notice:** Employee must give 30 days' notice of foreseeable leave for the birth or placement of a child or for planned medical treatment; if 30 days' notice cannot be given, employee must give such notice as is practicable.

- **Certification:** The employer may require an employee who takes leave for a serious health condition to provide a certification from a health care provider. The state has its own certification form.

- **Paid Leave:** The employee may request, or the employer may require the employee, to substitute accrued paid leave, except that accrued sick leave need not be used for any purpose not included in the employer's policy.

- **Benefits:** Employer is not required to provide continued benefits while employee is on leave.

- **Reinstatement:** An employee must be reinstated to his or her original position; if it is not available, the employee may be returned to an equivalent position. An employee who is not medically able to perform his or her original job when leave ends has a right to be transferred to work suitable to the employee's physical condition, if such work is available.

Pregnancy Disability Leave (Conn. Gen. Stat. §§ 46a-60(7))

Covered Employers: Employers with at least three employees.

Eligible Employees: All employees of covered employers.

Reasons for Leave: Disability relating to pregnancy, childbirth, or related conditions.

Amount of Leave: A "reasonable" leave of absence.

Reinstatement: Employee is entitled to be restored to the same or an equivalent position, unless the employer's circumstances have so changed as to make this impossible or unreasonable.

District of Columbia

Family and Medical Leave (D.C. Code §§ 32-501 and following)

Covered Employers: Employers with at least 20 employees.

Eligible Employees: Employees who have worked for at least one year and at least 1,000 hours in the previous 12 months.

Types of Leave

- **Family Leave:** For the birth, adoption, or foster placement of a child; for the permanent placement of a child for whom the employee permanently assumes and discharges parental responsibility; or to care for a family member with a serious health condition.

- **Medical Leave:** For the employee's own serious health condition.

Amount of Leave: Sixteen weeks of family leave plus 16 weeks of medical leave in any 24-month period. Leave for birth, adoption, or placement of a child must be taken within 12 months of child's arrival. If two family members work for the same employer, they can be limited to a total of 16 weeks of family leave and can take no more than four weeks of such leave at the same time.

Family Members: Same as FMLA, plus anyone related by blood, custody, or marriage, and anyone sharing the employee's residence with whom the employee has a committed relationship.

Procedural Requirements

- **Notice:** If the need for leave is foreseeable, the employee must provide reasonable notice.

- **Certification:** The employer may require an employee taking leave for a serious health condition to provide a medical certification.

- **Paid Leave:** The employee may substitute accrued paid leave if the type of leave the employee is taking is covered by the employer's policy.

- **Reinstatement:** Similar to the FMLA, but key employees are defined as the top five highest-paid employees of an employer with fewer than 50 employees. Employer may deny reinstatement if it is under contract to provide work or services; the employee's absence prohibits the employer from completing the contract in accordance with its terms; failing to complete the contract will cause substantial economic injury; and the employer, after making reasonable attempts, could not find a temporary replacement for the employee.

Small Necessities Law (D.C. Code §§ 32-1201 and following)

Covered Employers: All employers.

Eligible Employees: Employees who have worked for the employer for at least 12 months.

Reasons for Leave: To participate in school-related events, including activities sponsored by either a school or an associated organization such as a parent-teacher association. Activities may include meetings with a teacher or counselor as well as student performances and sports activities in which the employee is a participant, not merely a spectator. Employer may deny a request for leave only if it would disrupt the employer's business and make the achievement of production or service delivery unusually difficult.

Family Members: Those who may take leave include not only parents, guardians, and stepparents, but also a child's aunts, uncles, and grandparents.

Amount of Leave: Twenty-four hours of unpaid leave in any 12-month period.

Procedural Requirements

- **Notice:** Employee must provide notice at least ten calendar days in advance, unless the need for leave cannot be reasonably foreseen.

- **Paid Leave:** Employee may substitute accrued paid vacation or other appropriate paid leave.

Hawaii

Family and Medical Leave (Haw. Rev. Stat. §§ 398-1 to 398-11)

Covered Employers: Employers with at least 100 employees.

Eligible Employees: Employees who have worked for at least six consecutive months.

Types of Leave: Employee may take leave to care for a family member with a serious health condition or to care for a newly born or adopted child. Leave is not provided for employee's own serious health condition. Leave for a new child must be taken within a year of the child's arrival.

Amount of Leave: Four weeks in any calendar year. Spouses who work for the same employer do not have to combine leave; each is entitled to four weeks.

Family Members: Same family members as FMLA, plus parents-in-law, grandparents, grandparents-in-law, and reciprocal beneficiaries.

Procedural Requirements

- **Notice:** If the need for leave is foreseeable, employee must give written notice 30 days in advance; if that isn't practicable, employee must give at least two days' advance verbal notice. For unforeseeable leave, employee must give leave as soon as practicable. Employee must provide notice of the reason, start date, and anticipated duration of leave.

- **Certification:** Employer may require employee to provide a written certification as follows: from health care provider or family court for the birth of a child; from a recognized adoption agency, the attorney handling the adoption, or the individual designated by the birth parent to select and approve the adopted family for the adoption of a child; or from a health care provider for leave to care for a family member. The state has its own certification form.

- **Paid Leave:** Employee may request, or employer may require employee, to use accrued paid leave, but employees may use no more than ten days of sick leave per year unless a collective bargaining agreement provides otherwise.

Benefits: Employers are not specifically required to continue benefits during leave.

Reinstatement: The state has no key employee exception.

Domestic Violence Leave (Haw. Rev. Stat. §§ 378-71-74)

Covered Employers: Employers with at least 50 employees.

Eligible Employees: Any employee who has worked at least six consecutive months and who is—or whose minor child is—a victim of domestic abuse, sexual assault, or stalking.

Reasons for Leave: Leave is allowed to:

- seek medical attention
- obtain victim services
- get counseling
- temporarily or permanently relocate, or
- take legal action.

Amount of Leave: A "reasonable period," up to 30 days in a calendar year if the employer has at least 50 employees, or up to five days for smaller employers.

Procedural Requirements

- **Notice:** Employee must give reasonable notice of need for leave unless prohibited by imminent danger. Employer may ask employee to report once a week on status and intent to return to work.

- **Certification:** If leave is sought for medical attention, employer may require certification from health care provider. If leave is for nonmedical reasons and lasts no more than five days, employer may require employee to provide a signed statement confirming that the reason for leave qualified under the law. Employee who takes more than five days of leave for nonmedical purposes may be required to provide a police or court record or a signed statement from a victim services organization, an attorney or advocate, or a medical or other professional from whom the victim has sought assistance for issues relating to domestic violence.

- **Paid Leave:** Employee must exhaust all other available paid and unpaid leave before these provisions apply.

Temporary Disability Insurance (TDI)

Hawaii has a state temporary disability insurance program. Eligible employees who are unable to work due to a temporarily disability (including pregnancy) can receive compensation. Employers may self-insure by adopting a particular type of sick/disability leave program. For detailed information, go to the state's TDI website, www.hawaii.gov/labor/dcd/abouttdi.shtml.

Illinois

Small Necessities Law (820 Ill. Comp. Stat. § 147/1)

Covered Employers: Employers with at least 50 employees.

Eligible Employees: Employees who have worked for at least six consecutive months immediately preceding the leave request, and for at least as many hours per week, on average, as one-half of a full-time position.

Reasons for Leave: To attend school conferences or classroom activities relating to their children if they cannot be rescheduled during nonwork hours.

Amount of Leave: Eight hours of unpaid leave in any school year, with no more than four hours in one day.

Procedural Requirements

- **Notice:** Employee must ask for leave in writing at least seven days in advance. In an emergency, no more than 24 hours' notice may be required.

- **Certification:** Employee must provide verification (to be provided in writing by the school) of the school visit to the employer within two business days after taking leave.

- **Paid Leave:** Employees may not take this leave unless they have exhausted their accrued vacation, personal leave, and any other type of time off except for sick or disability leave. If employee takes unpaid leave, employer must allow employee to make up the time, if employee requests it and there is a reasonable opportunity to do so.

Domestic Violence Leave (820 Ill. Comp. Stat. § 180/1)

Covered Employers: Employers with at least 50 employees.

Eligible Employees: Any full-time or part-time employee who is a victim of domestic or sexual violence or has a family or household member who is a victim of domestic or sexual violence.

Reasons for Leave: Leave is allowed to:

- seek medical treatment
- obtain services from a victim services organization
- get counseling

- engage in safety planning, relocate, or otherwise take steps to increase the victim's safety, or

- seek legal assistance or remedies.

Amount of Leave: Up to 12 weeks of leave in a 12-month period; the law states that it does not intend to create rights beyond those provided by the FMLA.

Procedural Requirements

- **Notice:** Employee must provide at least 48 hours' notice, unless it's not practicable.

- **Certification:** Employer may require employee to provide certification that employee or family member is a victim of domestic violence and the employee is taking leave for a covered purpose. Employee must provide a sworn statement and documents such as a police or court record, a written statement from a person or group from whom the employee has sought assistance, and other written corroboration of the employee's need for leave.

- **Paid Leave:** Employee may elect to substitute any type of accrued paid or unpaid leave.

Iowa

Pregnancy Disability Leave (Iowa Code § 216.6(2))

Covered Employers: Employers with at least four employees.

Eligible Employees: All employees of covered employers.

Reasons for Leave: Disability relating to pregnancy, childbirth, or related conditions.

Amount of Leave: Unless employee is otherwise entitled to time off via sick leave, disability leave, or temporary disability insurance, employer must allow employee to take leave for the period of time she is disabled by the above conditions or for eight weeks, whichever is shorter.

Procedural Requirements

- **Notice:** Employee must provide "timely" notice of need for leave, and employer must approve any change in the dates of leave.

- **Certification:** Employer may require employee to submit medical certification stating that she is unable to reasonably perform the job's duties due to pregnancy-related disability.

Kentucky

Adoption Leave (Ky. Rev. Stat. § 337.015)

Covered Employers: All employers.

Eligible Employees: All employees.

- **Types of Leave:** For placement of an adoptive child under the age of seven.

Amount of Leave: Reasonable personal leave, not to exceed six weeks.

Procedural Requirements

- **Notice:** Employee must make written request for leave.

Louisiana

Pregnancy Disability Leave (La. Rev. Stat. §§ 23:341 and 23:342)

Covered Employers: Employers with more than 25 employees.

Eligible Employees: All employees of covered employers.

Reasons for Leave: Disability relating to pregnancy, childbirth, or related conditions.

Amount of Leave: Up to six weeks for normal pregnancy and childbirth; up to four months for more-disabling pregnancies.

Procedural Requirements

- **Notice:** Employer may require employee to give reasonable notice of date leave will begin and estimated duration of leave.

- **Paid Leave:** Employee is entitled to use accrued vacation time during leave.

Small Necessities Law (La. Rev. Stat. §§ 23:1015 and following)

Covered Employers: All employers.

Eligible Employees: All employees.

Reasons for Leave: To attend, observe, or participate in conferences or classroom activities relating to their children (in school or daycare) if they cannot be rescheduled during nonwork hours.

Amount of Leave: Sixteen hours of unpaid leave in any 12-month period.

Procedural Requirements

- **Notice:** Employee must give reasonable notice of need for leave and make a reasonable effort to schedule leave so it doesn't unduly disrupt the employer's operations.

- **Paid Leave:** Employee may substitute accrued vacation or other appropriate paid leave for this time off.

Maine

Family and Medical Leave (Me. Rev. Stat. tit. 26, §§ 843 and following)

Covered Employers: Employers with at least 15 employees.

Eligible Employees: Employees who has worked for at least 12 consecutive months and works at a site with at least 15 employees.

Types of Leave: For the birth or adoption of a child; for the employee's own serious health condition; to care for a family member with a serious health condition; or to be an organ donor.

Amount of Leave: Ten consecutive weeks in a two-year period.

Family Members: Same family members as FMLA, plus parents-in-law.

Procedural Requirements

- **Notice:** Employee must give 30 days' notice of the date when leave will begin and end, unless a medical emergency prevents the employee from doing so.

- **Medical Certifications:** Employer may ask employee to provide a written certification from a physician verifying the amount of leave requested; if employee relies in good faith on treatment by prayer or spiritual means in accordance with the tenets or practice of a recognized church or religious denomination, employee may submit a certification from an accredited practitioner of those healing methods.

- **Benefits:** Employer must make it possible for the employee to continue health care coverage at employee's expense.

Domestic Violence Leave (Me. Rev. Stat. tit. 26, § 850)

Covered Employers: All employers.

Eligible Employees: Any employee who, or whose parent, spouse, or child, has been a victim of violence, assault, sexual assault, stalking, or domestic violence.

Reasons for Leave: For the employee to:

- prepare for and attend court proceedings
- receive medical treatment or attend to medical treatment for a victim who is the employee's child, spouse, or parent, or
- obtain necessary services to deal with a crisis caused by domestic violence, stalking, or sexual assault.

Amount of Leave: "Reasonable and necessary" leave. Employer does not have to grant leave if the employee's absence would cause undue hardship; the employee doesn't request leave within a reasonable time under the circumstances; or leave is impractical, unreasonable, or unnecessary under the circumstances.

Procedural Requirements

- **Notice:** Employee must give notice within a reasonable time under the circumstances.
- **Certification:** Employer may require documentation of a family relationship with the victim.

Maryland

Adoption Leave (Md. Code [Lab. & Empl.] § 3-802)

Covered Employers: All employers.

Eligible Employees: All employees.

Leave Provided: Employer that provides paid parental leave following the birth of a child must make the same amount of leave available to adoptive parents.

Massachusetts

Small Necessities Law (Mass. Gen. Laws ch. 149 § 52D)

Covered Employers: Employers with at least 50 employees.

Eligible Employees: Employees who are eligible under the FMLA.

Reasons for Leave: Employee may take leave to:

- participate in school activities directly related to the educational advancement of the employee's child, such as parent-teacher conferences or interviewing for a new school

- accompany the employee's child to routine medical or dental appointments, and

- accompany an elderly relative (someone who is related to the employee by blood or marriage and is at least 60 years old) to routine medical or dental appointments or appointments for other professional services relating to the relative's care.

This leave is in addition to FMLA leave.

Amount of Leave: Twenty-fours hours in any 12-month period.

Procedural Requirements

- **Notice:** Employee must ask for leave in writing at least seven days in advance; if the need for leave is not foreseeable, employee must provide as much notice as is practicable.

- **Certification:** Employer may require employee to provide certification of the need for leave.

- **Paid Leave:** Employees may substitute, or employer may require employee to substitute, accrued paid leave for this time off; paid sick leave may be used only as allowed by the employer's policies.

Maternity Leave (Mass. Gen. Laws ch. 149, § 105D)

Covered Employers: Employers with at least six employees.

Eligible Employees: Female employees who have completed the employer's probationary period or have worked for the employer for three months (if there is no probationary period).

Reasons for Leave: For birth or adoption of a child.

Amount of Leave: Up to eight weeks of leave.

Procedural Requirements

- **Notice:** Employee must provide at least two weeks' notice of her expected departure date and intent to return to work.

- **Benefits:** Employer need not pay to continue employee's benefits unless employer does so for employees on other types of leave.

Minnesota

Family and Medical Leave (Minn. Stat. §§ 181-940 and following)

Covered Employers: Employers with at least 21 employees.

Eligible Employees: Employees who have worked at least half-time for one year.

Types of Leave: For the birth or adoption of a child.

Amount of Leave: Six weeks. Leave must begin within six weeks of the child's arrival; if child has to stay in the hospital longer than the mother, leave may begin within six weeks of the child's discharge.

Procedural Requirements

- **Notice:** Leave must begin on date requested by employee, but employer may adopt reasonable policies regarding the timing of requests for leave. If employee has been on leave for more than a month, employee must give two weeks' notice of return to work.

- **Benefits:** Employer must make group health benefits available to employee during leave, but need not pay for them.

Small Necessities Law (Minn. Stat. Ann. § 181.9412)

Covered Employers: Employers with at least two employees.

Eligible Employees: Employees who have worked for the employer for at least 12 months.

Reasons for Leave: To attend school conferences or other school-related activities for the employee's child, if they cannot be scheduled during nonwork hours.

Amount of Leave: Sixteen hours of unpaid leave in any 12-month period.

Procedural Requirements

- **Notice:** If need for leave is foreseeable, employee must provide reasonable prior notice and attempt to schedule leave so as not to unduly disrupt the employer's operations.

- **Paid Leave:** Employee may substitute accrued paid vacation or other appropriate paid leave.

Montana

Pregnancy Disability Leave (Mont. Code Ann. §§ 49-2-310 and 49-2-311)

Covered Employers: All employers.

Eligible Employees: All employees.

Reasons for Leave: Pregnancy-related disability.

Amount of Leave: "Reasonable" leave of absence for pregnancy.

Reinstatement: Employer must reinstate employee to the same or an equivalent position, unless the employer's circumstances have changed so much that it would be impossible or unreasonable to do so.

Nebraska

Adoption Leave (Neb. Rev. Stat. § 48-234)

Covered Employers: All employers.

Eligible Employees: All employees.

Leave Provided: Employer that provides parental leave following the birth of a child must make the same leave available to parents who adopt a child under the age of nine or a special needs child under the age of 19. Employer does not have to provide leave for stepparent or foster parent adoptions.

Nevada

Small Necessities Law (Nev. Rev. Stat. § 392.490)

Covered Employers: All employers.

Eligible Employees: All employees.

Reasons for Leave: Employer may not fire, or threaten to fire, an employee who appears at a conference requested by an administrator of his or her child's school, or who is notified, during work hours, of an emergency regarding the child.

New Hampshire

Pregnancy Disability Leave (N.H. Rev. Stat. § 354-A:7)

Covered Employers: Employers with at least six employees.

Eligible Employees: All employees of covered employers.

Reasons for Leave: Disability relating to pregnancy, childbirth, or related conditions.

Amount of Leave: The period of time during which the employee has a disability relating to the above conditions.

Reinstatement: Employee is entitled to be restored to the same or a comparable position, unless business necessity makes this impossible or unreasonable.

New York

Adoption Leave (N.Y. Lab. Law § 201-c)

Covered Employers: All employers.

Eligible Employees: All employees.

Leave Provided: Employer that provides parental leave for the birth of a biological child must make the same amount of leave available to adopt a child who is preschool age or younger, or up to age 18, if the child is disabled.

Temporary Disability Benefits (TDI)

New York has a state temporary disability insurance program. Eligible employees who are unable to work due to a temporarily disability (including pregnancy) can receive up to 50% of their wages. For detailed information, go to the state website for workers' compensation, www.wcb.state.ny.us. Select "Employers," then "Disability Benefits Coverage."

North Carolina

Domestic Violence Leave (N.C. Gen. Stat. § 50B-5.5)

Covered Employers: All employers.

Eligible Employees: All employees.

Amount of Leave: Employer may not fire, discipline, demote, or refuse to promote an employee who takes "reasonable time" off work.

Reasons for Leave: To obtain or attempt to obtain an order of protection from domestic violence for the employee or a minor child.

Procedural Requirements

- **Notice:** Employee must follow employers' usual time-off procedures, including advance notice, except in an emergency.

- **Certification:** Employer may require documentation of an emergency that prevented the employee from following usual time-off procedures, or any other information available to the employee that supports the reason for leave.

Small Necessities Law (N.C. Gen. Stat. § 95-28.3)

Covered Employers: All employers.

Eligible Employees: All employees.

Reasons for Leave: To attend or otherwise be involved in a child's school.

Amount of Leave: Four hours of unpaid leave per year.

Procedural Requirements

- **Notice:** Employer may require employee to provide written request for leave, 48 hours in advance. Leave shall be taken at a time mutually agreed upon by employer and employee.

- **Certification:** Employer may require employee to provide written verification from the child's school that the employee attended or was otherwise involved when leave was taken.

Oregon

Family and Medical Leave (Or. Rev. Stat. §§ 659A.150 and following)

Covered Employers: Employers with at least 25 employees.

Eligible Employees

- **Parental Leave:** Employee must have worked at least 180 days for the employer before leave is scheduled to begin.

- **All Other Types of Leave:** Employee must have worked at least 180 days for the employer and at least 25 hours per week during the 180 days immediately preceding the start of leave.

Types of Leave

- **Parental Leave:** For the birth or adoption of a child, or the placement of a foster child.

- **Serious Health Condition Leave:** To care for a family member with a serious health condition or for the employee's own serious health condition.

- **Pregnancy Disability Leave:** For prenatal care or pregnancy disability.

- **Sick Child Leave:** To care for a sick child who does not have a serious health condition but requires home care. Employer does not have to allow employee to take sick child leave if another family member is willing and able to care for the child.

Amount of Leave: Twelve weeks within any one-year period, with the following additional entitlements:

- An employee who takes 12 weeks of any other leave may take an additional 12 weeks of pregnancy disability leave.

- An employee who takes 12 weeks of parental leave may take an additional 12 weeks of sick child leave.

- An employee may combine these entitlements to take up to 36 weeks of leave: 12 for pregnancy disability, 12 for parental leave, and 12 for sick child leave.

Two family members (including spouses) who work for the same employer are each entitled to 12 weeks of leave, but the employer does not have to allow them to take this leave at the same time unless (1) both have serious health conditions; (2) one has a serious health condition and the other needs to care for him or her; or (3) one has a serious health condition and the other needs to care for a child who has a serious health condition.

Family Members: Same family members as FMLA, plus parents-in-law, domestic partners, and the parents and children of domestic partners.

Procedural Requirements

- **Notice:** Employee must give 30 days' advance written notice, including an explanation of the need for leave, unless leave is taken for an emergency, which requires written or verbal notice within 24 hours of start of leave. If employee fails to give notice as required, the employer may reduce the employee's remaining leave entitlement by up to three weeks.

- **Certification:** Employer may request medical verification of the need for leave (other than parental leave and sick child leave); employer must pay any costs not covered by insurance. For sick child leave, employer may request medical verification after the employee has taken leave on three separate occasions within the leave year.

- **Paid Leave:** Employee may use, and employers may require employees to use, accrued vacation for any type of leave and accrued sick leave for any reason allowed by the employer's policy and for parental leave.

- **Benefits:** Employer may, but is not required to, continue health benefits during leave. If employer chooses to continue benefits, employee may be required to pay only the employee's usual share of the premium.

Reinstatement: If the employee's job was eliminated during leave, the employee is entitled to any available, equivalent position. If no equivalent position is available at the employee's former worksite, the employee may be restored to an equivalent position within 20 miles.

Rhode Island

Family and Medical Leave (R.I. Gen. Laws §§ 28-41-1 and following)

Covered Employers: Employers with at least 50 employees.

Eligible Employees: Full-time employees who average at least 30 hours of work per week and have been employed for at least 12 consecutive months.

Types of Leave

- **Family Leave:** For the employee's own serious illness or to care for a family member with a serious illness.
- **Parental Leave:** For the birth or adoption of a child.

Amount of Leave: Thirteen weeks in any two calendar years.

Family Members: Same family members as FMLA, plus parents-in-law.

Procedural Requirements

- **Notice:** Employee must give 30 days' advance notice of the date when parental or family leave shall begin and end, unless a medical emergency prevents the employee from doing so. Notice must be in writing, must verify the truthfulness of the employee's factual statements, and must include a detailed description of the circumstances the entitle the employee to leave.
- **Certification:** Employer may ask employee to provide a written certification from a physician caring for the employee or family member.
- **Paid Leave:** Employer that allows employees to use sick leave following the birth of a child must also allow adoptive parents to use sick leave for the placement of a child.
- **Benefits:** Before starting leave, the employee must pay the employer what it will cost to pay the premiums to keep the employee's health benefits in effect during leave; the employer must return this payment to the employee within ten days after the employee returns to work.

Small Necessities Law (R.I. Gen. Laws §§ 28-41-12)

Covered Employers: Employers that have at least 50 employees.

Eligible Employees: Full-time employees who average at least 30 hours of work per week and have been employed by the same employer for at least 12 consecutive months.

Reasons for Leave: To attend school conferences or other school-related activities for the employee's child.

Amount of Leave: Ten hours of unpaid leave in any 12-month period.

Procedural Requirements

- **Notice:** Employee must provide at least 24 hours' notice of need for leave and must make a reasonable effort to schedule leave so as not to unduly disrupt employer's operations.

- **Paid Leave:** Employee may substitute accrued paid vacation or other appropriate paid leave.

Temporary Disability Insurance (TDI)

Rhode Island has a state temporary disability insurance program, funded by withholdings from employees' paychecks. Eligible employees who are unable to work due to a temporarily disability (including pregnancy) can receive up to 4.62% of their wages for 30 full weeks. Employees may also receive salary, paid sick leave, or vacation time from their employer while receiving temporary disability payments, and may receive benefits while working part-time due to a temporary disability. For detailed information, go to the state's TDI website, www.dlt.ri.gov/tdi.

Tennessee

Family and Medical Leave Law (Tenn. Code § 4-21-408)

Covered Employers: Employers with at least 100 full-time employees at the job-site or location where the employee works.

Eligible Employees: Employees who have worked full-time for at least 12 months.

Types of Leave: For pregnancy, childbirth, nursing an infant, and adoption.

Amount of Leave: Up to four months.

Procedural Requirements

- **Notice:** Employee must give at least three months' notice to be entitled to reinstatement; employee who cannot give three months' notice because of a medical emergency or change in the placement date shall not be denied reinstatement.

- **Benefits:** Employer need not pay to continue health benefits, unless it does so for employees on other types of leave.

Reinstatement: Reinstatement is not required in either of the following cases:

- The employee's job is so unique that the employer could not obtain a temporary replacement.

- The employee worked for another employer during leave.

The employer must notify the employee if it denies reinstatement for one of these reasons.

Vermont

Family and Medical Leave Law (21 Vt. Stat. §§ 470 and following)
Covered Employers

- **Parental Leave:** Employers with at least 10 employees.
- **Family Leave:** Employers with at least 15 employees.

Eligible Employees: Employees who have been continuously employed for one year, for an average of at least 30 hours per week.

Types of Leave

- **Parental Leave:** (1) During the employee's pregnancy and following the birth of an employee's child, (2) within a year after the initial placement of a child up to 16 years old for adoption.
- **Family Leave:** For the employee's own illness or to care for the employee's family member.

Amount of Leave: 12 weeks in a 12-month period. Spouses working for same employer are entitled to 12 weeks each; they need not combine leave.

Family Members: Includes all family members covered by FMLA plus parents-in-law and employee's civil union partner.

Procedural Requirements

- **Notice:** Employee must give reasonable written notice of intent to take leave, including the date leave is expected to begin and the expected duration; employer may not require more than six weeks' notice for birth or adoption of a child. Employee must provide reasonable notice of need to extend leave.
- **Certification:** Employer may require certification.
- **Paid Leave:** Employee may substitute up to six weeks of accrued paid leave for unpaid parental and family leave; employer may not require substitution.
- **Benefits:** All benefits continue during leave, not just health insurance; employee must pay usual share of the premiums.

Small Necessities Law (21 Vt. Stat. § 472a)

Covered Employers: Employers with at least 15 employees.

Eligible Employees: Employees who have been continuously employed for one year, for an average of at least 30 hours per week.

Amount of Leave: Twenty-four hours in a 12-month period; not more than four hours may be taken in any 30-day period. Employer may require employee to take at least two hours of leave at a time.

Reasons for Leave: For the employee to:

- participate in school activities directly related to the academic educational advancement of the employee's child, stepchild, foster child, or ward

- attend or accompany a family member to routine medical or dental appointments

- accompany the employee's parent, spouse, or parent-in-law to appointments for professional services related to their care and well-being, and

- respond to a medical emergency involving a family member.

Procedural Requirements

- **Notice:** Employee must provide the earliest possible notice, no fewer than seven days in advance, except for an emergency.

- **Paid Leave:** Employee may use accrued paid leave at the employer's discretion.

Washington

Family and Medical Leave Law (Wash. Rev. Code 49.78.010 and following)

Covered Employers: Employers with at least 50 employees.

Eligible Employees: Employees who have worked for at least a year and at least 1,250 hours during the previous year.

Types of Leave: For the birth, adoption, or foster placement of a child; for the employee's own serious health condition; or to care for a family member with a serious health condition. Parental leave must be taken within one year of the child's arrival.

Amount of Leave: Twelve weeks in a 12-month period. Spouses who work for the same employer may be limited to a combined total of 12 weeks of leave for the birth, adoption, or foster placement of a child and care for a parent with a serious health condition.

Procedural Requirements

- **Notice:** Employee must give 30 days' notice if the need for leave is foreseeable; such notice as is practicable otherwise.

- **Certification:** The employer may require the employee to provide a certification.

- **Benefits:** Unless required by a collective bargaining agreement or employer policy, the employee need not pay to continue the employee's health benefits. However, the employer must allow the employee to continue coverage, at the employee's expense.

Reinstatement: Employee who is reinstated to an equivalent position must be reinstated within 20 miles of the employee's original worksite.

Pregnancy Disability Leave (Wash. Admin. Code § 162-30-020)

Covered Employers: Employers with at least eight employees.

Eligible Employees: All employees of covered employers.

Reasons for Leave: Disability relating to pregnancy, childbirth, or related conditions.

Amount of Leave: For the period of disability. This time is in addition to the time provided under the FMLA and Washington's family and medical leave law.

Wisconsin

Family and Medical Leave Law (Wis. Stat. 103.10)

Covered Employers: Employers with at least 50 permanent employees.

Eligible Employees: Employees who have worked for more than 52 consecutive weeks and at least 1,000 hours in the preceding 52 weeks.

Types of Leave

- **Family Leave:** For birth, adoption, or to care for a family member with a serious health condition; does not cover foster care placements.

- **Medical Leave:** For the employee's own serious health condition that makes him or her unable to do the job.

Amount of Leave

- **Family Leave:** Up to eight weeks total, consisting of up to:

  - six weeks in a calendar year for birth or adoption (leave must begin within 16 weeks of the child's birth or placement), and

  - two weeks in a calendar year to care for a family member with a serious health condition.

- **Medical Leave:** Two weeks in a calendar year for the employee's serious health condition.

Family Members: Same family members as FMLA, plus parents-in-law.

Procedural Requirements

- **Notice:** Must be given in advance in a reasonable and practicable manner for planned medical treatment, birth, or placement of a child.

- **Certification:** Employer may require employee to submit certification.

- **Paid Leave:** Employee may elect to substitute accrued paid or unpaid leave of any other type provided by the employer.

Reinstatement: Wisconsin has no key employee exception.

State Departments of Labor

Alabama
Department of Industrial Relations
Montgomery, AL
334-242-8990
www.dir.state.al.us

Alaska
Department of Labor and Workforce
Development
Juneau, AK
907-465-5980
www.labor.state.ak.us

Arizona
Industrial Commission
Phoenix, AZ
602-542-4411
www.ica.state.az.us

Arkansas
Department of Labor
Little Rock, AR
501-682-4500
www.state.ar.us/labor

California
Department of Industrial Relations
San Francisco, CA
415-703-5070
www.dir.ca.gov

Colorado
Department of Labor and Employment
Denver, CO
303-318-8000
www.coworkforce.com

Connecticut
Labor Department
Wethersfield, CT
860-263-6505
www.ctdol.state.ct.us

Delaware
Department of Labor
Wilmington, DE
302-761-8000
www.delawareworks.com

District of Columbia
Department of Employment Services
Washington, DC
202-724-7000
http://does.ci.washington.dc.us

Florida
Agency for Workforce Innovation
Tallahassee, FL
850-245-7105
www.floridajobs.org or
www.myflorida.com

Georgia
Department of Labor
Atlanta, GA
404-232-7300
877-709-8185
www.dol.state.ga.us

Hawaii
Department of Labor and Industrial
Relations
Honolulu, HI
808-586-8844
http://hawaii.gov/labor

Idaho
Department of Labor
Boise, ID
208-332-3570
www.labor.state.id.us

Illinois
Department of Labor
Chicago, IL
312-793-2800
800-478-3998
www.state.il.us/agency/idol

Indiana
Department of Labor
Indianapolis, IN
317-232-2655
www.in.gov/labor

Iowa
Iowa Workforce Development
Des Moines, IA
515-281-5387
800-JOB-IOWA
www.iowaworkforce.org/labor

Kansas
Department of Human Resources
Office of Employment Standards
Topeka, KS
785-296-5000
www.dol.ks.gov

Kentucky
Department of Labor
Frankfort, KY
502-564-3070
http://labor.ky.gov

Louisiana
Department of Labor
Baton Rouge, LA
225-342-3111
www.ldol.state.la.us

Maine
Department of Labor
Augusta, ME
207-624-6400
www.state.me.us/labor

Maryland
Department of Labor, Licensing, and
Regulation
Division of Labor and Industry
Baltimore, MD
410-230-6001
www.dllr.state.md.us/labor

Massachusetts
Department of Labor and Workforce
Development
Boston, MA
617-727-6573
www.mass.gov/dol

Michigan
Department of Labor and Economic
Growth
Lansing, MI
517-373-1820
www.cis.state.mi.us or
www.michigan.gov/cis

Minnesota
Department of Labor and Industry
St. Paul, MN
651-284-5005
800-342-5354
www.doli.state.mn.us

Mississippi
Department of Employment Security
Jackson, MS
601-321-6000
www.mdes.ms.gov

Missouri
Department of Labor and Industrial
Relations
Jefferson City, MO
573-751-4091
www.dolir.mo.gov

Montana
Department of Labor and Industry
Helena, MT
406-444-2840
http://dli.state.mt.us

Nebraska
Department of Labor
Nebraska Workforce Development
Lincoln, NE
402-471-2239
Omaha, NE
402-595-3095
www.dol.state.ne.us

Nevada
Division of Industrial Relations
Carson City, NV
775-684-7260
http://dirweb.state.nv.us

New Hampshire
Department of Labor
Concord, NH
603-271-3176
www.labor.state.nh.us

New Jersey
Department of Labor and Workforce
Development
Labor Standards and Safety Enforcement
Trenton, NJ
609-292-2323
www.state.nj.us/labor

New Mexico
Labor and Industrial Division
Department of Labor
Santa Fe, NM
505-827-6875
Albuquerque, NM
505-222-4667
www.dol.state.nm.us

New York
Department of Labor
Albany, NY
518-457-9000
800-HIRE-992
www.labor.state.ny.us

North Carolina
Department of Labor
Raleigh, NC
919-733-7166
800-625-2267 (800-NC-LABOR)
www.nclabor.com

North Dakota
Department of Labor
Bismarck, ND
701-328-2660
800-582-8032
www.state.nd.us/labor

Ohio
Division of Labor and Worker Safety
Department of Commerce
Columbus, OH
614-644-2239
www.com.state.oh.us

Oklahoma
Department of Labor
Oklahoma City, OK
405-528-1500
888-269-5353
www.okdol.state.ok.us

Oregon

Bureau of Labor and Industries
Portland, OR
971-673-0761
www.boli.state.or.us

Pennsylvania

Department of Labor and Industry
Harrisburg, PA
717-787-5279
www.dli.state.pa.us

Rhode Island

Department of Labor and Training
Cranston, RI
401-462-8000
www.dlt.state.ri.us

South Carolina

Department of Labor, Licensing, and
Regulation
Columbia, SC
803-896-4300
www.llr.state.sc.us

South Dakota

Division of Labor and Management
Pierre, SD
605-773-3681
www.state.sd.us/dol/dlm/dlm-home.htm

Tennessee

Department of Labor and Workforce
Development
Nashville, TN
615-741-6642
www.state.tn.us/labor-wfd

Texas

Texas Workforce Commission
Austin, TX
800-832-9344 (Employer's hotline)
800-832-2829 (Employee's hotline)
www.twc.state.tx.us

Utah

Labor Commission
Salt Lake City, UT
801-530-6801
800-222-1238
http://laborcommission.utah.gov

Vermont

Department of Labor and Industry
Montpelier, VT
802-828-4000
www.doli.virginia.gov

Virginia

Department of Labor and Industry
Richmond, VA
804-371-2327
www.dli.state.va.us

Washington

Department of Labor and Industries
Olympia, WA
800-547-8367
www.lni.wa.gov

West Virginia

Division of Labor
Charleston, WV
304-558-7890
www.labor.state.wv.us

Wisconsin

Department of Workforce Development
Madison, WI
608-266-3131
www.dwd.state.wi.us

Wyoming

Department of Employment
Cheyenne, WY
307-777-7672
http://wydoe.state.wy.us

Current as of February 2007

Company Policies Regarding FMLA Leave

As explained throughout the book, your company's policies can affect its rights and obligations—and the rights and obligations of its employees—regarding FMLA leave. What you say in your FMLA policy and other company policies relating to leave is therefore very important.

This appendix explains how various policy choices affect your responsibilities under the FMLA. Here, we provide:

- A sample FMLA policy. As explained in Chapter 2, covered companies must include accurate, complete information about the FMLA in their employee handbooks, written policies, or other documents describing leave, wages, absences, and similar matters. The policy provided in this appendix will help you meet this obligation.

- A guide explaining how your company's FMLA policy affects its rights and obligations. You will have some choices to make when creating your company's policy; this section explains the ramifications of these choices. Use the guide in conjunction with the sample policy.

This appendix will help you draft a family and medical leave policy that complies with the FMLA, but remember—you may have additional obligations under state laws. Appendix A summarizes each state's family and medical leave laws. If the family or medical leave law of a state in which your company has employees is more generous than the FMLA or your policies, you must comply with the state law.

As a practical matter, if you company has employees in more than one state, it may be simpler to draft your family and medical leave policy to comply with the most generous of the state laws that apply and adopt that as the company-wide policy. This way, you won't have to draft separate policies for offices in the different states. You should consult with a lawyer for help devising a family and medical leave policy that meets both the FMLA's requirements and the legal requirements imposed by the state(s) where your company does business.

Family and Medical Leave Policy

It is our policy to grant family and/or medical leave to employees eligible under the Family and Medical Leave Act of 1993 ("FMLA") or any other applicable law.

Definitions

Alternative Position: A position to which an eligible employee may be temporarily reassigned during a period of intermittent or reduced-schedule leave. The alternative position will have the same pay and benefits as the employee's original position.

Child: The son or daughter of an eligible employee who is under 18 years of age, or 18 years or older and incapable of self-care as a result of physical or mental disability. For purposes of this policy, "child" includes the eligible employee's biological child, adopted child, foster child, stepchild, or legal ward.

Eligible Employee: An employee who has: 1) been employed by the company for at least 12 months; 2) worked at least 1,250 hours in the 12 months immediately preceding the start date of requested family or medical leave; and 3) worked at a worksite within a 75-mile radius of 50 or more employees of the company as of the date of the leave request.

Equivalent Position: A position: 1) with pay equivalent to the employee's original job; 2) with benefits equivalent to the employee's original job; 3) with job duties and responsibilities "substantially similar" to the employee's original job; 4) with a schedule that is the same as or equivalent to that of the employee's original job; and 5) located at the same worksite or one that is geographically proximate to the employee's original worksite.

Family Member: The eligible employee's spouse, child, or parent.

Health Care Providers: Doctors of osteopathy, podiatrists, dentists, optometrists, chiropractors (only for manual manipulation of the spine to treat a subluxation of the spine—that is, misalignment of vertebrae—identified by x-ray), clinical psychologists, nurse practitioners, nurse midwives, clinical social workers, and Christian Science practitioners.

Key Employee: A salaried employee in the highest-paid 10% of the company's employees working within 75 miles of the employee's worksite.

Parent: The eligible employee's biological, adoptive, or foster mother or father, or an individual who was the legal guardian of the eligible employee when the employee was a child.

Parenting Leave: Leave following birth, adoption, or foster placement of an eligible employee's child, including bonding leave.

Reinstatement: Restoration of employee to his or her original position when the employee returns from family or medical leave.

Serious Health Condition: Illness, injury, impairment, or physical or mental condition that involves one of the following: 1) inpatient care at a hospital, hospice, or residential medical care facility; 2) incapacity for more than three calendar days with continuing treatment by a health care provider; 3) incapacity due to pregnancy or prenatal care; 4) incapacity or treatment for a chronic serious health condition; 5) permanent or long-term incapacity for a condition for which treatment may not be effective (such as a terminal illness); or 6) absence for multiple treatments for either restorative surgery following an injury or accident or a condition that would require an absence of more than three days if not treated.

Spouse: A person of the opposite sex to whom the eligible employee is legally married.

Twelve-Month Leave Year: The rolling 12-month period measured backward from the first day that an eligible employee takes family or medical leave.

1. Leave Available

[Option 1—if company policy provides for more than 12 weeks of leave] An eligible employee may take up to ____ weeks (__ days) of family or medical leave in the 12-month leave year for any of the following reasons:

- because the employee's own serious health condition makes the employee unable to work

- to care for a spouse, child, or parent who has a serious health condition, or

- to care for a newborn or newly adopted son or daughter or a recently placed foster child.

SAMPLE

[Option 2—if company policy does not provide for more than 12 weeks of leave]
An eligible employee may take up to 12 weeks (60 work days) of family or medical leave in the 12-month leave year for any of the following reasons:

- because the employee's own serious health condition makes the employee unable to work

- to care for a spouse, child, or parent who has a serious health condition, or

- to care for a newborn or newly adopted son or daughter or a recently placed foster child.

If you have questions about how much leave time is available to you, please contact _____.

2. Serious Health Condition—Examples

Here are some examples of serious health conditions for which an eligible employee may take family or medical leave (Note: this is not an exhaustive list, but is for purposes of illustration):

- A condition requiring inpatient care includes, for example, medically necessary surgery.

- A condition that results in incapacity for three or more days and treatment by a health care provider includes, for example, a stroke.

- Incapacity due to pregnancy or prenatal care includes, for example, hypertension requiring bed rest.

- A chronic condition includes, for example, epilepsy.

- A condition for which treatment may not be effective includes, for example, terminal cancer.

- Absence for multiple treatments for restorative surgery includes, for example, skin grafts following a burn.

- A condition that could require an absence of more than three days if not treated includes, for example, kidney disease requiring dialysis.

3. Notice Requirements

To request family or medical leave, you are required to give notice of the need for leave at least 30 days in advance of the start date of the leave if the need for leave is foreseeable. If you fail to do so, we may delay the start of your leave. In emergencies and unexpected situations, you must give as much notice as is practicable under the circumstances.

To request family or medical leave, inform _____ that you need leave, when the leave will begin, and the reason for the leave (for example, for a serious medical condition or for parenting leave).

[Option—if the company requires written requests for other types of leave]
You must submit the reasons (for example, for a serious medical condition or for parenting leave) for the requested leave, the anticipated duration of the leave, and the anticipated start date of the leave in writing within the notice period described above. We will provide a form for this purpose.

4. Medical Certification

You may be required to provide a form from a health care provider certifying the need for leave when you request leave for your own or a family member's serious health condition. We will request medical certification from you in writing and provide you with a medical certification form to be used for this purpose. The company also has the right to seek a second opinion and periodic recertifications.

The company may also require that employees provide documentation or certification of parental status when requesting parental leave. Such documentation includes, for example, birth certificates, adoption decrees, or court orders.

5. Designation as FMLA Leave

Soon after you request family or medical leave, we will designate the leave as FMLA leave if we believe it qualifies as such, and notify you of this designation in writing. If we need more information to make a final FMLA designation, we will request that information from you and issue a preliminary designation until we receive sufficient information to make a final designation. Leave designated as FMLA leave will be deducted from your available FMLA leave for that leave year.

6. [Option] Substitution of Paid Leave

FMLA leave is unpaid leave. However, under this policy, if you are an eligible employee who has accrued paid time off, you [Option 1] may [Option 2] must use these benefits to receive pay for all or a portion of family or medical leave.

If you take paid sick leave, vacation leave, or other leave for a reason that qualifies for family or medical leave under the FMLA, the company will designate that time off as such and will count it against your 12-week leave entitlement.

7. Parenting Leave

An eligible employee taking parenting leave must complete this leave within one year of the birth, adoption, or foster placement of the employee's child.

[Option 1] Married parents of a new child who are both employed with the company may take a combined 12 weeks of leave in connection with the birth, adoption, or foster placement of their child. Unmarried parents of a new child who are both employed with the company may each take 12 weeks of leave in connection with the birth, adoption, or foster placement of their child.

[Option 2] Parents of a new child who are both employed with the company may each take 12 weeks of leave in connection with the birth, adoption, or foster placement of their child.

8. Intermittent and Reduced-Schedule Leave

An eligible employee may take leave all at one time or intermittently–that is, a day or two at a time–for his or her own serious health condition or to care for a family member with a serious health condition (for example, to attend doctor appointments or chemotherapy), if it is medically necessary to do so. An eligible employee may also take leave in the form of reduced hours for his or her own serious health condition or to care for a family member with a serious health condition, if it is medically necessary to do so (for example, to recover from an illness or medical treatment).

If you need intermittent or reduced-schedule leave, you must try to schedule the leave so it doesn't unduly disrupt the company's operations. We may temporarily reassign you to an alternative position to accommodate the intermittent or reduced-schedule leave.

[**Option 1**] Intermittent and reduced-schedule leaves are not available to employees seeking parental leave.

[**Option 2**] The company will consider requests for intermittent or reduced-schedule parenting leave on a case-by-case basis and will grant such requested leave if the leave does not create an undue hardship to the operations and work schedules of the company.

9. Employees Who Work Part Time or Irregular Hours

An eligible part-time employee or an employee who works variable or irregular hours may take intermittent or reduced-schedule leave in proportion to the amount of time he or she normally works. For example, if you usually work 20 hours per week and want a work schedule reduction to 10 hours per week, that amounts to one-half of your normal working hours. You would use up your entitlement to 12 weeks of leave in 24 weeks under that reduced schedule leave.

If your schedule varies from week to week, the leave workweek is measured by calculating the weekly average hours worked in the 12 weeks prior to the start of the leave. We will calculate this average and put it in writing for your review and signature.

10. Health Insurance

During an approved family or medical leave, the company will continue your health care benefits. You must continue to pay any share of the premium for which you are currently responsible by the usual due date of payment. If your premium payments are more than 30 days late, we may discontinue your coverage for the rest of your leave. If you choose not to return to work at the end of your leave, you will be required to reimburse the company for its share of the premiums paid during your leave.

11. Other Benefits

[**Option 1—if the company does not allow employee benefits to continue or accrue during other types of leave, including paid leave**] With the exception of health care benefits, discussed above, employee benefits will not continue or accrue during the period of your family or medical leave. These benefits will be restored when you return from leave at the same level as before the leave.

SAMPLE

[Option 2—if the company allows employee benefits to continue and/or accrue, but only during paid leave] If your family or medical leave is paid leave, discussed above, all employee benefits will continue and accrue during the period of the paid family or medical leave.

[Option 3—if the company allows employee benefits to continue and/or accrue during all types of leave] In addition to the health care benefits discussed above, employee benefits continue and accrue during the family or medical leave period. You will be required to reimburse the company for the portion of the benefits' premiums for which you are usually responsible for but which the company paid during the leave.

12. Premium Payments

Any premium payments for which you are responsible during the leave period must be paid on or before your regular payday. If you fail to make timely payment of the premiums, your benefit coverage, including insurance coverage, may be discontinued.

13. [Option] Status Reports

You must periodically contact the human resources manager during your leave and inform the manager of your status and intent to return to work.

14. [Option] Moonlighting

You may not work for another employer while on family or medical leave. Such outside employment is grounds for immediate termination.

15. Reinstatement

When you return from family or medical leave, you have the right to return to your former position or an equivalent position, except:

- You have no greater right to reinstatement than you would have had if you had not been on leave. If your position is restructured for reasons unrelated to your leave, for example, you have no right to reinstatement to the exact same position you held before leave.

> - The company is not obligated to reinstate you if you are a key employee—that is, if you are among the highest-paid 10 % of our workforce—and holding your job open during your leave would cause the company substantial economic harm. If the company classifies you as a key employee under this definition, you will be notified soon after you request leave.
>
> - Two weeks prior to your intended return date, you should notify the human resources manager of your intent to return to work. And, if anything has changed concerning your return to work while you have been on leave, you should notify human resources of the change.
>
> If you are returning from leave for your own serious health condition, the company may ask you to provide a fitness-for-duty report from your health care provider before you return to work. We will provide a form to be used for this purpose.

How Your FMLA Policy Affects Company Obligations

As we've explained, your company has to comply with its own leave policy if its terms are more generous or less strict than the FMLA. If your company's leave policy is less generous or stricter than the FMLA, you must follow the FMLA with respect to FMLA-eligible employees or FMLA-qualified leaves. Here are a few areas of particular importance—review them while using the sample policy above to create your own policy.

Definitions

Your company may define terms more broadly than the FMLA. If it does, it may extend the FMLA's protections to employees who would not otherwise be eligible.

- **Eligible employee.** Your company can offer family and medical leave to employees who don't meet the FMLA's eligibility requirements (12 months' employment/1,250 hours in 12 months preceding leave). However, such a decision has ramifications. For example, you can deduct reduced-schedule FMLA leave time (less than a full week of leave) from an eligible, exempt employee's pay without affecting the employee's exempt status. But, if you grant reduced-schedule leave to an exempt employee who is not eligible under the FMLA, you risk eliminating the employee's exempt status and violating the Fair Labor Standards Act.

- **Family member.** Your company can also elect to include in its family and medical leave policy family members not included under the FMLA, for example, siblings, grandparents, or domestic partners. But, if so, you cannot deduct the leave granted for such individuals' care from the employee's available FMLA leave time.

- **Twelve-month leave year.** The rolling leave year method is the most advantageous to employers, because it limits employees' ability to be out of work for more than 12 weeks in a 12-month period. However, you are free to calculate the leave year using one of the alternative methods. In fact, some state laws may mandate a different calculation.

Clause 1: Leave Available

Your company can offer more leave than the FMLA's 12 weeks. You may want to consider this option if your company has employees in more than one state, including a state that requires you to provide more leave time. By offering the leave time required under the state law to all employees in all states, you can adopt a single, uniform leave policy for all company locations.

Clause 3: Notice Requirements

Your company can require employees seeking family and medical leave to comply with the usual and customary notice requirements and procedures (for example, requiring that the employee notify you of the need for leave in writing) that it imposes for other types of leave requests.

However, you cannot require more notice (in other words, more than 30 days for foreseeable leave) or more information (in other words, more than leave dates and general statement of reason for leave) than the FMLA requires. And, you cannot impose stricter requirements on employees seeking family or medical leave than you impose on employees seeking other types of leave.

If an employee doesn't give the required leave notice, you can delay the start of an employee's leave, but only if you have informed the employee of the duty to provide notice.

Clause 4: Medical Certification

You have to give an employee seeking leave for a serious health condition an individual written request for medical certification, even if your company's family and medical leave policy states that medical certification will be required.

Clause 6: Substitution of Paid Leave

If your company has a paid leave policy, an employee's use of it during family or medical leave is subject to its terms. For example, if your company offers paid sick leave for the employee's own illness, you must allow an employee taking FMLA leave for his or her own serious health condition to use the paid sick leave available. However, you do not have to let the employee use that paid sick leave policy to care for family members, since the sick leave policy does not provide for that.

If your company paid leave policy requires less information than the FMLA does, you have to limit your request for information to that required by your policy. Conversely, you cannot require more information from employees using paid leave for FMLA leave than the FMLA requires, even if your company usually requests more information for paid leave requests.

Remember, it's not really a substitution, but an overlap. The employee isn't using paid leave instead of FMLA leave but is using the two types of leave at the same time. So, don't forget to deduct the paid leave taken from the employee's available FMLA leave time.

Clause 7: Parenting Leave

Even though the FMLA requires you to offer only 12 weeks of combined parenting leave to married employees when both are employed by the company, your company can offer 12 full weeks of leave to each parent.

Clause 8: Intermittent or Reduced-Schedule Leave

Your company can allow employees to take intermittent or reduced schedule parenting leave, but the FMLA doesn't require it. On the other hand, you can impose restrictions on the leave that you usually can't impose on intermittent FMLA leave, such as requiring the employee to take the leave in larger increments than those your company uses for payroll.

Clause 10: Health Insurance

You can terminate an employee's health coverage if the employee is required to pay a portion of the premium and fails to do so. However, the date that an employee's coverage officially terminates depends, in part, on your policies for other types of paid leave. If your company has an established policy that allows it to terminate coverage retroactively to the date of the missed payment, it may do so. If it doesn't have this type of policy, it may terminate coverage effective 30 days after the missed payment.

Clause 11: Other Benefits

If your company usually allows employee benefits to continue and accrue during other types of leave, you have to follow that practice when an employee takes FMLA leave. If your company usually does not continue employee benefits during leave, you do not have to continue benefits (other than health benefits) during FMLA leave. However, regardless of company policy, you must restore all employee benefits to the employee upon return from leave. The benefits must be restored to the same level as before leave and without any requalification. For this reason, it may be easier and less costly to simply continue the benefits during leave, regardless of company policy on other types of leave.

You have to follow your company's policy regarding the continuation and accrual of benefits during paid leave for employees who substitute paid leave for FMLA leave. So, if your company's employee benefits continue to accrue during paid leave, they must also continue to accrue during an FMLA leave that is taken as paid leave.

Clause 12: Premium Payments

You can require employees to pay premiums for benefits during FMLA leave, but you must inform them of this requirement in your policies and you must also inform them when premium payments are due and the possible consequences of failing to pay. You can seek reimbursement of premiums paid by your company during leave from the employee upon return from leave, except that your company can't recover its premium payments if the employee fails to return from paid leave.

Clause 13: Status Reports

You can request periodic status reports during an employee's FMLA leave, asking whether the employee intends to return and, if so, when. Just make sure you are reasonable: Don't ask too often, and don't ask for more information than is allowed. Avoid the appearance of bullying the employee to return from leave earlier than the employee is ready to. Don't try to get additional medical information via the status reports.

Clause 14: Moonlighting

You can prohibit an employee from working for another employer during FMLA leave, as long as your company has a uniform policy against moonlighting that applies for all employees.

Forms and Checklists

Your Rights
under the
Family and Medical Leave Act of 1993

FMLA requires covered employers to provide up to 12 weeks of unpaid, job-protected leave to "eligible" employees for certain family and medical reasons. Employees are eligible if they have worked for their employer for at least one year, and for 1,250 hours over the previous 12 months, and if there are at least 50 employees within 75 miles. The FMLA permits employees to take leave on an intermittent basis or to work a reduced schedule under certain circumstances.

Reasons for Taking Leave:

Unpaid leave must be granted for *any* of the following reasons:
- to care for the employee's child after birth, or placement for adoption or foster care;
- to care for the employee's spouse, son or daughter, or parent who has a serious health condition; or
- for a serious health condition that makes the employee unable to perform the employee's job.

At the employee's or employer's option, certain kinds of *paid* leave may be substituted for unpaid leave.

Advance Notice and Medical Certification:

The employee may be required to provide advance leave notice and medical certification. Taking of leave may be denied if requirements are not met.
- The employee ordinarily must provide 30 days advance notice when the leave is "foreseeable."
- An employer may require medical certification to support a request for leave because of a serious health condition, and may require second or third opinions (at the employer's expense) and a fitness for duty report to return to work.

Job Benefits and Protection:

- For the duration of FMLA leave, the employer must maintain the employee's health coverage under any "group health plan."

- Upon return from FMLA leave, most employees must be restored to their original or equivalent positions with equivalent pay, benefits, and other employment terms.
- The use of FMLA leave cannot result in the loss of any employment benefit that accrued prior to the start of an employee's leave.

Unlawful Acts by Employers:

FMLA makes it unlawful for any employer to:
- interfere with, restrain, or deny the exercise of any right provided under FMLA:
- discharge or discriminate against any person for opposing any practice made unlawful by FMLA or for involvement in any proceeding under or relating to FMLA.

Enforcement:

- The U.S. Department of Labor is authorized to investigate and resolve complaints of violations.
- An eligible employee may bring a civil action against an employer for violations.

FMLA does not affect any Federal or State law prohibiting discrimination, or supersede any State or local law or collective bargaining agreement which provides greater family or medical leave rights.

For Additional Information:

If you have access to the Internet visit our FMLA website: **http://www.dol.gov/esa/whd/fmla**. To locate your nearest Wage-Hour Office, telephone our Wage-Hour toll-free information and help line at 1-866-4USWAGE (1-866-487-9243): a customer service representative is available to assist you with referral information from 8am to 5pm **in your time zone;** or log onto our Home Page at **http://www.wagehour.dol.gov**.

U.S. Department of Labor
Employment Standards Administration
Wage and Hour Division
Washington, D.C. 20210

WH Publication 1420
Revised August 2001

*U.S. GOVERNMENT PRINTING OFFICE 2001-476-344/49051

Sus Derechos
bajo
La Ley de Ausencia Familiar y Médica de 1993

La Ley de Ausencia Familiar y Médica de 1993 (LAFM) requiere que patrones sujetos a la ley provean a sus empleados 12 semanas de ausencia del trabajo sin paga por ciertas razones familiares médicas, con protección del empleo a empleados "elegibles." Se consideran elegibles a los empleados de dicho patrón quienes hayan trabajado un año, y trabajado 1,250 horas o más en los últimos 12 meses, y trabajan dentro de un área de 75 millas donde se ocupan a 50 empleados o más del mismo patrón.

Razones para Solicitar Ausencia:

Tiene derecho un empleado de tomar ausencia del trabajo sin paga por cualquiera de las siguientes razones:

- para cuidar a un niño recién nacido, o llevar a cabo una adopción o crianza, de un niño del empleado;
- para cuidar a un cónyuge (esposo/a), hijo/a, o *cualquiera* de los padres, quien padezca de un estado de salud grave, o;
- por un estado de salud grave que le impide a un empleado desempeñar su trabajo.

Se puede elegir por parte del empleado o el patrón substituir una ausencia sin paga por una ausencia pagada si el empleado tiene el tiempo pagado acumulado.

Notificación por Adelantado y Certificado Médico:

Se le puede exigir a un empleado que notifique por adelantado la necesidad de estar ausente, y además exigirle que provea certificado médico. Se puede negar el permiso si el empleado no cumple con estos requisitos.

- Por lo general se requiere que el empleado notifique al patrón con 30 días por adelantado cuando la ausencia es "anticipada."
- El patrón puede exigirle un certificado médico al empleado que pide tomar ausencia por motivo de un estado de salud grave, y puede exigir una segunda o tercera opinión médica (a cuenta del patrón), y además puede exigir un certificado médico de la salud, estado físico y capacidad del empleado para regresar al trabajo.

Beneficios y Protección del Empleo:

Durante una ausencia, el patrón tendrá que mantener en vigor el seguro de salud del empleado bajo cualquier "plan de salud de grupo" en existencia.

- Al regresar de una ausencia los empleados tienen el derecho a su trabajo original o a un trabajo equivalente con sueldo, beneficios, y otras condiciones de empleo equivalentes.
- Una ausencia no puede resultar en la pérdida de ningún beneficio acumulado antes de que el empleado comenzara la ausencia del trabajo.

Actos Ilegales Por Parte del Patrón:

La LAFM le prohibe al patrón lo siguiente:

- que interfiera, restrinja, o niegue que se ejercite cualquier derecho estipulado por la LAFM;
- que se despida o se discrimine en contra de cualquier persona que se oponga a una práctica prohibida por la LAFM, o se involucre en cualquier procedimiento relacionado a esta ley.

Ejecución:

- El "Department of Labor" tiene la autoridad de investigar y resolver quejas de infracciones de la LAFM.
- El empleado elegible puede demandar a un patrón por medio de acción civil por infracciones de la LAFM.

La LAFM no afecta ninguna ley federal o estatal que prohiba la discriminación, ni reemplaza ninguna ley estatal o local, o convenio sindical que provea más amplios derechos de ausencia familiar o médica.

Para Más Información:

Si tiene acceso al internet, visite la pagina de la LAFM: **http://www.dol.gov/esa/whd/fmla**. Para localizar la oficina de horarios y salarios más cercana, llame a nuestra linea gratis de información y ayuda al 1-866-4USWAGE (1-866-487-9243). Representantes estan disponibles para asistir con información desde 8am a 5pm **en su zona horaria**; o visite nuestra pagina de internet **http://www.wagehour.dol.gov**.

 US Department of Labor
Employment Standards Administration
Wage and Hour Division
Washington, D.C. 20210

WH Publication 1420SP
Revised August 2001

*U.S. GOVERNMENT PRINTING OFFICE 2001-476-344/49051

Form Regarding FMLA Leave to Care for a Family Member

I, _____ have requested time off work to care for
_____. I have read the definitions below and I confirm
that this person qualifies as my _____.

I have attached a copy of the following documents confirming this relationship:

_____

_____

_____

_____

(List any documents you can provide, such as a birth certificate, papers confirming an adoption or foster care placement, marriage certificate, and so on. If you don't have any documents, please write that in the space provided.)

_____

_____

_____

_____

Date: _____

Signature: _____

Definitions

Spouse: A husband or wife to whom you are legally married.

Parent: Your legal parent, or someone who had day-to-day responsibility for supporting your financially and taking care of you when you were a child.

Child: Your biological child, adopted child, stepchild, foster child, or legal ward, or a child whom you have the day-to-day responsibility to support financially and take care of. Children are covered only until they reach the age of 18, unless they are incapable of taking care of themselves because of a physical or mental disability.

FMLA Hours Worked

Fill out this worksheet for each employee who requests leave, to verify that the employee is eligible under the FMLA. Don't put more than one name on the worksheet—the information should go in each employee's confidential file. If an employee requests multiple leaves in the same year, simply add rows to the worksheet.

Employee Name	Start Date	Hours Worked in the 12 Months Prior to Requested Leave	Dates FMLA Leave Taken

FMLA Leave Tracking for [*employee name*]

Use this form if your company uses the rolling year to calculate leave eligibility.

1. In the first column, write the date the employee's FMLA leave began.

2. In the second column, write the total amount of leave taken during each FMLA leave.

3. In the third column, write the date the employee will be eligible to take more leave.

   • If the employee takes 12 weeks all at once, the employee will not be eligible to take more leave for a full year from the first date the leave was taken.

   • If the employee has taken less than 12 weeks in the previous year (based on the first date of leave requested the current year), the employee is immediately eligible to take some leave. How much depends on the amount of leave taken during the 12 months prior to the current leave request.

   • If the employee has taken 12 weeks of leave in the previous year (based on the start date of the current leave), the employee will be eligible for additional leave one year from the start of the first leave taken in the previous year.

4. In the fourth column, write the amount of leave the employee will be eligible to take on the next eligible leave date.

   • If the employee takes less than 12 weeks of leave at once, the employee is eligible for 12 weeks less the amount of leave taken counting backward from the date the leave is requested. For example, assume today's date is March 1, 2007. If the employee took a four-week leave beginning on January 1, 2006, and another eight-week leave beginning on April 1, 2006, the employee currently has four weeks of leave available.

Date Leave Commenced	Amount of Leave Taken	Date Eligible for Additional Leave	Amount of Leave Available

Calculating Intermittent/Reduced-Schedule Leave

Use this worksheet to calculate how long it will take an employee to use up available intermittent or reduced-schedule leave.

1. In the first column, insert the employee's name and the number of hours the employee normally works. If the employee doesn't work a set number of hours each week, you can calculate an average based on the 12 weeks immediately prior to the employee's request for leave, but get the employee's signature verifying that average is correct.

2. Multiply that number by 12, and put it in the second column. This tells you how many hours the employee has available for FMLA leave.

3. In the third column, write the number of hours of leave the employee has requested for each week.

4. In column four, divide the number in the second column by the number in the third column.

5. The result (in column 5) is the number of calendar weeks the employee has to exhaust leave, assuming equal amounts of time are taken each week and the employee has not already used any of his or her leave entitlement.

Regular Workweek	Available FMLA Leave	Leave Needed (hrs./wk.)	Available Leave/ Leave Needed	Number of Calendar Weeks to Exhaust FMLA Leave
(Employee Name): hrs./wk.	X 12 wks.=hrs.	hrs./wk.	hrs./hrs.	=weeks
(Employee Name): hrs./wk.	X 12 wks.=hrs.	hrs./wk.	hrs./hrs.	=weeks
(Employee Name): hrs./wk.	X 12 wk.=hrs.	hrs./wk.	hrs./hrs.	=weeks

FMLA Designation (Preliminary)

TO: ___*[employee's name]*___ :

You have requested leave from ___*[date]*___ to ___*[date]*___ . Based on the information you provided, the leave you requested is preliminarily designated as FMLA leave.

Please provide the following additional information:

[other information requested, such as medical certification, proof of family relationship, and so on]

Once you have provided this information, we will determine whether your leave is covered by the FMLA. If so, we will issue a final designation to that effect, and the leave you take will be counted against your available FMLA leave time. If not, we will withdraw this preliminary designation, in writing.

___*[your name]*_____   ___*[date]*_____

FMLA Designation (Final)

TO: ___[employee's name]___ :

You have requested leave from ___[date]___ to ___[date]___ . Based on the information you provided, the leave you requested is designated as FMLA leave and will count against your available FMLA leave time.

___[your name]_____ ___[date]_____

Employer Response to Employee
Request for Family or Medical Leave
(Optional Use Form -- See 29 CFR § 825.301)

U.S. Department of Labor
Employment Standards Administration
Wage and Hour Division

(Family and Medical Leave Act of 1993)

Date:

OMB No. : 1215-0181
Expires : 08-31-07

To: _____
(Employee's Name)

From: _____
(Name of Appropriate Employer Representative)

Subject: REQUEST FOR FAMILY/MEDICAL LEAVE

On _____ , you notified us of your need to take family/medical leave due to:
(Date)

☐   The birth of a child, or the placement of a child with you for adoption or foster care; or

☐   A serious health condition that makes you unable to perform the essential functions for your job: or

☐   A serious health condition affecting your ☐ spouse, ☐ child, ☐ parent, for which you are needed to
provide care.

You notified us that you need this leave beginning on _____ and that you expect
(Date)
leave to continue until on or about _____ .
(Date)

Except as explained below, you have a right under the FMLA for up to 12 weeks of unpaid leave in a 12-month
period for the reasons listed above. Also, your health benefits must be maintained during any period of unpaid
leave under the same conditions as if you continued to work, and you must be reinstated to the same or an
equivalent job with the same pay, benefits, and terms and conditions of employment on your return from leave. If
you do not return to work following FMLA leave for a reason other than: (1) the continuation, recurrence, or onset
of a serious health condition which would entitle you to FMLA leave; or (2) other circumstances beyond your
control, you may be required to reimburse us for our share of health insurance premiums paid on your behalf during
your FMLA leave.

This is to inform you that: *(check appropriate boxes; explain where indicated)*

1. You are ☐ eligible ☐ not eligible for leave under the FMLA.

2. The requested leave ☐ will ☐ will not be counted against your annual FMLA leave entitlement.

3. You ☐ will ☐ will not be required to furnish medical certification of a serious health condition. If required,
you must furnish certification by _____ *(insert date)* (must be at least 15 days
after you are notified of this requirement), or we may delay the commencement of your leave until the certification
is submitted.

4. You may elect to substitute accrued paid leave for unpaid FMLA leave. We ☐ will ☐ will not require that
you substitute accrued paid leave for unpaid FMLA leave. If paid leave will be used, the following conditions will
apply: *(Explain)*

Form WH-381
Rev. June 1997

5. (a) If you normally pay a portion of the premiums for your health insurance, these payments will continue during the period of FMLA leave. Arrangements for payment have been discussed with you, and it is agreed that you will make premium payments as follows: *(Set forth dates, e.g., the 10th of each month, or pay periods, etc. that specifically cover the agreement with the employee.)*

(b) You have a minimum 30-day *(or, indicate longer period, if applicable)* grace period in which to make premium payments. If payment is not made timely, your group health insurance may be cancelled, *provided* we notify you in writing at least 15 days before the date that your health coverage will lapse, or, at our option, we may pay your share of the premiums during FMLA leave, and recover these payments from you upon your return to work. We ☐ will ☐ will not pay your share of health insurance premiums while you are on leave.

(c) We ☐ will ☐ will not do the same with other benefits *(e.g., life insurance, disability insurance, etc.)* while you are on FMLA leave. If we do pay your premiums for other benefits, when you return from leave you ☐ will ☐ will not be expected to reimburse us for the payments made on your behalf.

6. You ☐ will ☐ will not be required to present a fitness-for-duty certificate prior to being restored to employment. If such certification is required but not received, your return to work may be delayed until certification is provided.

7. (a) You ☐ are ☐ are not a "key employee" as described in § 825.217 of the FMLA regulations. If you are a "key employee:" restoration to employment may be denied following FMLA leave on the grounds that such restoration will cause substantial and grievous economic injury to us as discussed in § 825.218.

(b) We ☐ have ☐ have not determined that restoring you to employment at the conclusion of FMLA leave will cause substantial and grievous economic harm to *us. (Explain (a) and/or (b) below. See §825.219 of the FMLA regulations.)*

8. While on leave, you ☐ will ☐ will not be required to furnish us with periodic reports every _____ _____ *(indicate interval of periodic reports, as appropriate for the particular leave situation)* of your status and intent to return to work *(see § 825.309 of the FMLA regulations).* If the circumstances of your leave change and you are able to return to work earlier than the date indicated on the reverse side of this form, you ☐ will ☐ will not be required to notify us at least two work days prior to the date you intend to report to work.

9. You ☐ will ☐ will not be required to furnish recertification relating to a serious health condition. *(Explain below. if necessary, including the interval between certifications as prescribed in §825.308 of the FMLA regulations.)*

This optional use form may be used to satisfy mandatory employer requirements to provide employees taking FMLA leave with Written notice detailing specific expectations and obligations of the employee and explaining any consequences of a failure to meet these obligations. (29 CFR 825.301(b).)

Note: Persons are not required to respond to this collection of information unless it displays a currently valid OMB control number.

Public Burden Statement

We estimate that it will take an average of 5 minutes to complete this collection of information, including the time for reviewing instructions. searching existing data sources, gathering and maintaining the data needed, and completing and reviewing the collection of information. If you have any comments regarding this burden estimate or any other aspect of this collection of information, including suggestions for reducing this burden. send them to the Administrator, Wage and Hour Division, Department of Labor, Room S-3502. 200 Constitution Avenue, N.W., Washington. D.C. 20210.

DO NOT SEND THE COMPLETED FORM TO THE OFFICE SHOWN ABOVE.

Certification of Health Care Provider
(Family and Medical Leave Act of 1993)

U.S. Department of Labor
Employment Standards Administration
Wage and Hour Division

(When completed, this form goes to the employee, __Not to the Department of Labor.__)

OMB No.: 1215-0181
Expires: 08-31-2007

---

1. Employee's Name

2. Patient's Name *(If different from employee)*

---

3. Page 4 describes what is meant by a **"serious health condition"** under the Family and Medical Leave Act. Does the patient's condition[1] qualify under any of the categories described? If so, please check the applicable category.

(1) _____ (2) _____ (3) _____ (4) _____ (5) _____ (6) _____ , or None of the above _____

4. Describe the **medical facts** which support your certification, including a brief statement as to how the medical facts meet the criteria of one of these categories:

---

5. a. State the approximate **date** the condition commenced, and the probable duration of the condition (and also the probable duration of the patient's present **incapacity**[2] if different):

   b. Will it be necessary for the employee to take work only **intermittently or to work on a less than full schedule** as a result of the condition (including for treatment described in Item 6 below)?

   If yes, give the probable duration:

   c. If the condition is a **chronic condition** (condition #4) or **pregnancy**, state whether the patient is presently incapacitated[2] and the likely duration and frequency of **episodes of incapacity**[2]:

---

[1] Here and elsewhere on this form, the information sought relates **only** to the condition for which the employee is taking FMLA leave.

[2] "Incapacity," for purposes of FMLA, is defined to mean inability to work, attend school or perform other regular daily activities due to the serious health condition, treatment therefor, or recovery therefrom.

Form WH-380
Revised December 1999

6. a. If additional **treatments** will be required for the condition, provide an estimate of the probable number of such treatments.

If the patient will be absent from work or other daily activities because of **treatment** on an **intermittent** or **part-time** basis, also provide an estimate of the probable number of and interval between such treatments, actual or estimated dates of treatment if known, and period required for recovery if any:

b. If any of these treatments will be provided by **another provider of health services** (e.g., physical therapist), please state the nature of the treatments:

c. **If a regimen of continuing treatment** by the patient is required under your supervision, provide a general description of such regimen (*e.g.*, prescription drugs, physical therapy requiring special equipment):

7. a. If medical leave is required for the employee's **absence from work** because of the **employee's own condition** (including absences due to pregnancy or a chronic condition), is the employee **unable to perform work** of any kind?

b. If able to perform some work, is the employee **unable to perform any one or more of the essential functions of the employee's job** (the employee or the employer should supply you with information about the essential job functions)? If yes, please list the essential functions the employee is unable to perform:

c. If neither a. nor b. applies, is it necessary for the employee to be **absent from work for treatment**?

8. a. If leave is required to **care for a family member** of the employee with a serious health condition, **does the patient require assistance** for basic medical or personal needs or safety, or for transportation?

   b. If no, would the employee's presence to provide **psychological comfort** be beneficial to the patient or assist in the patient's recovery?

   c. If the patient will need care only **intermittently** or on a part-time basis, please indicate the probable **duration** of this need:

Signature of Health Care Provider

Type of Practice

Address

Telephone Number

Date

To be completed by the employee needing family leave to care for a family member:

State the care you will provide and an estimate of the period during which care will be provided, including a schedule if leave is to be taken intermittently or if it will be necessary for you to work less than a full schedule:

Employee Signature

Date

A **"Serious Health Condition"** means an illness, injury impairment, or physical or mental condition that involves one of the following:

1. Hospital Care

   Inpatient care (*i.e.*, an overnight stay) in a hospital, hospice, or residential medical care facility, including any period of incapacity[2] or subsequent treatment in connection with or consequent to such inpatient care.

2. Absence Plus Treatment

   (a) A period of incapacity[2] of **more than three consecutive calendar days** (including any subsequent treatment or period of incapacity[2] relating to the same condition), that also involves:

   (1) **Treatment**[3] **two or more times** by a health care provider, by a nurse or physician's assistant under direct supervision of a health care provider, or by a provider of health care services (*e.g.*, physical therapist) under orders of, or on referral by, a health care provider; or

   (2) **Treatment** by a health care provider on **at least one occasion** which results in a **regimen of continuing treatment**[4] under the supervision of the health care provider.

3. Pregnancy

   Any period of incapacity due to **pregnancy**, or for **prenatal care**.

4. Chronic Conditions Requiring Treatments

   A **chronic condition** which:

   (1) Requires **periodic visits** for treatment by a health care provider, or by a nurse or physician's assistant under direct supervision of a health care provider;

   (2) Continues over an **extended period of time** (including recurring episodes of a single underlying condition); and

   (3) May cause **episodic** rather than a continuing period of incapacity[2] (*e.g.*, asthma, diabetes, epilepsy, etc.).

5. Permanent/Long-term Conditions Requiring Supervision

   A period of **Incapacity**[2] which is **permanent or long-term** due to a condition for which treatment may not be effective. The employee or family member must be **under the continuing supervision of, but need not be receiving active treatment by, a health care provider**. Examples include Alzheimer's, a severe stroke, or the terminal stages of a disease.

6. Multiple Treatments (Non-Chronic Conditions)

   Any period of absence to receive **multiple treatments** (including any period of recovery therefrom) by a health care provider or by a provider of health care services under orders of, or on referral by, a health care provider, either for **restorative surgery** after an accident or other injury, **or for a condition that would likely result in a period of Incapacity**[2] **of more than three consecutive calendar days in the absence of medical intervention or treatment**, such as cancer (chemotherapy, radiation, etc.), severe arthritis (physical therapy), and kidney disease (dialysis).

This optional form may be used by employees to satisfy a mandatory requirement to furnish a medical certification (when requested) from a health care provider, including second or third opinions and recertification (29 CFR 825.306).

Note: Persons are not required to respond to this collection of information unless it displays a currently valid OMB control number.

---

[3] Treatment includes examinations to determine if a serious health condition exists and evaluations of the condition. Treatment does not include routine physical examinations, eye examinations, or dental examinations.

[4] A regimen of continuing treatment includes, for example, a course of prescription medication (*e.g.*, an antibiotic) or therapy requiring special equipment to resolve or alleviate the health condition. A regimen of treatment does not include the taking of over-the-counter medications such as aspirin, antihistamines, or salves; or bed-rest, drinking fluids, exercise, and other similar activities that can be initiated without a visit to a health care provider.

Public Burden Statement

We estimate that it will take an average of 20 minutes to complete this collection of information, including the time for reviewing instructions, searching existing data sources, gathering and maintaining the data needed, and completing and reviewing the collection of information. If you have any comments regarding this burden estimate or any other aspect of this collection of information, including suggestions for reducing this burden, send them to the Administrator, Wage and Hour Division, Department of Labor, Room S-3502, 200 Constitution Avenue, N.W., Washington, D.C. 20210.

DO NOT SEND THE COMPLETED FORM TO THIS OFFICE; IT GOES TO THE EMPLOYEE.

*U.S. GPO: 2000-461-954/25505

Request for Medical Certification

To: __[employee's name]__

From: __[manager's name]__

Date: __[today's date]__

On [date], you informed us of your need to take leave for a serious health condition.

You will be required to submit a medical certification of a serious health condition from [your or your [family member]'s] health care provider. The medical certification form is attached to this letter. Please note that you will have to complete a portion of the form if you are seeking leave to care for a family member.

You must return this form to us by [date 15 calendar days after employee receives the letter]. If you fail to return this form on time, we may delay the start of your leave, or postpone the continuation of your leave, until we receive your certification. If you are unable to return the form on time due to circumstances beyond your control, please contact me right away.

Feel free to contact me if you have any questions about this requirement.

Sincerely,

__[your name]_____   __[date]_____

Notice to Key Employee of Substantial and Grievous Economic Injury

To: ___[Employee name]_____

As indicated by written notice dated *[date employee was given individual notice form]*, you are a key employee of this company. This means that you can be denied reinstatement following FMLA leave if such reinstatement would cause substantial and grievous economic injury to the company.

We have determined that reinstating you would cause substantial and grievous economic injury to the company, because *[explain reasons for determination]*.

We cannot deny you the right to take FMLA leave, or discontinue your health benefits, based on this determination. However, we intend to deny you reinstatement once your leave is finished.

If you wish to avoid these consequences, you must return to work no later than *[date employee must return; also indicate why this date was chosen—for example, "this is the latest we can afford to have you out without hiring a permanent replacement."]* If you do not return to work by *[date employee must return]*, we intend to replace you and deny you reinstatement.

Please contact me immediately if you have any questions.

Sincerely,

___[your name]_____

___[your title]_____

Dated:

Notice of Termination of Group Health Coverage

[date]

[employee's name]

[employee's address]

Dear _[employee's name]_,

As I informed you by written notice when you first requested FMLA leave, you are required to pay your share of the premium for group health insurance. We agreed that you would pay these amounts by _[explain method and amount—for example, "sending me a check on the first of each month in the amount of $65.25"]_. I have attached a copy of the written notice explaining this requirement, for your reference. _[explain how payment was missed—for example, "I have not yet received your payment that was due on May 1."]_ I am writing to inform you that we are going to terminate your health insurance coverage if we do not receive your _[date of missed payment]_ payment by _[deadline for submitting missed payment]_.

Please take care of this right away. If you have any questions, feel free to call me at _[phone number]_.

Sincerely,

[your name]

[your title]

✓ Managers' Checklist	Does the FMLA Apply to My Company?

❏ My company had 50 or more employees on payroll during each of 20 workweeks in this or the last calendar year.

    ❏ I included all employees on leave in this count.

    ❏ I included all part-time employees on payroll during any workweek.

    ❏ I did not include employees hired or fired during any workweek in the count for that workweek.

    ❏ I did not include employees working outside the U.S. or its territories in this count.

    ❏ I counted all employees jointly employed by my company and joint employer(s), including temp agency employees.

    ❏ I counted all employees of my company and any other company that is integrated with it.

✓ Managers' Checklist	Is the Employee Eligible for FMLA Leave?

❏ There are 50 or more employees working within 75 miles of the leave-seeking employee's worksite.

    ❏ I counted telecommuting or other employees not physically present at the worksite where they report or where they receive work assignments.

    ❏ I measured the 75-mile radius based on the most direct surface travel routes, like roads, highways, and waterways.

    ❏ I counted all buildings within a reasonable geographic vicinity as a single worksite and measured the 75-mile radius from those buildings.

❏ The employee worked for the company for at least 12 months (or 52 weeks) prior to the first day of the requested leave.

    ❏ I counted the employee as working in any week when the employee was on company payroll, even if the employee worked intermittently or part time.

    ❏ I counted the employee as working in any week when the employee was on leave and getting pay or benefits from my company.

    ❏ I did not count the employee as working in any week when the employee was suspended or should otherwise have been working but wasn't.

❏ Company records show that the employee worked at least 1,250 hours in the 12 months prior to the first day of the requested leave.

    ❏ I counted only the hours that the employee actually worked, whether paid or not.

    ❏ Because my company does not count time on leave when calculating hours for overtime pay purposes, I did not count any hours that the employee was on leave.

| ✓ | Managers' Checklist | **Leave for a New Child** |

❑ I confirmed that the employee requesting parenting leave is eligible for FMLA leave (see Chapter 3).

❑ I have informed the employee that he or she must substitute paid company vacation, personal, or family leave for unpaid FMLA leave, and

　❑ I have subtracted the paid leave from the employee's available FMLA leave for the leave year.

❑ I have noted the deadline by which the employee must take the full 12 weeks of parenting leave (365 days after birth, adoption, or foster placement).

For Pregnancy Leave:

❑ If the employee is requesting leave for her own pregnancy before delivery, I have:

　❑ requested medical certification of a serious medical condition

　❑ designated the leave as leave for the employee's own medical condition and notified the employee

　❑ noted in the employee's FMLA file that the employee may still request parenting leave within the one-year deadline.

❑ If a pregnant employee is requesting leave to begin before delivery, I have:

　❑ asked if the leave is for her own medical condition (including prenatal care) or for parenting, and

　❑ if for her own medical condition, I have followed the steps in the preceding list entry, and

　❑ if for parenting, I have denied the request for leave prior to delivery.

❑ If an employee is requesting leave to care for his pregnant spouse, I have:

　❑ requested appropriate certification of serious medical condition

　❑ designated the leave as leave for the spouse's serious medical condition and notified the employee, and

　❑ noted that the employee may still request parenting leave within the 365-day deadline.

Managers' Checklist | **Leave for a New Child, continued**

For Parenting Leave:

❏ If the employee is requesting parenting leave, I have confirmed that the leave is:

    ❏ to begin after the birth of the child

    ❏ not for the employee's own medical condition, and

    ❏ full time and not intermittent or reduced-schedule leave, unless company policy or state law permits such leave.

❏ If the employee is requesting parenting leave for the birth of a child, I have requested appropriate certification (birth certificate).

❏ If the employee is requesting parenting leave for adoption or foster placement, I have:

    ❏ requested appropriate certification of adoption or placement (for example, a court order)

    ❏ allowed time off before adoption or foster placement if necessary to attend proceedings or meetings related to placement.

Where Both Parents Work for Your Company:

❏ For parents who are married and are both seeking parenting leave, I have:

    ❏ confirmed in writing to the parents that they get no more than a combined total of 12 weeks of parenting leave, and

    ❏ subtracted the parenting time from each employee's FMLA time and noted the remainder for use for other types of FMLA leave.

❏ For parents who are not married and are both seeking leave, I have:

    ❏ confirmed in writing to the parents that each parent has a full 12 weeks of parenting leave available

    ❏ subtracted the parenting time from each employee's FMLA time and noted the remainder for use for other types of FMLA leave

---

✓ **Managers' Checklist** | **Duration of Leave**

For All Employees Requesting Leave:

- ❏ I confirmed that my company's method for defining the FMLA leave year is in writing, in our FMLA leave policy.

- ❏ If our company has not yet defined its leave year or has decided to change methods of defining the leave year, I either
  - ❏ provided all employees with notice of this change at least 60 days before they requested leave, or
  - ❏ gave employees the benefit of whichever leave year calculation method provided them with the most leave.

- ❏ I calculated the FMLA leave time available to the employee requesting leave according to my company's leave-year method.

- ❏ I recorded all FMLA leave the employee has taken, but I have not included the following types of time off as FMLA leave:
  - ❏ time the employee actually spent working
  - ❏ time taken off for the company's convenience, and
  - ❏ weeks during which the company was shut down.

For Employees Requesting Intermittent or Reduced-Schedule Leave

- ❏ I determined that the employee's requested intermittent or reduced-schedule leave is medically necessary.

- ❏ I determined that the employee is able to perform the essential functions of his or her job.

- ❏ If the employee works the same number of hours each week, I used that schedule to calculate the FMLA leave available to the employee.

✓ Managers' Checklist	Duration of Leave, continued

- ❏ If the employee's hours are irregular, I calculated the average hours worked per week by the employee requesting FMLA leave, and

    - ❏ I have a written agreement of the average workweek signed by the employee, and

    - ❏ I calculated the pro rata time off that the employee is entitled to under the FMLA.

- ❏ If the employee is exempt from overtime, the employee and I reached an agreement as to the employee's average weekly hours, and

    - ❏ I have the employee's sign-off on this average.

- ❏ I included all mandatory overtime hours in the workweek hours of the employee requesting FMLA leave.

Managers' Checklist — Giving Notice and Designating Leave

❏ I have given a written designation form letter to the employee requesting leave. The designation form letter includes:

  ❏ a statement that the leave is FMLA leave and will reduce the employee's available FMLA leave time, or

  ❏ a statement that the leave is preliminarily designated FMLA leave and will reduce the employee's available FMLA leave time, pending investigation into whether the need for leave falls under the FMLA, or

  ❏ a statement that the leave is not FMLA leave.

❏ After giving the preliminary designation, I have asked the employee requesting leave or his or her spokesperson to tell me the reason for the leave, and

  ❏ the employee has informed me that the employee needs the leave because of a serious health condition, and I have confirmed the FMLA designation in writing

  ❏ the employee has given me some information that leads me to believe that the need for leave falls under the FMLA, and I have requested additional information, including medical certification, or

  ❏ the need for leave does not fall under the FMLA, and I have withdrawn the preliminary FMLA designation in writing.

❏ Where an employee's behavior reveals the employee might have a serious health condition, I have placed the employee on FMLA leave with a preliminary designation and have conducted an inquiry into whether the employee actually has a serious health condition.

❏ I have granted an employee's request for leave and preliminarily designated the leave as FMLA leave even though the employee did not mention the FMLA, where

  ❏ the employee gave me enough information to believe that the need for leave might fall under the FMLA, or

  ❏ I have information from another source that the employee's need for leave falls under the FMLA.

✓	**Managers' Checklist**	**Giving Notice and Designating Leave, continued**

❑ Where I have learned information during an employee's leave that leads me to believe it falls under the FMLA, I have given the employee a written FMLA designation.

❑ I have informed any employee requesting FMLA leave that

    ❑ he or she may use paid leave during FMLA leave (where appropriate) and informed the employee that the leave time will reduce available FMLA leave time, or

    ❑ Company policy requires that paid leave be substituted and informed the employee that the leave time will reduce available FMLA leave time.

❑ I have designated workers' compensation leave as FMLA leave, where the workplace injury is a serious health condition under the FMLA.

❑ When the employee requests leave for an unforeseeable, FMLA-covered reason, I have granted the leave and designated it as FMLA leave even though the employee did not give 30-days' notice.

❑ I have made sure not to require more employee notice for FMLA leave than is required by state law.

❑ I have made sure not to require more employee notice for FMLA leave than is required by a collective bargaining agreement covering the requesting employee.

❑ I have given the employee going out on FMLA leave an individualized notice with FMLA information specific to his or her situation.

❑ I have given additional notices to the employee on leave when

    ❑ an employee has requested FMLA leave six months or more after his or her first request for leave

    ❑ the information I initially gave the employee in the individualized notice has changed, or

    ❑ the company requires a medical certification or fitness-for-duty certification prior to the employee returning to work..

| ✓ | **Managers' Checklist** | **Medical Certifications** |

❏ I requested a medical certification as soon as I learned that the employee was seeking leave for a potentially serious health condition.

❏ I made the request in writing, dated and signed.

❏ The request explained the consequences of failing to return the certification on time.

❏ I gave the employee a medical certification form.

❏ I did not request any information that goes beyond what's required by the form.

❏ I worked with the employee to get a complete medical certification.

❏ If the form was not returned on time, I contacted the employee immediately to find out why and explain the importance of getting the form in.

❏ If the form was returned incomplete, I told the employee about the problem and provided an opportunity to correct it.

❏ I requested a second opinion if I had doubts about the initial medical certification.

    ❏ I did not send the employee to a health care provider who is regularly employed by my company.

    ❏ While the second opinion was pending, I provided FMLA benefits to the employee.

    ❏ I provided a copy of the second opinion to the employee, within two days after receiving his or her request.

    ❏ Before acting on a second opinion that contradicts the first, I consulted with an attorney.

    ❏ I requested recertifications as appropriate.

    ❏ I requested recertification only every 30 days or when the employee's initial certification expired, unless an exception allowed me to request one more often.

    ❏ I requested recertification whenever the employee's situation changed or I learned information that cast doubt on the employee's reasons for leave.

    ❏ I placed the medical certification(s) and any recertifications in confidential medical files, not the employee's regular personnel file.

✓ Managers' Checklist	Managing FMLA Leave

Scheduling

❏ I calendared the start and end dates of the employee's leave, if I know them.

❏ If the employee did not give 30 days' notice of foreseeable leave, I considered whether to require the employee to delay the start of his or her leave.

❏ If I didn't let the employee take leave as a date requested because the employee didn't provide enough notice, I put that decision in writing and gave it to the employee.

❏ If the employee is taking parenting leave, I made sure the employee's leave will be complete within one year of the child's arrival.

❏ If the employee's foreseeable leave will cause undue disruption to the company's operations, I asked the employee to try to reschedule (subject to the approval of his or her health care provider).

❏ If the employee had to take unforeseeable leave, I made initial contact with the employee or a family member to gather information and made plans to follow up in a few days.

Handling the Employee's Work

❏ If the employee was available, I talked to the employee and came up with a plan to cover his or her job duties during leave.

❏ If the employee's coworkers will pick up some extra work, I made any changes necessary to ensure that they will not be stretched too thin.

❏ I determined which, if any, of the employee's responsibilities I will handle and made the necessary arrangements to do so.

❏ If we will bring on temporary help, I made the necessary arrangements to hire a temp.

❏ If we will be using an outside consultant or company, I took any steps necessary to start the process.

❏ I informed everyone who needs to know about these arrangements, such as my manager, the employee's coworkers, vendors, clients, and so on.

✓	Managers' Checklist	Managing FMLA Leave, continued

Benefits

❏ I made arrangements to continue the employee's group health benefits—including medical, dental, and vision coverage—during FMLA leave.

❏ I applied any benefits changes to the employee, just as if he or she were not on leave.

❏ If the employee chose not to continue benefits, I made sure that we can reinstate those benefits immediately, without any requalification requirements, when the employee returns to work; if not, I continued the employee's benefits, arranged to pay the employee's share of the premium, and sought reimbursement from the employee after his or her return to work.

❏ I collected the employee's share of the premium as permitted by the FMLA and provided written notice, in advance, of how and when to make these payments.

❏ Before terminating the employee's coverage for failing to pay the premiums, I sent the employee written notice, including the following information:

    ❏ The employee's payment hasn't been received.

    ❏ The company intends to terminate the employee's coverage if payment isn't received by a specified date, at least 15 days after the date I sent the letter.

❏ Before terminating the employee's coverage for failing to pay the premiums, I made sure we could reinstate the employee's coverage without any requalification requirements.

❏ For other benefits, I followed my company's usual policies for employees on unpaid leave.

❏ Before discontinuing any life, disability, or other insurance benefits, I made sure that we could reinstate the employee's coverage without any requalification requirements; if not, I continued the employee's coverage, arranged to pay the employee's share of the premium, and sought reimbursement from the employee after his or her return to work.

Managers' Checklist   Reinstating an Employee

If the Employee Was Reinstated

❑ I reinstated the employee to the position he or she held prior to taking leave or to an equivalent position.

    ❑ The position has the same base pay, and the same opportunities to earn extra pay, as the former position.

    ❑ The position offers the same benefits, at the same levels, that the employee used to receive.

    ❑ The position has the same or substantially similar job duties as the employee's former job.

    ❑ The position has the same or a substantially similar shift or schedule as the employee worked before taking leave.

    ❑ The position is at the same worksite, or one that is geographically proximate to, where the employee worked before taking leave.

❑ I reinstated the employee immediately upon his or her return from leave or within two working days of receiving notice of intent to return to work from the employee.

❑ I restored the employee's pay, including base pay, opportunities to earn extra pay, and any across-the-board raises (such as cost-of-living increases) that became effective during the employee's leave.

❑ I did not count the employee's FMLA leave time against him or her when determining eligibility for bonuses based on an absence of negative occurrences, such as attendance or safety bonuses.

❑ I restored the employee's benefits, including any across-the-board changes that took effect during the employee's leave.

    ❑ I did not count the employee's FMLA leave as a break in service for purposes of our pension plan

    ❑ I counted the employee as "employed" while on leave if our pension plan requires employees to be employed on a particular date for purposes of contributions, eligibility, or vesting.

| ✓ | Managers' Checklist | **Reinstating an Employee, continued** |

❑ I restored the employee's seniority-based benefits.

❑ If our company's policies allow employees to accrue seniority-based benefits while on unpaid leave, I added these accrued benefits to the employee's total.

❑ I required the employee to provide a fitness-for-duty certification, but only if:

  ❑ I gave the employee notice that a certification would be required.

  ❑ Company policy requires it for all similarly situated employees.

  ❑ It was job-related and consistent with business necessity.

If the Employee Was Not Reinstated:

❑ I did not reinstate the employee because one of the following occurred:

  ❑ The employee was unable to perform an essential function of the position.

    ❑ I researched our company's obligations under the Americans With Disabilities Act and/or workers' compensation law.

  ❑ The employee's position was eliminated, for reasons unrelated to his or her FMLA leave.

  ❑ The employee was fired for reasons unrelated to his or her FMLA leave.

    ❑ If the employee was fired for attendance problems, I made sure that the employee's FMLA leave was not counted against him or her.

    ❑ I talked to a lawyer to make sure that we are on legally safe ground in taking this action.

✓	Managers' Checklist	Reinstating an Employee, continued

❏ The employee was fired for reasons unrelated to his or her FMLA leave.

    ❏ If the employee was fired for attendance problems, I made sure that the employee's FMLA leave was not counted against him or her.

    ❏ I talked to a lawyer to make sure that we are on legally safe ground in taking this action.

❏ The employee's job or work was temporary and has been completed.

    ❏ The employee committed fraud in obtaining FMLA leave.

    ❏ If the employee was not reinstated because he or she worked another job while on FMLA leave, I made sure our company policies prohibit moonlighting.

    ❏ The employee gave unequivocal notice that he or she did not intend to return from FMLA leave.

    ❏ The employee is a key employee, and reinstating him or her would cause our company substantial and grievous economic injury.

    ❏ The employee is among the highest-paid 10% of employees within a 75-mile radius.

    ❏ I notified the employee, when he or she requested leave or shortly thereafter, of this key employee status.

    ❏ I notified the employee when the company determined that reinstatement would cause substantial and grievous economic injury and gave the employee a reasonable time frame to return to work.

    ❏ If the employee requested reinstatement, I reevaluated whether reinstating him or her would cause substantial and grievous economic injury and notified the employee of my conclusions.

 **Managers' Checklist**

If an Employee Doesn't Return From Leave

❑ I determined why the employee did not come back to work.

❑ If the employee did not return to work because of the continuation of a serious health condition, I

    ❑ asked the employee to provide a medical certification, and

    ❑ did not seek reimbursement for premiums the company paid to continue the employee's health insurance.

❑ I did not seek reimbursement for health insurance premiums if the employee could not return to work for reasons beyond the employee's control.

❑ If the employee's failure to return from work was voluntary, I determined what amount (if any) we can recover from the employee for what we spent on benefit premiums while the employee was on leave.

    ❑ I included in this amount our company's share of the premium for health insurance continuation during the employee's leave.

    ❑ If the employee did not pay his or her share of the premium for health insurance, I included any part of the employee's share that we paid during the employee's leave.

    ❑ If we continued any other insurance benefits (such as life or disability coverage), I included any amounts we paid towards the employee's share of the premium during the employee's leave.

    ❑ I did not include the company's share of the premium for any other insurance benefits.

❑ Regardless of whether or not we are entitled to seek reimbursement from the employee, I offered the employee continued health care coverage under COBRA and, if we are self-insured, paid any claims the employee incurred while on FMLA leave.

❑ Before seeking reimbursement via withholding from money we still owe the employee, I made sure that this is allowed by state law.

| ✓ | **Managers' Checklist** | **Record Keeping** |

❑ I have collected all FMLA forms and documents for the employee and have put the documents into files separate from the employee's personnel files, including:

   ❑ payroll records (showing FMLA eligibility or noneligibility)

   ❑ charts showing FMLA leave time taken and FMLA leave time available (for intermittent or reduced-schedule leave, in hours or days, depending on how the leave was taken)

   ❑ preliminary FMLA designation forms

   ❑ forms confirming or withdrawing preliminary FMLA designations

   ❑ individualized FMLA notices

   ❑ medical certifications and second and third opinions

   ❑ six-month notices (issued when the employee takes FMLA leave more than six months after first taking leave or when there is a change in leave information)

   ❑ fitness-for-duty certifications and requests for such certifications, and

   ❑ periodic reports of employee status while on leave.

❑ I have kept a chart showing the running total in hours or days (depending on how the leave was taken) of intermittent or reduced-schedule FMLA leave time taken by the employee taking such leave.

❑ I have kept all employee (or employee family member) medical information in separate files and

❑ I have treated these records and the information in them as confidential, barring others from gaining access to them except to supervisors and managers to provide necessary accommodations or first aid personnel if a condition might require emergency medical treatment.

How to Use the CD-ROM

The tear-out forms in Appendix C are included on a CD-ROM in the back of the book. This CD-ROM, which can be used with Windows computers, installs files that you use with software programs that are already installed on your computer. It is *not* a standalone software program. Please read this appendix and the README.TXT file included on the CD-ROM for instructions on using the Forms CD-ROM.

Note to Mac users: This CD-ROM and its files should also work on Macintosh computers. Please note, however, that Nolo cannot provide technical support for non-Windows users.

How to View the README File

If you do not know how to view the file README.TXT, insert the Forms CD-ROM into your computer's CD-ROM drive and follow these instructions:

- **Windows 2000, XP, and Vista:** (1) On your PC's desktop, double click the My Computer icon; (2) double click the icon for the CD-ROM drive into which the Forms CD-ROM was inserted; (3) double click the file README.TXT.
- **Macintosh:** (1) On your Mac desktop, double click the icon for the CD-ROM that you inserted; (2) double click on the file README.TXT.

While the README file is open, print it out by using the Print command in the File menu.

Four different kinds of forms are on the CD-ROM:

- Word processing (RTF) forms that you can open, complete, print, and save with your word processing program (see "Using the Word Processing Files to Create Documents," below),
- Government forms (PDF) that can be viewed only with Adobe Acrobat Reader 4.0 or higher (see "Using Government Forms," below). Some of these forms have "fill-in" text fields and can be completed using your computer. You will not, however, be able to save the completed forms with the filled-in data. PDF forms without fill-in text fields must be printed out and filled in by hand or with a typewriter.

- Financial planning spreadsheets in Microsoft Excel format (XLS), which you can use with Microsoft's Excel or another spreadsheet program that can read XLS files (see "Using the Financial Planning Spreadsheets," below).
- MP3 audio files that you can listen to using your computer's media or MP3 player (see "Listening to the Audio Files," below).

See below for a list of forms, their file names, and their file formats.

Listening Without Installing

If you don't want to copy 44 MB of audio files to your hard disk, you can "play" the CD-ROM on your computer. For details, see "Playing the Audio Files Without Installing," below.

Installing the Form Files Onto Your Computer

Before you can do anything with the files on the CD-ROM, you need to install them onto your hard disk. In accordance with U.S. copyright laws, remember that copies of the CD-ROM and its files are for your personal use only.

Insert the Forms CD-ROM and do the following:

Windows 2000, XP, and Vista Users

Follow the instructions that appear on the screen. (If nothing happens when you insert the Forms CD-ROM, then (1) double click the My Computer icon; (2) double click the icon for the CD-ROM drive into which the Forms CD-ROM was inserted; (3) double click the file WELCOME.EXE.)

By default, all the files are installed to the \FMLA Guide Resources folder in the \Program Files folder of your computer. A folder called "FMLA Guide Resources" is added to the "Programs" folder of the Start menu.

Macintosh Users

Step 1: If the "FMLA Guide CD" window is not open, open it by double clicking the "FMLA Guide CD" icon.

Step 2: Select the "FMLA Guide Resources" folder icon.

Step 3: Drag and drop the folder icon onto the icon of your hard disk.

Using the Word Processing Files to Create Documents

This section concerns the files for forms that can be opened and edited with your word processing program.

All word processing forms come in rich text format. These files have the extension ".RTF." For example, the form for the FMLA Policy discussed in Chapters 2 and 3 is on the file Policy.rtf. All forms, their file names, and their file formats are listed at the end of this appendix.

RTF files can be read by most recent word processing programs including all versions of MS Word for Windows and Macintosh, WordPad for Windows, and recent versions of WordPerfect for Windows and Macintosh.

To use a form from the CD-ROM to create your documents you must: (1) open a file in your word processor or text editor; (2) edit the form by filling in the required information; (3) print it out; (4) rename and save your revised file.

The following are general instructions. However, each word processor uses different commands to open, format, save, and print documents. Please read your word processor's manual for specific instructions on performing these tasks.

Do not call Nolo's technical support if you have questions on how to use your word processor or your computer.

Step 1: Opening a File

There are three ways to open the word processing files included on the CD-ROM after you have installed them onto your computer:

- Windows users can open a file by selecting its "shortcut" as follows: (1) Click the Windows "Start" button; (2) open the "Programs" folder; (3) open the "FMLA Guide Resources" subfolder; (4) click the shortcut to the form you want to work with.

- Both Windows and Macintosh users can open a file directly by double clicking it. Use My Computer or Windows Explorer (Windows 2000, XP, or Vista) or the Finder (Macintosh) to go to the folder you installed or copied the CD-ROM's files to. Then, double click the specific file you want to open.

- You can also open a file from within your word processor. To do this, you must first start your word processor. Then, go to the File menu and choose the Open command. This opens a dialog box where you will tell the program (1) the type of file you want to open (*.RTF) and (2) the location and name of the file (you will need to navigate through the directory tree to get to the folder on your hard disk where the CD-ROM's files have been installed).

Where Are the Files Installed?

Windows Users: RTF files are installed by default to a folder named \FMLA Guide Resources in the \Program Files folder of your computer.

Macintosh Users: RTF files are located in the "FMLA Guide Resources" folder.

Step 2: Editing Your Document

Fill in the appropriate information according to the instructions and sample agreements in the book. Underlines are used to indicate where you need to enter your information, frequently followed by instructions in brackets. Be sure to delete the underlines and instructions from your edited document. You will also want to make sure that any signature lines in your completed documents appear on a page with at least some text from the document itself.

Editing Forms That Have Optional or Alternative Text

Some of the forms have optional or alternate text:

- With optional text, you choose whether to include or exclude the given text.
- With alternative text, you select one alternative to include and exclude the other alternatives.

When editing these forms, we suggest you do the following:

Optional text

If you don't want to include optional text, just delete it from your document.

If you do want to include optional text, just leave it in your document.

In either case, delete the italicized instructions.

Alternative text

First delete all the alternatives that you do not want to include, then delete the italicized instructions.

Step 3: Printing Out the Document

Use your word processor's or text editor's "Print" command to print out your document.

Step 4: Saving Your Document

After filling in the form, use the "Save As" command to save and rename the file. Because all the files are "read-only," you will not be able to use the "Save" command. This is for your protection. *If you save the file without renaming it, the underlines that indicate where you need to enter your information will be lost, and you will not be able to create a new document with this file without recopying the original file from the CD-ROM.*

Using Government Forms

Electronic copies of useful government forms are included on the CD-ROM in Adobe Acrobat PDF format. You must have Adobe Reader installed on your computer to use these forms. Adobe Reader is available for all types of Windows and Macintosh systems. If you don't already have this software, you can download it for free at www.adobe.com.

All forms, their file names, and their file formats are listed in appendix. These form files were created by the Department of Labor, not by Nolo.

Some of these forms have fill-in text fields. To create your document using these files, you must: (1) open a file; (2) fill in the text fields using either your mouse or the Tab key on your keyboard to navigate from field to field; (3) print it out.

Saving a filled-in form: Newer government forms are enabled with "document rights" that allow you to save your filled-in form to your hard disk. Version 5.1 or later of Adobe Reader is required. When you open these government forms in Reader, you'll see a document rights message box if this feature is available. If you are using an earlier version of Adobe Reader, you will be prompted to download a newer version that will allow you to save. You will not be able to save government forms that do not have document rights enabled, but you can still print out completed versions of these forms.

Forms without fill-in text fields cannot be filled out using your computer. To create your document using these files, you must: (1) open the file; (2) print it out; (3) complete it by hand or typewriter.

Step 1: Opening a Form

PDF files, like the word processing files, can be opened one of three ways:

- Windows users can open a file by selecting its "shortcut" as follows: (1) Click the Windows "Start" button; (2) open the "Programs" folder; (3) open the "FMLA Guide Resources" subfolder; (4) click on the shortcut to the form you want to work with.

- Both Windows and Macintosh users can open a file directly by double clicking it. Use My Computer or Windows Explorer (Windows 2000, XP, or Vista) or the Finder (Macintosh) to go to the folder you created and copied the CD-ROM's files to. Then, double click the specific file you want to open.

- You can also open a PDF file from within Adobe Reader. To do this, you must first start Reader. Then, go to the File menu and choose the Open command. This opens a dialog box where you will tell the program the location and name of the file (you will need to navigate through the directory tree to get to the folder on your hard disk where the CD-ROM's files have been installed).

Where Are the PDF Files Installed?

- **Windows Users:** PDF files are installed by default to a folder named \FMLA Guide Resources in the \Program Files folder of your computer.

- **Macintosh Users:** PDF files are located in the "PDF" folder within the "FMLA Guide Resources" folder.

Step 2: Filling in a Form

Use your mouse or the Tab key on your keyboard to navigate from field to field within these forms.

- If document rights are enabled, you can save your completed form to disk using Adobe Reader 5.1 or higher.

- If document rights are not enabled, be sure to have all the information you will need to complete a form on hand, because you will not be able to save a copy of the filled-in form to disk. You can, however, print out a completed version.

NOTE: This step is applicable only to forms that have been created with fill-in text fields. Forms without fill-in fields must be completed by hand or typewriter after you have printed them out.

Step 3: Printing a Form

Choose "Print" from the Acrobat Reader "File" menu. This will open the Print dialog box. In the "Print Range" section of the Print dialog box, select the appropriate print range, then click "OK."

Using the Financial Planning Spreadsheets

This section concerns the files for the financial planning spreadsheets that can be opened and completed with Microsoft Excel or another spreadsheet program that understands XLS files.

These spreadsheets are in Microsoft Excel format. These files have the extension ".XLS". For example, the Cash Flow Forecast spreadsheet discussed in Chapter 7 is on the file CashFlow.xls. All forms and their filenames are listed below.

To complete a financial planning spreadsheet you must: (1) open the file in a spreadsheet program that is compatible with XLS files; (2) fill in the needed fields; (3) print it out; (4) rename and save your revised file.

The following are general instructions. However, each spreadsheet program uses different commands to open, format, save, and print documents. Please read your spreadsheet program's manual for specific instructions on performing these tasks.

Step 1: Opening a File

There are three ways to open the spreadsheet files included on the CD-ROM after you have installed them onto your computer:

- Windows users can open a file by selecting its "shortcut" as follows: (1) Click the Windows "Start" button; (2) open the "Programs" folder; (3) open the "FMLA Guide Resources" subfolder; and (4) click the shortcut to the spreadsheet you want to work with.

- Both Windows and Macintosh users can open a file directly by double clicking it. Use My Computer or Windows Explorer (Windows 2000, XP, or Vista) or the Finder (Macintosh) to go to the folder you installed or copied the CD-ROM's files to. Then, double click the specific file you want to open.

- You can also open a file from within your spreadsheet program. To do this, you must first start your spreadsheet program. Then, go to the File menu and choose the Open command. This opens a dialog box where you will tell the program (1) the type of file you want to open (*.XLS) and (2) the location and name of the file (you will need to navigate through the directory tree to get to the folder on your hard disk where the CD-ROM's files have been installed). If these directions are unclear you will need to look through the manual for your spreadsheet program—Nolo's technical support department will not be able to help you with the use of your spreadsheet program.

Where Are the Files Installed?

Windows Users: XLS files are installed by default to a folder named \FMLA Guide Resources in the \Program Files folder of your computer.

Macintosh Users: XLS files are located in the "FMLA Guide Resources" folder.

Step 2: Entering Information Into the Spreadsheet

Fill in the appropriate information according to the instructions and sample spreadsheets in the book. As you fill in these spreadsheets, numeric calculations are performed automatically. If you do not know how to use your spreadsheet program to enter information into an XLS file, you will need to look through the manual for your spreadsheet program—Nolo's technical support department will *not* be able to help you with the use of your spreadsheet program.

Step 3: Printing Out the Spreadsheet

Use your spreadsheet program's "Print" command to print out your document. If you do not know how to use your spreadsheet program to print a document, you will need to look through the manual for your spreadsheet program—Nolo's technical support department will *not* be able to help you with the use of your spreadsheet program.

Step 4: Saving Your Spreadsheet

After filling in the form, use the "Save As" command to save and rename the file. Because all the files are "read-only," you will not be able to use the "Save" command. This is for your protection. *If you save the file without renaming it, you will overwrite the original financial planning spreadsheet, and you will not be able to create a new document with this file without recopying the original file from the CD-ROM.*

If you do not know how to use your spreadsheet program to save a document, you will need to look through the manual for your spreadsheet program—Nolo's technical support department will *not* be able to help you with the use of your spreadsheet program.

Listening to the Audio Files

This section explains how to use your computer's media player to listen to the audio files. All audio files are in MP3 format. (Most computers come with a media player that plays MP3 files.) For example, "FMLA: The Human Side" is on the file TheHumanSide.mp3. At the end of this appendix, you'll see a list of the audio files and their file names.

You can listen to files that you have installed on your computer, or you can listen without having installed the files to your hard disk (see "Playing the Audio Files Without Installing," below).

Please keep in mind that these are general instructions—because every media player is unique, these steps may not mirror the steps you need to follow to use your player. *Please do not contact Nolo's technical support if you are having difficulty using your media player.*

Listening to Audio Files You've Installed on Your Computer

There are two ways to listen to the audio files that you have installed on your computer:

- Windows users can open a file by selecting its "shortcut" as follows: (1) Click the Windows "Start" button, (2) open the "Programs" folder; (3) open the "FMLA Guide Resources" subfolder; (4) open the "Audio" subfolder; (5) click the shortcut to the audio segment you want to hear.

- Both Windows and Macintosh users can open a file directly by double clicking it. Use My Computer or Windows Explorer (Windows 2000, XP, and Vista) or the Finder (Macintosh) to go to the folder in which you installed or copied the CD-ROM's files. Then, double click the MP3 file you want to hear.

Where Are the Files Installed?

Windows Users: MP3 files are installed by default to a folder named \FMLA Guide Resources\Audio in the \Program Files folder of your computer.

Macintosh Users: MP3 files are located in the "FMLA Guide Audio" folder.

Playing the Audio Files Without Installing

If you don't want to copy 44 MB of audio files to your hard disk, you can "play" the CD-ROM on your computer. Here's how:

Windows users

Step 1: Insert the Forms CD-ROM to view the "Welcome to FMLA Guide CD" window. (If nothing happens when you insert the Forms CD-ROM, double click the My Computer icon, double click the icon for the CD-ROM drive into which the Forms CD-ROM was inserted, and double click the file WELCOME.EXE.)

Step 2: Click "Listen to Audio."

Mac users

Step 1: Insert the Forms CD-ROM. If the "FMLA Guide CD" window does not open, open it by double clicking the "FMLA Guide CD" icon.

Step 2: Open the "FMLA Guide Audio" folder by double clicking the "FMLA Guide Audio" icon.

Step 3: Double click the audio file you want to hear.

List of Forms Included on the Forms CD-ROM

The following files are in rich text format (RTF):

FILE NAME	FORM TITLE
Policy.rtf	FMLA Policy
LeaveForm.rtf	Form Regarding FMLA Leave to Care for a Family Member
WorkHours.rtf	FMLA Hours Worked
Tracking.rtf	FMLA Leave Tracking
DesignationPrelim.rtf	FMLA Designation (Preliminary)
DesignationFinal.rtf	FMLA Designation (Final)
MedCertifRequest.rtf	Request for Medical Certification
NoticeEconInjury.rtf	Notice to Key Employee of Substantial and Grievous Economic Injury
CoverageTerm.rtf	Notice of Termination of Group Health Coverage

The following files are in portable document format (PDF):

FILE NAME	FORM TITLE
Fmlaen.pdf	Family and Medical Leave Act Poster (English)
Fmlasp.pdf	Family and Medical Leave Act Poster (Spanish)
WH-380.pdf	Certification of Health Care Provider
WH-381.pdf	Employer Response to Employee Request for Family or Medical Leave
Apply.pdf	Does the FMLA Apply to My Company?
Eligible.pdf	Is the Employee Eligible for FMLA Leave?
ChildLeave.pdf	Leave for a New Child
LeaveDuration.pdf	Duration of Leave
LeaveNotice.pdf	Giving Notice and Designating Leave
Certifications.pdf	Medical Certifications
ManagingLeave.pdf	Managing FMLA Leave
Reinstatement.pdf	Reinstating an Employee
EmployeeDeparture.pdf	If an Employee Doesn't Return From Leave
RecordKeeping.pdf	Record Keeping

The following spreadsheet is in Microsoft Excel Format (XLS):

FILE NAME	FORM TITLE
CalculateLeave.xls	Calculating Intermittent/Reduced Schedule Leave

The following files are Audio (MP3):

FILE NAME	FORM TITLE
PolicyandEnforcement.mp3	FMLA: Policy and Enforcement
ManagementandReqs.mp3	FMLA: Management and Requirements
TheHumanSide.mp3	FMLA: The Human Side
Scenario1.mp3	The Essential Guide to Family and Medical Leave: Scenario 1
Scenario2.mp3	The Essential Guide to Family and Medical Leave: Scenario 2

Index

CATALOG
...more from Nolo

BUSINESS	PRICE	CODE
Business Buyout Agreements (Book w/CD-ROM)	$49.99	BSAG
The CA Nonprofit Corporation Kit (Binder w/CD-ROM)	$69.99	CNP
California Workers' Comp: How to Take Charge When You're Injured on the Job	$34.99	WORK
The Complete Guide to Buying a Business (Book w/CD-ROM)	$24.99	BUYBU
The Complete Guide to Selling a Business (Book w/CD-ROM)	$24.99	SELBU
Consultant & Independent Contractor Agreements (Book w/CD-ROM)	$29.99	CICA
The Corporate Records Handbook (Book w/CD-ROM)	$69.99	CORMI
Create Your Own Employee Handbook (Book w/CD-ROM)	$49.99	EMHA
Dealing With Problem Employees	$44.99	PROBM
Deduct It! Lower Your Small Business Taxes	$34.99	DEDU
Effective Fundraising for Nonprofits	$24.99	EFFN
The Employer's Legal Handbook	$39.99	EMPL
Essential Guide to Federal Employment Laws	$39.99	FEMP
Form a Partnership (Book W/CD-ROM)	$39.99	PART
Form Your Own Limited Liability Company (Book w/CD-ROM)	$44.99	LIAB
Home Business Tax Deductions: Keep What You Earn	$34.99	DEHB
How to Form a Nonprofit Corporation (Book w/CD-ROM)—National Edition	$49.99	NNP
How to Form a Nonprofit Corporation in California (Book w/CD-ROM)	$49.99	NON
How to Form Your Own California Corporation (Binder w/CD-ROM)	$59.99	CACI
How to Form Your Own California Corporation (Book w/CD-ROM)	$34.99	CCOR
How to Write a Business Plan (Book w/CD-ROM)	$34.99	SBS
Incorporate Your Business (Book w/CD-ROM)	$49.99	NIBS
Investors in Your Backyard (Book w/CD-ROM)	$24.99	FINBUS
The Job Description Handbook	$29.99	JOB
Legal Guide for Starting & Running a Small Business	$34.99	RUNS
Legal Forms for Starting & Running a Small Business (Book w/CD-ROM)	$29.99	RUNSF
LLC or Corporation?	$24.99	CHENT
The Manager's Legal Handbook	$39.99	ELBA
Marketing Without Advertising	$20.00	MWAD
Music Law (Book w/CD-ROM)	$39.99	ML
Negotiate the Best Lease for Your Business	$24.99	LESP
Nolo's Guide to Social Security Disability (Book w/CD-ROM)	$29.99	QSS
Nolo's Quick LLC	$29.99	LLCQ
The Performance Appraisal Handbook	$29.99	PERF
The Small Business Start-up Kit (Book w/CD-ROM)	$24.99	SMBU
The Small Business Start-up Kit for California (Book w/CD-ROM)	$24.99	OPEN
Starting & Running a Successful Newsletter or Magazine	$29.99	MAG
Tax Deductions for Professionals	$34.99	DEPO
Tax Savvy for Small Business	$36.99	SAVVY
Whoops! I'm in Business	$19.99	WHOO
Working for Yourself: Law & Taxes for Independent Contractors, Freelancers & Consultants	$39.99	WAGE
Working With Independent Contractors (Book w/CD-ROM)	$29.99	HICI
Your Crafts Business: A Legal Guide (Book w/CD-ROM)	$26.99	VART
Your Limited Liability Company: An Operating Manual (Book w/CD-ROM)	$49.99	LOP
Your Rights in the Workplace	$29.99	YRW

Prices subject to change.

CONSUMER

	PRICE	CODE
How to Win Your Personal Injury Claim	$29.99	PICL
Nolo's Encyclopedia of Everyday Law	$29.99	EVL
Nolo's Guide to California Law	$24.99	CLAW

ESTATE PLANNING & PROBATE

8 Ways to Avoid Probate	$19.99	PRAV
Estate Planning Basics	$21.99	ESPN
The Executor's Guide: Settling a Loved One's Estate or Trust	$34.99	EXEC
How to Probate an Estate in California	$49.99	PAE
Make Your Own Living Trust (Book w/CD-ROM)	$39.99	LITR
Nolo's Simple Will Book (Book w/CD-ROM)	$36.99	SWIL
Plan Your Estate	$44.99	NEST
Quick & Legal Will Book (Book w/CD-ROM)	$19.99	QUIC
Special Needs Trust: Protect Your Child's Financial Future (Book w/CD-ROM)	$34.99	SPNT

FAMILY MATTERS

Always Dad	$16.99	DIFA
Building a Parenting Agreement That Works	$24.99	CUST
The Complete IEP Guide	$34.99	IEP
Divorce & Money: How to Make the Best Financial Decisions During Divorce	$34.99	DIMO
Divorce Without Court	$29.99	DWCT
Do Your Own California Adoption: Nolo's Guide for Stepparents & Domestic Partners (Book w/CD-ROM)	$34.99	ADOP
Every Dog's Legal Guide: A Must-Have for Your Owner	$19.99	DOG
Get a Life: You Don't Need a Million to Retire Well	$24.99	LIFE
The Guardianship Book for California	$34.99	GB
A Legal Guide for Lesbian and Gay Couples	$34.99	LG
Living Together: A Legal Guide (Book w/CD-ROM)	$34.99	LTK
Nolo's IEP Guide: Learning Disabilities	$29.99	IELD
Parent Savvy	$19.99	PRNT
Prenuptial Agreements: How to Write a Fair & Lasting Contract (Book w/CD-ROM)	$34.99	PNUP
Work Less, Live More	$17.99	RECL

GOING TO COURT

Beat Your Ticket: Go To Court & Win! (National Edition)	$21.99	BEYT
The Criminal Law Handbook: Know Your Rights, Survive the System	$39.99	KYR
Everybody's Guide to Small Claims Court (National Edition)	$29.99	NSCC
Everybody's Guide to Small Claims Court in California	$29.99	CSCC
Fight Your Ticket & Win in California	$29.99	FYT
How to Change Your Name in California	$29.99	NAME
Nolo's Deposition Handbook	$29.99	DEP
Represent Yourself in Court: How to Prepare & Try a Winning Case	$39.99	RYC
Win Your Lawsuit: A Judge's Guide to Representing Yourselfin California Superior Court	$29.99	SLWY

HOMEOWNERS, LANDLORDS & TENANTS

California Tenants' Rights	$27.99	CTEN
Deeds for California Real Estate	$24.99	DEED
Every Landlord's Legal Guide (National Edition, Book w/CD-ROM)	$44.99	ELLI
Every Landlord's Guide to Finding Great Tenants (Book w/CD-ROM)	$19.99	FIND
Every Landlord's Tax Deduction Guide	$34.99	DELL
Every Tenant's Legal Guide	$29.99	EVTEN
For Sale by Owner in California	$29.99	FSBO
How to Buy a House in California	$29.99	BHCA
The California Landlord's Law Book: Rights & Responsibilities(Book w/CD-ROM)	$44.99	LBRT
The California Landlord's Law Book: Evictions (Book w/CD-ROM)	$44.99	LBEV
Leases & Rental Agreements	$29.99	LEAR

	PRICE	CODE
Neighbor Law: Fences, Trees, Boundaries & Noise	$26.99	NEI
Renters' Rights (National Edition)	$24.99	RENT

IMMIGRATION

	PRICE	CODE
Becoming A U.S. Citizen: A Guide to the Law, Exam and Interview	$24.99	USCIT
Fiancé & Marriage Visas (Book w/CD-ROM)	$34.99	IMAR
How to Get a Green Card	$29.99	GRN
Student & Tourist Visas	$29.99	ISTU
U.S. Immigration Made Easy	$39.99	IMEZ

MONEY MATTERS

	PRICE	CODE
101 Law Forms for Personal Use (Book w/CD-ROM)	$29.99	SPOT
Chapter 13 Bankruptcy: Repay Your Debts	$39.99	CHB
Credit Repair (Book w/CD-ROM)	$24.99	CREP
How to File for Chapter 7 Bankruptcy	$29.99	HFB
IRAs, 401(k)s & Other Retirement Plans: Taking Your Money Out	$34.99	RET
Solve Your Money Troubles	$19.99	MT
Stand Up to the IRS	$29.99	SIRS

PATENTS AND COPYRIGHTS

	PRICE	CODE
All I Need is Money: How to Finance Your Invention	$19.99	FINA
The Copyright Handbook: How to Protect and Use Written Works (Book w/CD-ROM)	$39.99	COHA
Copyright Your Software (Book w/CD-ROM)	$34.95	CYS
Getting Permission: How to License & Clear Copyrighted Materials Online & Off (Book w/CD-ROM) RIPER	$34.99	
How to Make Patent Drawings	$29.99	DRAW
The Inventor's Notebook	$24.99	INOT
Nolo's Patents for Beginners	$24.99	QPAT
Patent, Copyright & Trademark	$39.99	PCTM
Patent It Yourself	$49.99	PAT
Patent Pending in 24 Hours	$34.99	PEND
Patenting Art & Entertainment: New Strategies for Protecting Creative Ideas	$39.99	PATAE
Profit from Your Idea (Book w/CD-ROM)	$34.99	LICE
The Public Domain	$34.99	PUBL
Trademark: Legal Care for Your Business and Product Name	$39.99	TRD
Web and Software Development: A Legal Guide (Book w/ CD-ROM)	$44.99	SFT
What Every Inventor Needs to Know About Business & Taxes (Book w/CD-ROM)	$21.99	ILAX

RESEARCH & REFERENCE

	PRICE	CODE
Legal Research: How to Find & Understand the Law	$39.99	LRES

SENIORS

	PRICE	CODE
Long-Term Care: How to Plan & Pay for It	$19.99	ELD
Social Security, Medicare & Goverment Pensions	$29.99	SOA

SOFTWARE Call or check our website at www.nolo.com for special discounts on Software!

	PRICE	CODE
Incorporator Pro	89.99	STNC1
LLC Maker—Windows	$89.95	LLP1
Patent Pending Now!	$199.99	PP1
PatentEase—Windows	$349.00	PEAS
Personal RecordKeeper 5.0 CD—Windows	$59.95	RKD5
Quicken Legal Business Pro 2007—Windows	$109.99	SBQB7
Quicken WillMaker Plus 2007—Windows	$79.99	WQP7

Special Upgrade Offer
Save 35% on the latest edition of your Nolo book

Because laws and legal procedures change often, we update our books regularly. To help keep you up-to-date, we are extending this special upgrade offer. Cut out and mail the title portion of the cover of your old Nolo book and we'll give you 35% off the retail price of the New Edition of that book when you purchase directly from Nolo. This offer is to individuals only. Prices and offer subject to change without notice.

ORDER 24 HOURS A DAY @ www.nolo.com
Call 800-728-3555 • Mail or fax the order form in this book

Order Form

Name	
Address	
City	
State, Zip	
Daytime Phone	
E-mail	

Our "No-Hassle" Guarantee

Return anything you buy directly from Nolo for any reason and we'll cheerfully refund your purchase price. No ifs, ands or buts.

☐ Check here if you do not wish to receive mailings from other companies

Item Code	Quantity	Item	Unit Price	Total Price

Method of payment

☐ Check ☐ VISA

☐ American Express

☐ MasterCard

☐ Discover Card

Subtotal	
Add your local sales tax (California only)	
Shipping: RUSH $12, Basic $9 (See below)	
"I bought 3, ship it to me FREE!" (Ground shipping only)	
TOTAL	

Account Number

Expiration Date

Signature

Shipping and Handling

Rush Delivery—Only $12

We'll ship any order to any street address in the U.S. by UPS 2nd Day Air* for only $12!

* Order by noon Pacific Time and get your order in 2 business days. Orders placed after noon Pacific Time will arrive in 3 business days. P.O. boxes and S.F. Bay Area use basic shipping. Alaska and Hawaii use 2nd Day Air or Priority Mail.

Basic Shipping—$9

Use for P.O. Boxes, Northern California and Ground Service.

Allow 1-2 weeks for delivery.

U.S. addresses only.

For faster service, use your credit card and our toll-free numbers

Call our customer service group Monday thru Friday 7am to 7pm PST

 Phone
1-800-728-3555

 Fax
1-800-645-0895

 Mail
Nolo
950 Parker St.
Berkeley, CA 94710

Order 24 hours a day @ www.nolo.com

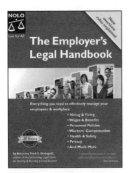

Get the Latest in the Law

① **Nolo's Legal Updater**
We'll send you an email whenever a new edition of your book is published!
Sign up at **www.nolo.com/legalupdater**.

② **Updates at Nolo.com**
Check **www.nolo.com/update** to find recent changes in the law that
affect the current edition of your book.

③ **Nolo Customer Service**
To make sure that this edition of the book is the most recent one, call us at
800-728-3555 and ask one of our friendly customer service representatives
(7:00 am to 6:00 pm PST, weekdays only). Or find out at **www.nolo.com**.

④ **Complete the Registration & Comment Card ...**
... and we'll do the work for you! Just indicate your preferences below:

- -

Registration & Comment Card

NAME   DATE

ADDRESS

CITY   STATE   ZIP

PHONE   EMAIL

COMMENTS

WAS THIS BOOK EASY TO USE?   (VERY EASY)   5   4   3   2   1   (VERY DIFFICULT)

☐ Yes, you can quote me in future Nolo promotional materials. *Please include phone number above.*

☐ Yes, send me **Nolo's Legal Updater** via email when a new edition of this book is available.

Yes, I want to sign up for the following email newsletters:

  ☐ **NoloBriefs** (monthly)
  ☐ **Nolo's Special Offer** (monthly)
  ☐ **Nolo's BizBriefs** (monthly)
  ☐ **Every Landlord's Quarterly** (four times a year)

☐ Yes, you can give my contact info to carefully selected
partners whose products may be of interest to me.

NOLO
⚖ ⚖

FMLA 1.0

Nolo
950 Parker Street
Berkeley, CA 94710-9867
www.nolo.com

NOLO

YOUR LEGAL COMPANION